Rebuilding Community

Rebuilding Community

Displaced Women and the Making of a Shia Ismaili Muslim Sociality

SHENILA KHOJA-MOOLJI

OXFORD
UNIVERSITY PRESS

Oxford University Press is a department of the University of Oxford. It furthers
the University's objective of excellence in research, scholarship, and education
by publishing worldwide. Oxford is a registered trade mark of Oxford University
Press in the UK and certain other countries.

Published in the United States of America by Oxford University Press
198 Madison Avenue, New York, NY 10016, United States of America.

Library of Congress Cataloging-in-Publication Data
Names: Khoja-Moolji, Shenila, 1982– author.
Title: Rebuilding community : displaced women and the making of a Shia
Ismaili Muslim sociality / Shenila Khoja-Moolji.
Description: 1. | New York : Oxford University Press, 2023. | Includes
bibliographical references and index.
Identifiers: LCCN 2023006056 (print) | LCCN 2023006057 (ebook) |
ISBN 9780197642030 (paperback) | ISBN 9780197642023 (hardback) |
ISBN 9780197642054 (epub)
Subjects: LCSH: Muslim women—United States—Attitudes. | Muslim
women—Religious life—United States. | Women in Islam—United States. |
Muslims—United States—Social conditions. | Women—United
States—Social conditions. | Ismailites—United States. | Women
refugees—Bangladesh—Social conditions. | Women refugees—Africa,
East—Social conditions.
Classification: LCC BP67 .A3 W665 2023 (print) | LCC BP67 .A3 (ebook) | DDC
305.48/6970973—dc23/eng/20230210
LC record available at https://lccn.loc.gov/2023006056
LC ebook record available at https://lccn.loc.gov/2023006057

DOI: 10.1093/oso/9780197642023.001.0001

Paperback printed by Marquis Book Printing, Canada
Hardback printed by Bridgeport National Bindery, Inc., United States of America

For my beloved MHI

Contents

Acknowledgments

It has been my privilege to write *Rebuilding Community*. The book has received innumerable *barakah* in the form of fortuitous introductions to Ismaili women, lost photographs suddenly found, grant funds awarded, a last-minute offer for the cover image, and thoughtful and generous engagement from readers and reviewers. In fact, I have experienced this book as a gift that has enabled me to discover the lives of incredible Muslim women— their hardships but also their sheer will to bring joy to themselves, their families, and their *jamat*. I have learned how faith (*iman*) expands, narrows, overcomes, halts, and persists. *Alhamdulillah.*

Many women and men from the Ismaili Muslim community, mentors, friends, and colleagues have supported this endeavor. I am grateful to the over ninety Ismailis who shared their life stories with me, welcomed me into their homes, showered me with love, and fed me *chola*, *thepla*, *chai*, and biscuits. I interviewed several of my interlocutors multiple times and then WhatsApped and called them with further questions. They were extremely patient with my inquiries. No words of gratitude are enough: this book is as much theirs as mine. I have not been able to include every one of the hundreds of accounts and stories shared with me, but they have informed my interpretations.

I am grateful in particular to my family, who are always there for me with their prayers and encouragement. Special thanks to my mother, Farida Khoja, who has been on this book-writing journey with me for years, sharing her stories, introducing me to other women, joining me for some interviews, helping me interpret *ginans*, reading drafts of chapters, and even asking me on several occasions to rewrite them!

I am lucky to have found the most generous mentors in the academy: Lila Abu-Lughod, Ali Asani, Leila Ahmed, Hussein Rashid, and Nargis Virani. Their advice and gentle critiques have guided many projects. I am indebted to the inspired teaching of Jane I. Smith and Ann Braude at Harvard University; Nancy Lesko, Monisha Bajaj, and Neferti Tadiar at Columbia University; and my early mentor Reverend Janet Cooper Nelson at Brown University.

I am grateful to the many colleagues who read entire drafts or parts of the manuscript and shared their helpful feedback: Lila Abu-Lughod, Ali Asani, Juliane Hammer, Celene Ibrahim, Farouk Mitha, Neelam Khoja, Zahra Ayubi, Alyssa Niccolini, Mary Ann Chacko, Omar Kasmani, Uzair Ibrahim, Karishma Desai, Mariam Durrani, Julia Boss, Laura Portwood-Stacer, Tashif Kara, Sahir Dewji, and the anonymous reviewers at Oxford University, New York University, and University of North Carolina Presses. Conversations with Parin Dossa, Zayn Kassam, Hussain Jasani, Nazira Mawji, Zahra Jamal, Natasha Merchant, Fariyal Ross-Sheriff, Rizwan Mawani, and Kamaluddin Ali Muhammad were extremely fruitful. Zahir Dhalla, Malik Merchant, and Shezan Muhammadi were most helpful in sharing archival materials; Hafiz Lakhani generously responded to my numerous queries about *ginans*.

My writing group with Oyman Basaran, Shruti Devgan, and Jay Sosa has been truly generative; I am thankful for their close readings and friendship. I thank other colleagues at Georgetown University and Bowdoin College who took a keen interest in the book: in particular, John Esposito, Jonathan A. C. Brown, Jen Scanlon, Marilyn Reizbaum, and Jill Smith. My friends have cheered me along in life-affirming ways: Laila Moolji, Furhana Husani, Warda Ali, Zahra Somani, Meena Naik, Anar Amin, Nuhad Pirani, Nusrat Vastani, Ayesha Khurshid, Erum Jaffer, Norin Taj, Raheem Haji, Murad Abdulla, Asif Makhani, Ahmed Chagani, Zahra Kassam, Shaista Patel, Saima Gowani, and Raheel Lakhani.

This project was accomplished with the support of grants from Georgetown University, Bowdoin College, and Indiana University's Muslim Philanthropy Initiative. Research assistance from Hina Hussain, Shanil Khoja, Rimsha Hirani, Inara Allahwala, Elise Hocking, Ziana Sundrani, Rahul Prabhu, and Ziyanah Ladak was invaluable. Many thanks also to my editors, Cynthia Read, Theo Calderara, and Brent Matheny, and to other staff at Oxford University Press, who have supported this book with great enthusiasm. Lauren Bauschard, Chirin Dirani, and Andrew Condon at the Prince Alwaleed Bin Talal Center for Muslim-Christian Understanding at Georgetown University provided invaluable support. And Wafi Momin and Naureen Ali at the Special Collections Unit of the Aga Khan Library were exceedingly helpful. I benefited from the engagement of those who attended lectures and keynotes where I presented early findings from the book, including audiences at Harvard Divinity School, Princeton University, Bard Berlin, the EnGender conference, the University of Pennsylvania, Tufts

University, and the Institute of Ismaili Studies. Nermeen Mouftah and Megan Robb provided helpful feedback when I shared a chapter at the American Academy of Religion's Islam, Gender, Women program unit.

Finally, my deep gratitude to the Ismaili *jamats* of Pakistan and the United States that have nurtured me in innumerable ways, and to the Ismaili volunteers whose *seva* has benefited me directly.

Alhamdu li-llahi rabbil alamin.

Note on Translation

My interlocutors spoke to me in Gujarati, Urdu, Sindhi, Kuchchhi, and English, with a majority of conversations embracing multiple languages on this list. Unless otherwise stated, all translations are mine.

For the sake of readability, diacritical marks have been kept to a minimum. For terms shared across Arabic, Persian, and Urdu, I privilege the form used in the spoken language of the interlocutor (for instance, the Urdu *moujza* over its Arabic counterpart *mu'jiza*).

Arabic, Persian, Urdu, Sindhi, or Kuchchhi terms that have been incorporated into English (such as Ismaili, Shia, Muslim, Imam, and jamatkhana) are not italicized. Translation of other terms (such as *jamat, seva, moujza, ginan, farman, Mawla, juro,* and *sukrit*) is provided only on their first appearance.

1

Introduction

Rebuilding Community

[Atlanta, Georgia, 2019. The phone rings.]

FARIDA, IN URDU: Hello, *kaisay ho* (How are you)? [Farida listens closely as Zarina, the woman on the other end, responds in a mix of English and Urdu.]

FARIDA: Yes, I will bring the application forms to jamatkhana and we can complete them together. If your application gets approved, you will then only have to pay $10 for your visit to the doctor. They will provide you medicine for free, and free visits to specialists, too. This service is provided by the DeKalb County, you see, and run by volunteer doctors. Let's meet in jamatkhana. I will explain more.

[Farida returns to her cooking. That evening at the jamatkhana, she helps Zarina, who has recently migrated from India, complete the forms to enroll as a patient at the DeKalb County Physicians' Care Clinic.]

ZARINA: Will you please take me to the clinic, too? My son works at the gas station all day and I can't drive. There is no one to take me.

[Farida quickly reconfigures her weekly schedule in her head.]

FARIDA: *Theek hai*, no problem.

Farida gets up daily at 4:00 a.m. to drive to a nearby jamatkhana for morning prayers. Jamatkhana, a Persian word meaning community house, is the site of congregational worship and gathering for Shia Ismaili Muslims. After prayers, when other congregants have left this community house, Farida stays behind with a handful of other women to wash the objects used during rituals. Back home by 6:30 a.m., she prepares and packs lunches for

Rebuilding Community. Shenila Khoja-Moolji, Oxford University Press. © Oxford University Press 2023.
DOI: 10.1093/oso/9780197642023.003.0001

her husband and son. Lunch is often a sandwich, but everyone wants something different: her seventy-year-old husband likes one piece of bread instead of two and fruit on the side; her son, in his mid-thirties, is happy with two slices and even some extra meat. Farida takes an hour-long nap, then leaves for work. Until 3:00 p.m., at a shop a few blocks from her house, she scoops ice cream, rings up customers, and makes cakes. Back at home, she cooks dinner so that it is ready for her husband and son when they return from work in the evening. She takes a thirty-minute nap and then heads out to drive sixty-five-year-old Zarina to the county's free clinic. Farida tries not to miss the 7:30 p.m. evening prayers at the jamatkhana but sometimes, when the clinic is crowded with patients, she has to make that sacrifice. Farida says she is known in her local Ismaili community as the "*baima* (older sister) who helps newcomers get free healthcare": "They think I am some healthcare worker [laughs]."

Sixty-one-year-old Farida migrated to the United States from Pakistan just over two decades ago. She made the move so her children could have a better chance at life, particularly access to a higher quality of education. Her family left behind a stable middle-class life in Karachi for Atlanta where, at first, they struggled professionally and economically in the unfamiliar environment. Members of the local Ismaili *jamat* (community) came to their aid: one woman helped Farida open a bank account; another helped her get a driver's license; yet another introduced Farida to the Salvation Army where she could buy discounted furniture and directed her to a job opening at the local ice cream shop where she would work for the next two decades.

Her relocation to Atlanta in 2001 was not the first time Farida had benefited from such forms of community support. In 1971, as a twelve-year-old, she was displaced from her childhood home when East Pakistan (now Bangladesh) became a site of ethno-national war. She fled Dhaka with her mother and sister and found herself at a camp established by local Ismailis at a jamatkhana in Karachi. An ad hoc Ismaili volunteer committee came together to support displaced families like hers. The committee helped her widowed mother find housing and subsidized their rent for a year; a local Ismaili business owner offered her older sister a job, and the Ismailia Youth Services paid Farida's tuition at an Ismaili-run boarding school (Figure 1.1). The Ismaili *jamat* of Karachi formed a protective web, an infrastructure of care, around this displaced family and saved it from sinking deeper into poverty.

Figure 1.1 Farida (back row in white hairband), together with other children who had fled East Pakistan with their families, photographed in summer 1971 at the Muhammadi Girls Academy, Karachi. Children arriving from East Pakistan had been asked to remain at school during the summer holiday to take classes in Urdu, the language predominantly used in West Pakistan. Farida recalls that at the time she moved to Karachi she knew English and some Bangla but only spoken Urdu.
Courtesy of Farida Khoja.

There is a cyclical quality to Farida's life story, and to her family's story as well. Her mother, Shakar Juma, also lived through numerous geographic dislocations. Shakar was born sometime during the early 1930s into an impoverished family then living in the peninsular region of Kathiawar in western India. As the region was ravaged by famines, floods, and epidemics, Ismailis were advised by their Imam (spiritual leader) to move elsewhere in India or to East Africa. Shakar's family migrated first to Bombay and then when she was in her twenties to Calcutta, where she married a day laborer named Juma Qurban Ali Chagani. Mounting tensions between Hindus and Muslims during the late 1940s and early 1950s, as the British colonizers departed, meant she soon had to leave

Figure 1.2 Shakar Juma with her husband, Juma Qurban Ali Chagani, and four of their children; Farida is seated on the floor. Shakar is pregnant with her fifth child. Dhaka, 1962.
Courtesy of Farida Khoja.

Calcutta as well. This time, Shakar and Juma settled in Dhaka in East Pakistan (Figures 1.2 and 1.3). Juma found work at a chocolate factory, while Shakar did odd jobs. In addition to caring for their own four children, the couple was also responsible for Juma's three younger siblings and his father. When Juma passed away of tuberculosis in 1963—while Shakar was pregnant with their fifth child—she suddenly had to care for the entire household. An Ismaili woman from her jamatkhana helped her find employment as a cook and housekeeper. Another, in 1965, facilitated young Farida's admission to an Ismaili girls' hostel. When in 1971 Shakar fled from Dhaka to Karachi with her children, including Farida, the cycle of vulnerability repeated—but so did, as we have seen, the cycle of care from members of her faith community. These acts of support reinforced the sense of affinity Shakar felt with other Ismailis and the reassurance

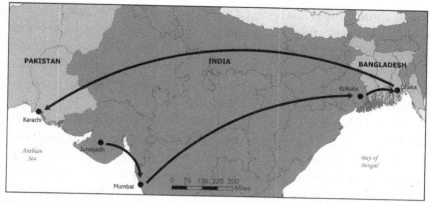

Figure 1.3 Shakar Juma's movements between 1930 and 1971: successive displacements across the region due to poverty and war; map shows present-day boundaries and place names.

she drew from her own faith: "*Shukar Mawla* (thanks to our Lord)," says eighty-one-year-old Shakar, who now resides in Karachi.[1]

Modern secular observers might interpret Farida's efforts for Ismaili newcomers arriving in Atlanta as "paying forward" the generosity of those who helped her family through multiple displacements and forced migrations. But this framing fails to capture the spiritual and worldmaking dimensions of her actions. Perhaps slightly irritated at the need to elaborate on something so obvious, she explains to me, "It is *seva*. It is *khidmat*. This is what it means to be a part of the Ismaili *jamat*. It is how we make it possible for other Ismailis to find a place here [in the United States]." *Seva* is a Sanskrit word used to express devotion and service to a supreme deity with whom the devotee has a personal relationship, and the word *khidmat* is used by speakers of the Urdu language to express similar sentiments.[2] Among contemporary Ismaili Muslims of South Asian descent, *seva* and *khidmat* denote service to the Imam as well as to individuals and institutions of the Ismaili community and beyond. Farida's invocation of *seva/khidmat* to describe her care for Zarina thus points to a set of spiritual commitments that exceed the idea of serial reciprocity conveyed by "paying it forward." We instead see an ethical act of support that is set apart from expectation of exchange or calculation of ends. It is deemed virtuous in and of itself. Such everyday acts of care, from Farida's perspective, help new migrants find a foothold in unfamiliar environments (Atlanta) while reinforcing affiliation with the

Ismaili community ("This is what it means to be a part of the Ismaili *jamat*"). Ordinary ethics like these that respond to the experience of displacement are highly visible in the life stories of the Ismailis I consider in this project. But as I hope to demonstrate in the pages that follow, it has been the ongoing and pervasive exercise of ordinary ethics of care and support that has produced an Ismaili sociality beyond moments of crisis as well.

Farida is my mother. This book occasionally returns to her narrative but works more broadly to uncover the stories of care, help, and support that dozens of Ismaili Muslim women have extended to coreligionists against the dislocating effects of wars and forced migration. My interlocutors fall into two cohorts: one that fled East Pakistan in the early 1970s due to civil war, and the other that was forced to leave East Africa during the same time, when Idi Amin expelled Asians from Uganda and anti-Asian sentiments intensified in Kenya and Tanzania.[3] Although separated by thousands of miles of land and sea prior to these dislocations, the women in these cohorts share not only a religious tradition (Shia Ismaili) but also ethnicity and languages, as they trace their ancestors to the Sindh-Gujarat region in India. On leaving their homes in East Pakistan and East Africa, looking to resettle in West Pakistan (today's Pakistan), England, Canada, and the United States, they began the individual and collective work of navigating the unfamiliar environments of new places. I follow the trajectories of these women and contemplate larger questions about the formation of religious community, women's care practices, and placemaking after displacement.[4]

Religious community is a repository of meaning and a marker of identity for many individuals, but it is not a given. Vered Amit and Brian Alleyne have suggested that we explain *how* community is empirically formed.[5] To offer the help she does to new Ismaili arrivals, for example, Farida had to learn to navigate the healthcare system of DeKalb County. She investigated the kinds of documents the clinic would require to provide financial assistance to patients. She began printing copies of forms and carrying them in her purse so she would have the right paperwork handy when someone in jamatkhana asked for help with healthcare. She maintains active connections with the clinic staff by remembering to give them gifts at Christmas. She makes phone calls to schedule appointments, drives fellow Ismailis to the clinic, and translates between Gujarati and English. She even learned some words in Farsi to communicate with new arrivals from Afghanistan. She listens intently to the women who come to her with their problems and provides emotional care in the process. And she offers these forms of support on days when she has also, as usual, sacrificed her sleep to clean the jamatkhana after morning prayers—sharing in a gendered practice to care for ritual space that, as we will see in the chapters that follow, has been central to building a sense of community for displaced Ismailis.

Such forms of care produce what Todne Thomas calls "spiritualized socialities" or communities that are bound together through a shared orientation to the Divine.[6] Relationalities like these can bridge and even transcend ethnic differences. Their salience is heightened in moments of dislocation as forced migration disrupts the bonds people enjoy to a fixed place, crucial to a sense of self and for accessing support. Anthropologist John Gray therefore sees the aftermath of displacement as a "predicament of emplacement."[7] Care activities like Farida's are particularly visible in these moments, not least because they have an emplacing effect. But when we study such practices of support undertaken by numerous women over time, we uncover a collective record that has bound Ismailis into a spiritual sociality or *jamat*, intergenerationally.[8]

While women's labor of assembling community is central to maintaining religio-spiritual lifeworlds, this labor remains underappreciated and in its routine forms can be largely invisible.[9] Stories of support offered by women like Farida (and by those who cared for her own family half a century earlier) circulate primarily as family memories; they are not considered worthy of archiving within national or even religious histories. Relatedly, studies of refugee placemaking often narrow in on the contractual obligations between states and citizens and on the resources that the state or other agencies provide to displaced people.[10] Less attention has been paid to the labor that displaced people themselves undertake to rebuild their communities. The tasks of social, cultural, and spiritual reproduction—often performed by women—are comparatively absent as concerns of workforce participation take prominence.[11] By attending to the tasks of community formation as they occur in the context of displacement, we can deepen our understanding of the refugee experience; we can also use the heightened visibility of care work in displacement to better understand how that work supports spiritual communities during more ordinary circumstances. Indeed, while migrant placemaking is often about subjective attachment to a physical site, the book expands this definition to include a consideration of attachment to people and symbols as well, and situates those placemaking activities within the framework of spiritual acts that have more broadly defined and sustained the Ismaili sociality.

The acts of care that I archive in this book are not inevitable: Farida was not required to give Zarina a ride to the clinic, nor, two decades earlier, did the woman who took Farida to the DMV to get her license have to do so. While my interlocutors share ethnic and cultural ties, their expressions of care for each other cannot be reduced to these bonds, frayed after decades of living in the cities of the United States and Canada. Women's actions instead spring from a shared religious covenant. Scholars have used the lens of spiritual kinship to describe such practices of religious community formation.[12] This lens is indeed helpful here, as the Ismaili Imams have frequently guided their followers to think of each other as brothers and sisters. Younger Ismailis often call older community members "uncle" and "aunty" even when not biologically related to them. But aside from these linguistic significations, we find another mode of subjectivation in the language of ethical conduct (kindness, care, support, help), as evident in the following directive (*farman*) from the Imam that Ismailis regularly hear in jamatkhanas:

> I remind my spiritual children, here in India but [also] around the world, that you are brothers and sisters. Help where help is needed. Be generous where generosity is needed. Be strong where strength is needed. Be kind where kindness is needed. So that you build within the *jamat*, a sense, a strong sense, of brotherhood and sisterhood. So that no *murid* (committed initiate of the Imam) feels isolated, feels lost. Every *murid* should know that he and she has thousands of brothers and sisters around the world, so no *murid* is alone. And, in addition to which I am with all my *murids* around the world.[13]

Directives like these assert a normative force, keeping Ismailis orientated to each other. To explore the making and remaking of Ismaili sociality, then, entails examining a range of voluntary ethical acts that involve sharing time, knowledge, and material resources.

There is an ongoingness and ordinariness to this ethical conduct that extends beyond current analyses of Muslim charity and religiosity, which, as Amira Mittermaier observes, are dominated by "the hegemonic paradigm of self-cultivation."[14] Ismailis practice their *din* (faith) both by working on their selves (their souls, bodies, thoughts) *and* by working intersubjectively to create community (cooking meals for coreligionists, visiting the sick, offering rides, storytelling). Of course, such modes of religious intersubjectivity are not distinct to Ismailis; Muslims globally engage in ethical community making. But unlike other Muslim groups, within Ismailis, the Imam acts as a centripetal force that gives this community a distinct route to ethical action. The Ismaili landscape of religiosity has a strong collectivist impetus that is sustained intergenerationally and transnationally, due in part to the Imam's continuous guidance on interpersonal ethical conduct for community making. Identifying an Ismaili ethics of care is not to argue that the community's particular understanding of spiritual obligation, honed in the diaspora, is wholly distinct from modes of care developed in other communities. It is, rather, a close examination of one manner of living a Muslim life in which members of other communities—or the scholars who study them—may identify points of commonality as well as difference.

In the book I cover a large range of women's activities, but reproductive work—such as cleaning jamatkhanas, cooking during religious festivals, assisting an elder with a bedpan at a refugee camp, and washing ritual objects—is a recurring theme. Even though such work is necessary for the propagation of society, it is generally viewed as a property of women's biology and is therefore under- or devalued. Marxist feminists have consequently regarded housework as a quintessential site for gendered exploitation and have sought to demonstrate its value by moving it into the realm of waged labor.[15] Instead of pointing out the economic value of women's work for the *jamat* (although there is certainly a basis for that), I reconceptualize this work in spiritual and relational terms, aligning with those feminist scholars who refuse to reduce women's work to productivist logics.[16] I mobilize a different logic altogether, viewing women's reproductive activities as producing sociability, repairing past trauma, and furnishing continuity from one generation to the next. This approach retains "care" as a useful framework for interpreting relationalities, kinships, and coalitions previously excluded from view. The challenge for me, then, is to emphasize the salience of care work, and the importance of those who undertake it, while also pointing out the circumstances and scenarios when it becomes a site of subjugation.

Ultimately, *Rebuilding Community* reframes the ordinary ethical practices of displaced women as the concrete spatiotemporal events that form religious community. In the process, we also learn about placemaking after displacement and re-evaluate care work. The book flashes back to their ancestors (chapter 2) and pays a visit to their descendants (chapter 6) to trace the transmutation of an Ismaili ethics of care. This broader view shows us that the *jamat*—and religious community, more generally—is not a given, but an ethical relation that is maintained daily and intergenerationally through everyday acts of care.

The Diasporic Movements of Ismailis

As Shia, my interlocutors belong to a religious minority that makes up less than fifteen percent of the world's Muslim population. As Ismailis, they are a marginal presence within this Shia minority. As displaced people, they are often unwelcome and pathologized as a drain on the resources of host countries. They are thus *multiply* minoritized—their lives strained by gender and minoritarian religion, and further constrained by their experience of displacement and racism in host countries. But in contrast to the more conventional articulation of displaced people as dependent and passive subjects, I follow bell hooks in reframing their position on the margins as a site of knowledge, possibility, and relationality.[17] I shift my attention to their rebuilding efforts in order to offer a multidimensional look into their lives—one that escapes easy categorizations of victim/agent or traumatized/empowered.

The Shia Muslim minority to which my interlocutors belong emerged in the seventh century following the death of Prophet Muhammad. A small group of the Prophet's followers sided with his son-in-law, Ali ibn Abi Talib, as the rightful legatee (*wasi*) to the Prophet. The majority favored the Prophet's old friend, Abu Bakr, who ultimately took on the leadership of Muslims as the first caliph. Ali's followers continued to seek guidance from him and his successors, and consolidated over time as the Shi'at Ali (party of Ali, also known as Shia), while the majoritarian interpretation of Islam coalesced into what is known today as the Ahl al-Sunna wa al-Jama'a (People of the Sunna and the Community) or Sunni. Within the Shia minority, several smaller groups emerged as schisms developed over rightful successors. One such major division occurred in the eighth century when, after the death of the then Imam, Ja'far al-Sadiq, one group pledged allegiance to his son Ismail while another followed his other son, Musa al-Kazim; the former would come to be known as the Ismailis. The Ismailis later experienced another schism over succession and split further into two groups, Musta'lian and Nizari. My study focuses on the Nizari line of Ismailis, estimated today to be twelve to fifteen million in number and spread globally.[18] Their present Imam, Karim al-Husseini Aga Khan IV, is the forty-ninth Imam in direct succession from Prophet Muhammad. Today, Nizari Ismailis use "*jamat*" as a self-referential term to denote a deterritorialized, transnational, trans-ethnic, and trans-caste formation uniting individuals into a single sociality characterized by its allegiance to the Shia Ismaili Imam of the time. While Nizari Ismailis can be found in over twenty-five countries, in this book I focus on a *specific* cohort of Nizari Ismailis, the Khojas (even as I use "Ismaili" for shorthand), who trace their ancestors to western India, and study their displacement and diasporic journeys over the course of the twentieth century that brought them to North America.

From the eleventh century onward, the Nizari Ismaili Imams, located first in Egypt and then in Persia, sent out *dais* and *pirs* to various regions, including to the Indian subcontinent.[19] These emissaries explained Ismaili doctrines within local Indic theologies and philosophies, and referred to their teachings as *satpanth*, "the true path."[20] They composed *ginans* (hymns) in local languages to convey their message. The fifteenth-century *pir*, Sadr al-Din, conferred the title of *khwajah* (an honorific in Persian for lord or master)—modified over time to "Khoja"—to a group of his *satpanthi* followers and also established the first jamatkhana.[21] Over the course of centuries, Khojas settled in the Sindh-Gujarat corridor and absorbed various lower-caste groups.[22] They even developed an original script *Khwajah Sindhi* (or Khojki) that connected them to their Sindhi heritage.[23] Khojas continued to migrate within the region for different reasons: some Khojas, for instance, migrated from Sindh to Kuchchh in the sixteenth century to escape religious persecution;[24] others during the nineteenth century migrated to Bombay and thrived in the emerging mercantile economy; and others established extensive trade networks connecting Bombay and Karachi to Muscat and Zanzibar. These Khojas—the ancestors of my interlocutors—functioned socially as a caste (*jnat*) group, practiced endogamy, and had their own council of elders that oversaw administrative, financial, and social matters.[25] Whereas *satpanthi* practices could be understood within both Islamic and Indic doctrinal frameworks, and appealed to individuals from a wide range of social backgrounds, as the British Raj entrenched in India during the nineteenth century, the colonizers demanded more clarity about the religious affiliations of their subject population. Colonial practices of governance such as the census surveys compelled Indians to identify themselves as either "Muslim" or "Hindu." It is in this social milieu, and over a period of some 150 years, that the identity of *satpanthi* Khojas transformed from a group that could be simultaneously understood as a caste, a trader's guild, and a *panth* to a distinctly Muslim *jamat*: Shia Ismaili Muslims.[26]

It is estimated that in the 1860s there were about 1,000 Khoja families in Bombay; 2,000 families in Sindh; 5,000 in Kathiawar; 450 in the East African coastal region, mainly Zanzibar; and 400 in Muscat.[27] Khojas residing in the regions of Kuchchh and Kathiawar (today's Gujarat) were engaged in subsistence farming or worked as petty traders and farm laborers.[28] Famines from 1876 to 1877 and again from 1895 to 1902 hit western India hard and significantly weakened the economic prospects of Khojas there.[29] These were only the most recent episodes; famines in 1812–1813 and 1833–1835 had previously precipitated migration out of rural Kuchchh toward urban Kathiawar and onward to Bombay.[30] Such crises combined with epidemics and increasing commercial activity in the Indian Ocean created the conditions for greater numbers of Khoja Ismailis to head to the Arabian Gulf, the Swahili coast, Gwadar, and Rangoon (see Figure 1.4 for trading routes).

In the Ismaili collective memory, it is remembered that Imam Hasan Ali Shah Aga Khan I (d. 1881) instructed Ismailis in western India to move to other regions of India and to the Gulf.[31] His son, Imam Aga Ali Shah Aga Khan II (d. 1885), and later his grandson, Imam Sultan Mahomed Shah Aga Khan III (d. 1947), advised them to migrate to East Africa as a way to escape the hardships of western India.[32] While there is evidence of Khojas in East Africa as early as the twelfth century, it is only in the nineteenth century that they became a sizable group.[33] When the Omani Sultan moved his capital from Muscat to Zanzibar in 1840, Asian merchants—including Khojas—who were already actively trading in the Arabian Gulf, followed suit to benefit from increased trade on the Swahili coast. In time, established Khoja merchants facilitated the move of other Khoja Ismailis by recruiting them to work for their expanding enterprises. Even larger numbers of Asians migrated to East Africa after the British established a protectorate in the 1890s over the territories that would later become Uganda and Kenya, and after the First World War over the future Tanzania. British colonizers encouraged Asians to migrate to the region as indentured laborers, artisans, and clerks to support railway and bridge projects, act as small traders, or serve as staff for the colonial civil service. By the early twentieth century, thousands of Indians, including Ismailis, had thus made East Africa their home.[34]

Relocation within India became easier when the Great Indian Peninsular Railway opened its first passenger line in 1853. Cities, especially Bombay, offered more economic opportunities, and already-established Khoja traders supported newcomers. Rashida Moolji (b. 1945) recalls that her family settled in the Dongri area because of its proximity to the Old Harbour and its goods

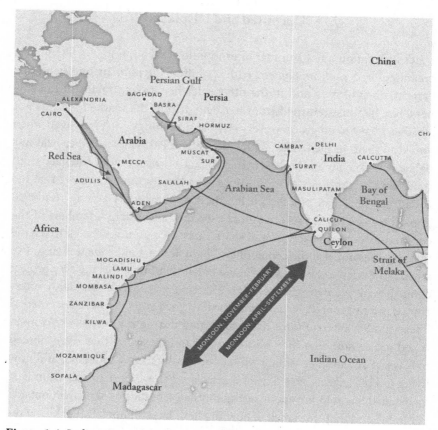

Figure 1.4 Indian Ocean, showing trade routes and monsoon winds.
Map by Willie Ryan, 2016 (used with permission), National Museum of African Art, Smithsonian Institution.

depot.[35] Newcomers still trying to find a footing in the city would work at shops by day and sleep in the Kandi Mola jamatkhana by night.[36] Yet prospects for long-term growth were limited even in major Indian cities; some young men thought they could earn more in East Africa. They thus headed to East African coastal towns such as Zanzibar, Lamu, or Mombasa, remaining in those cities or moving inland. After settling in, they often returned to India to marry Ismaili women and brought them back to Africa. Partition-related violence in India during the 1940s and 1950s, as well as the expulsion of Asians from Uganda and the Pakistani civil war in the 1970s, exposed Ismailis to precarity once again. They fled the regions they had made home, sometimes for generations, and headed to North America, Europe, and West Pakistan.

Uprooted and Displaced

I met Rehmat on a hot summer afternoon in Aliabad, Karachi. She wore a cream-colored *shalwar kameez* with a chiffon *dupatta*. In one hand she carried a bag of okra and in the other a leather wallet, fraying at the corners. She had just returned from her daily trip to the market: "In this hot weather I have to do grocery every day because things don't last, even when you keep them in the fridge."[37] The intensity of Pakistan's summer heat was palpably visible on our bodies, materializing as sweat on our foreheads and stains on our clothing. We sat near a fan in the community center that the Ismaili Council had established for the neighborhood's elderly residents. The center is open for several hours each day, and elderly members of the community come to exercise and share snacks. Rehmat was quick to tell me that she does not visit the center often: "I am not that old." She was sixty-five when I interviewed her. As I explained to her that I was working on a project about Ismaili women who fled East Pakistan in 1971, she suddenly interrupted me and roared, "*Hamain ukhar diya gaya tha!* (We were uprooted!)" These sudden interruptions happened often during my fieldwork. Women urged me to note that they "did *not* want to leave," that they were "forced to leave." S.A., another Ismaili woman originally from Chittagong and now living in Los Angeles, was sixteen years old when violence broke out in East Pakistan.[38] She told me about seeing mutilated bodies on the street outside her home and that "the smell of burning flesh has still not left [her]." She repeated, in English, "I was displaced. I was displaced," and when speaking of her early days in Karachi she recalled, "I did not feel at home." Laila Bandali, who fled Uganda in 1972 when Idi Amin expelled Asians, likewise stressed that her family did not want to emigrate: "Uganda was our home."[39] A better understanding of the women's vehement objections to these long-past dislocations begins with some political context.

Fleeing East Pakistan

When British rule over India ended in 1947, Pakistan was founded as two wings—East and West Pakistan—separated by a thousand miles of territory assigned to India (Figure 1.5). Although East Pakistanis outnumbered West Pakistanis, it was West Pakistan that wielded power as the center of government, defense, and industry; East Pakistan was underrepresented in

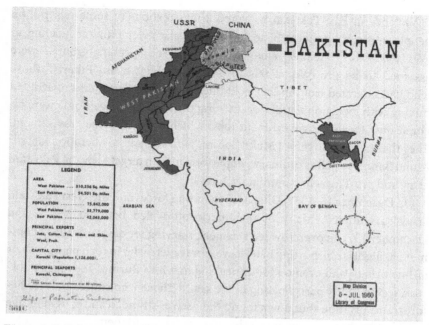

Figure 1.5 Pakistan ca. 1950s.
Source: Geography and Map Division, Library of Congress.

both the civil service and the army. Early governments continued to invest heavily in West Pakistan, causing the eastern half of the country to trail behind in economic development. Disillusionment and resentment grew among East Pakistanis, furthered by West Pakistan's refusal to recognize their language, Bengali, as a national language. These feelings intensified when the central government delayed relief following the November 1970 cyclone, which according to some estimates caused over 230,000 deaths.[40] The underlying fissures finally erupted into open conflict when, after the general elections of 1971, the government refused to hand over the mandate to Sheikh Mujibur Rahman, a politician from East Pakistan who had won an absolute majority of national seats. In March 1971, Rahman's East Pakistan–based party, the Awami League, declared independence and established the People's Republic of Bangladesh. The central state in West Pakistan immediately mobilized the army to quell what they saw as a rebellion. Conflict ensued and relations between east and west deteriorated further in December, when India intervened on behalf of Bangladesh, turning a civil war into an international one.

Violence in East Pakistan triggered a mass exodus of some ten million people, most of whom went to India, with a smaller number heading to West Pakistan.[41] Ismailis—along with other Urdu-speaking groups—were assumed to be pro–West Pakistan. Popularly known as "Biharis," those who had migrated from India (including Ismailis) to East Pakistan avoided mixing with local populations or learning the local language; some were favored over locals for government jobs, which created further resentment. They thus became targets of Mukti Bahini, the Bangladeshi liberation force.[42] Mukti Bahini as well as ordinary people were in turn targeted by the Pakistani army and pro-Pakistan paramilitary forces.

On December 16, 1971, Dhaka fell to Indian forces and the West Pakistani army surrendered. Many of my interlocutors fled between March and December 1971 in overcrowded steamers, starving for days on end; on commercial flights transporting betel leaves for traders who in turn paid for their airline tickets; and even on foot, sneaking first into Burma. They recall horrors, seeing "body parts floating in the sea."[43] Those who could not leave before transportation shut down found themselves stranded and sought refuge in jamatkhanas for weeks as riots happened all around them.

While scholars have examined the experience of displaced people who ended up at camps located on the Bangladesh-India border, less attention has been paid to those who fled to West Pakistan.[44] This project begins to reconstruct their story. My oral history interviews suggest that a few thousand Ismailis arrived in West Pakistan during the 1970–1974 period.[45] Many had relatives already established in the region who could support them, but at the height of the relocation numerous displaced families were accommodated in camps set up at various jamatkhanas in Karachi. My grandmother's was one such family; they spent weeks at a camp in the Garden East jamatkhana. Although the government initiated some efforts to support the refugees, primary responsibility for the new arrivals was left to private institutions. A volunteer-run Ismaili group, the Rehabilitation Committee for Ismailis from Uganda, Burma, and East Pakistan, provided subsidized housing to displaced families in the neighborhood of Karimabad and surrounding areas (Figure 1.6).[46] The committee settled over thirty-five families there, assisted them with rent for several months, helped them get their legal documents in order, located jobs for adults, and enrolled children in schools.

Figure 1.6 Y Building in Karimabad, Karachi, where several displaced families from East Pakistan, including Shakar Juma's, were resettled by the Ismaili volunteers.

Photo by author, 2020.

Fleeing East Africa

As noted earlier, Khoja Ismailis had been in East Africa much longer than in East Pakistan. This project takes as its point of departure the late nineteenth century when the British established a protectorate over Uganda, Zanzibar, and Kenya and would soon create one over Tanganyika. The British colonial government in East Africa treated the religiously and ethnically diverse Asian migrant group, which included Hindus, Sikhs, and Muslims, as a single entity and instituted policies to segregate them socially and economically from Africans and Europeans.[47] Domains of activity from education and health to farming, property ownership, and professional occupations were all organized along racial lines. Colonial policies permitted Asians to purchase cash crops from African farmers and sell them to the British for processing, and in turn sell goods imported from Britain to Africans. As anthropologist Mahmood Mamdani explains, colonial racial-economic policy was designed to restrict Africans to the agricultural sector and keep them away from the marketplace while allocating trading functions to an alien community that could easily be controlled.[48] Asians thus acted as middlemen in the trade between the British and Africans. Favorable treatment of one group over others in the service of capital is consistent with British colonial practice in other contexts too, including Europe. British racial capitalism relied on creating divisions among populations whose interests might otherwise, logically, lead them to work together against the ruling colonial regime.[49] Through trade licenses, administrative appointments, and land grants, English ruling elites enticed the Asian working class to identify with them. Accordingly, Asians resisted social commingling with Africans, often self-segregated by religious and communal allegiances, and emulated British social mores (more on this in chapter 2). British policies thus created a virtual Asian monopoly over business enterprise and produced social divisions, which local populations resented.[50] This resentment coalesced with movements for independence after the Second World War to create widespread anti-Asian sentiment and racial conflict.

In the 1960s, Zanzibar, Uganda, Tanganyika, and Kenya secured independence from the British, but conflicts ensued between Asians and Africans. In 1963, Zanzibar achieved independence from the British and governing functions passed onto the Sultan and his mainly Arab government, which was overthrown a year later by local revolutionaries. In the conflict, over twenty thousand Arabs and Asians were killed. Ismailis took shelter in the jamatkhana and fled in the ensuing years as land was nationalized and forced marriages between Asians and Africans became a pathway to racial integration. In Uganda, racial tensions escalated with Idi Amin's takeover in 1971. Amin, then a major general in Milton Obote's government, organized a military coup with British and Israeli support.[51] On August 4, 1972, he announced that all Asians would be required to leave Uganda within ninety days. There were, at the time, approximately eighty thousand Asians in the country.[52] Those who held British protected persons' or British subjects' passports headed to the United Kingdom, but others with Ugandan citizenship had their papers confiscated and became stateless.[53] Many Ismailis were part of the latter group as they had opted to become citizens of Uganda on their Imam's advice.[54] In fact, many of my interlocutors insisted that Africa was their home; they were second- or third-generation Africans and knew no other.[55]

In the years leading up to the expulsion, Asians in Uganda were harassed, kidnapped, and even tortured and killed. These anti-Asian attacks intensified during the ninety-day expulsion period.[56] Ultimately, more than 50,000 Asians fled Uganda between the day the expulsion order was issued and the November deadline; others had left the country earlier. The United Kingdom admitted 29,000 Ugandan Asians; 1,500 settled in the United States; and more than 7,000 were accepted as refugees by the Canadian government.[57] Smaller numbers headed to Australia, Austria, Belgium, Denmark, the Netherlands, New Zealand, Norway, Sweden, Switzerland, India, and Pakistan. Remaining behind in Uganda were those who lacked proper documentation to leave. In chapter 3 we will meet one of these "stateless" Asians, Laila Datoo, who lost her Ugandan citizenship as a result of Idi Amin's order. Some 3,600 newly stateless individuals were evacuated by the United Nations High Commissioner for Refugees after the deadline passed, flown to transit accommodations in European cities, and then settled in other countries. Asians were permitted by the Ugandan government to take with them only what they could carry, which often equated to two suitcases per person, plus fifty pounds in cash per family.[58] Their businesses, homes, and cars were confiscated without compensation and distributed to the dictator's favorites.

Like Uganda, Kenya and Tanzania had also seen Africanization fervor as those nations transitioned to independence, although neither country explicitly expelled Asians. The Arusha Declaration of 1967 committed Tanzania to socialism and self-reliance, a commitment that manifested first in the nationalization of banks, grain-milling plants, and manufacturing companies, and then in a government takeover of commercial buildings, including houses purchased as investments.[59] Among those I interviewed from Tanzania, many recalled losing their properties and businesses at this time. Others spoke of being overlooked for promotions as the nation shifted toward fostering the success of Africans through Africanization of the civil service and state apparatus.[60] Yet others shared incidents of harassment and bullying and recalled a general atmosphere of fear.[61] Historian Ned Bertz estimates that about half of the Muslim migrant population in Tanzania left during this time.[62] The experience of Asians in Kenya was similar. Like Uganda's, the Kenyan government passed a Trade Licensing Act to restrict the operation of non-African-owned businesses.[63] Many Asians lost their companies, were unable to find other ways to earn a living, and left Kenya as a result.[64] In the book, I use the term "displaced people" to denote both refugees and forced migrants, signaling the direct as well as indirect forms of expulsion that my interlocutors experienced. By the early 1970s, thousands of Ismailis from East Africa found themselves uprooted and displaced, often with no assets or savings.

Placemaking after Displacement

Within the limited scholarship on displaced Ismailis, we have seen a disproportionate emphasis on the experience of those who left East Africa. In contrast, we know little about the Ismailis who fled East Pakistan in the same period. One reason for this, perhaps, is that later in life some of these displaced East Africans, particularly men, published memoirs or shared their stories in other public fora. Yet whether they left East Africa or East Pakistan, Ismailis found themselves in unfamiliar environments in West Pakistan (today's Pakistan), England, Canada, and the United States.[65] In new cities they met fellow Ismailis at makeshift jamatkhanas; spoke Gujarati, Kuchchhi, and Urdu with each other; shared news of job possibilities; cooked heritage foods; and participated in religious rituals. Their children grew up together and later in life would look for common threads running through the patchwork of their parents' experiences. By combining the two groups in this study I both signal their intermingling in diasporic contexts and harken back to their common descent as Khojas from western India. This move is not meant to flatten out differences between Ismailis from East Africa and those from East Pakistan. While both experienced traumatic expulsions, for many of my East Pakistani interlocutors it took decades before they found stability. In contrast, many of my East African interlocutors report comparatively smooth transitions given their higher levels of educational attainment and facility in the English language prior to displacement. There is certainly heterogeneity within these cohorts too: differences in individual life circumstances, from family support to age, created marked disparities in their experience of displacement. While acknowledging the specificity of my interlocutors' experience, I consider them together as well for they reveal patterns of what was possible at a given conjunction of time and place, and as such they represent a collective situation of displaced Ismailis and their strivings for emplacement.

In the chapters that follow I will often refer to my interlocutors simply as Ismaili (instead of Shia Nizari Khoja Ismaili Muslims) and speak about Ismaili ethics and practices, but I remind readers that my arguments are not generalizable to all Ismailis or even to all Khoja Ismailis. What I offer is a look at the practices of care—and an articulation of an ethic of care—of a specific cohort that take shape within the historical trajectories of displacement and migratory routes recounted in the previous section.

Gender, Religion, and Placemaking

Studies about migrant and refugee placemaking often focus on the modifications that displaced people make to the built environment, establishing spaces of worship, commerce, and community centers.[66] Viewed through this lens, diasporic Ismailis have carved out a place for themselves by establishing jamatkhanas and social welfare institutions. Today we find prominent jamatkhanas that announce the presence of Ismailis in the several cities to which they migrated, including Dar es Salaam, Nairobi, Houston, Atlanta, Toronto, and Burnaby, British Columbia. Some of these jamatkhanas have acquired an unofficial ambassadorial status and have become hubs for connecting Ismailis to local communities as well as to governing bodies. These structures serve as concrete representations of Ismailis in urban landscapes. The East African landscape remains marked by additional architectural displays, including numerous Aga Khan Schools, Aga Khan Hospitals, and Aga Khan Sports Centers. In Toronto, Wynford Drive houses the majestic Aga Khan Museum. Ismailis have also claimed space by hosting Partnership Walks across major American and Canadian cities to raise funds for the Aga Khan Foundation, an Imamat agency that works to alleviate poverty in developing countries. Ismaili business owners often exhibit religious icons such as photographs of the Imam at their workplaces, and some even use naming conventions that mark their establishments as Ismaili—my interlocutors, for example, recall enjoying *bhajias* (vegetable fritters) at a hotel in Nairobi known as the Ismailia Hotel.[67] These are all examples of placemaking where built structures and material objects as well as public performances declare and facilitate diasporic belonging.

I take particular interest, however, in the more hidden and sometimes intangible practices of placemaking, focusing specifically on women's care for coreligionists. Consider the story of my interlocutor G.V.[68] When the Ugandan expulsion decree was announced in 1972, Ismailis, like other Asians, scrambled to secure travel documents and apply for refugee status. Those in rural towns traveled to Kampala as the embassies and airport were located there. But they often found themselves without housing or other support. G.V. remembers hosting many Ismailis in her apartment in Kampala while they waited for proper documentation or for flights. She recalls cooking for them, making their beds, cleaning up after them, and explaining to them how to stay safe after sunset, when she would be away from home managing her husband's shop. Her husband was a well-known member of the Ismaili Council for Uganda and had taken on the responsibility of helping Ismailis obtain proper documentation; G.V. managed the shop so he could help other Ismailis. While G.V.'s husband's efforts are known widely, given his position in the Council, G.V.'s are preserved only in the memories of her family and the people she helped.

G.V.'s endeavors in Uganda, or Farida's more recent efforts in Atlanta that we saw at the beginning of the chapter, are routine (cooking, cleaning, giving someone a ride, managing a shop) and therefore remain hidden. This book extends the concept of placemaking beyond the construction of physical infrastructures to include such ordinary acts of care that sustain connection among people and to ideas; it considers acts of care undertaken by women during flight and in host countries. These care tasks include activities for the biological reproduction of the community as well as those that facilitate its religio-cultural reproduction—such as telling stories about the Imam's miracles or writing cookbooks to transmit Ismaili food cultures. As noted earlier, the circumstances of displacement and migration help us see women's efforts more clearly. This book thus joins recent scholarly interventions that emphasize displaced women's agentic practices during flight and in asylum. Cindy Horst's study of Somali refugees at the Dadaab camps in Kenya is a case in point.[69] Horst elaborates on the networks of mutual aid that emerged in the camps to show "a level of agency, of transformative power and choice, that is not easily associated with refugees."[70] Likewise, Ma Vang reframes Hmong refugee women as carriers of communal histories and place-based knowledges.[71] These studies reclaim women's stories, embodiment, and practices to rewrite history and excavate refugee epistemologies. Relatedly, scholars are also emphasizing the salience of religious practice and places of worship in migrant and refugee placemaking. Whereas Greg Noble and Thomas Tweed explore how spaces of worship provide visibility and feelings of embeddedness to migrants, Manuel Vásquez and Kim Knott do the same by focusing on prayers and rituals.[72] We learn from Sarah Tobin about Syrian refugee women's mobilization of Islamic historical narratives to make sense of their exile, and Alisa Perkins's work shows how diasporic Muslims in Detroit use public and political space to fashion belonging.[73]

Rebuilding Community contributes to this emergent scholarly nexus of gender, religion, and placemaking not only by examining the built environments that displaced Ismailis have constructed but also by underlining the spiritual and sensory dimensions of placemaking. My interlocutors do not perceive cleaning jamatkhanas and cooking for coreligionists through a lens of gendered exploitation but rather regard these activities as blessings, privileges, and opportunities offered by the Imam. Because this book mobilizes nonproductivist logics, I am interested primarily in highlighting the intergenerational continuity, meaning, and joy that emerge in and through women's practices of care. Such an understanding of reproductive work underplays (although it does not deny) its usual connection with exploitation; it instead recuperates such work by viewing it as a domain through which Ismaili women have historically made substantial contributions to the social reproduction of their religious community. It also posits care work as a life-giving activity that should be shared by both men and women. In chronicling the lives and tireless care activities of Ismaili women that resituate the *jamat* in new locations, this book then also gestures toward the longer genealogy of women's labor that has sustained Ismaili religio-social lifeworlds.

Writing Women into Modern Ismaili History

Yasmin Alibhai-Brown calls Ismailis a "people in motion . . . who settle but cautiously . . . a people who leave no trace . . . [a people with a] nomadic history . . . [a] roaming tribe."[74] When Alibhai-Brown talks about "a people in motion," she means Ismailis like herself who were pushed out of East Africa during the 1970s—but she is also describing the extended collective memory of a minority people who have, for centuries, remained on the move to avoid persecution. Historian Farhad Daftary describes Ismailis as "among the most ruthlessly persecuted minorities of the Muslim world."[75] That history of persecution has for centuries forced Ismailis into an underground existence where they conceal their religious identity.[76] And ongoing persecution—with its corollaries of mobility and secrecy—means that little has survived in the written record documenting the history of Ismailis. Further complicating the lack of an Ismaili-authored literature is the survival of an abundant corpus of polemical writing against premodern Ismailis. This material documents their status as a persecuted group but for obvious reasons is of dubious value for scholars seeking to better understand early Ismaili culture and experience. Modern scholarly work on Ismailis has thus unsurprisingly focused on correcting anti-Ismaili polemics and recuperating Ismaili history by translating extant texts, archiving the movements of the Imams and *dawa* activities, and tracing the development of Ismaili doctrines.[77] We still know little, however, about the lives of ordinary Ismailis.

Nevertheless, scholarship on the modern period is growing. Several ethnographic studies of Ismaili communities, particularly in Central Asia and Pakistan, are underway.[78] And scholars are documenting the transmutation of Ismaili identity, the community's religious texts, the Imams' efforts to build social governance institutions, and the changes the community has experienced as a result of migrations, increasing access to education, and encounters with anti-Brown racism in the diaspora.[79] Through memoirs and other vernacular writing by community members, numerous community stories are being preserved.[80] Much of this is still about the activities of community leaders, traders, and *dais*—all groups largely composed of men—and comparatively little about Ismaili women and particularly, working-class women.[81] The story of Ismaili migration to East Africa, for example, is told through the lens of the "Ismaili pioneers" or "uncrowned kings"—men who traveled from India to Zanzibar and benefited from their position in the colonial economy.[82] These "pioneers" often facilitated the journeys of other Ismailis to East Africa, offering them their first jobs or business opportunities. They show up in community histories as exemplars of determination and obedience to the Imam (for instance, one of the earliest issues of the community's magazine in the United Kingdom, *Ismaili Forum*, published in 1979, features an image of Varas Allidina Visram on the cover, and a later issue in the same year provides the migration account of a Mukhi Somani).[83] Gendered and class-bound as these histories may be, they have accomplished the crucial task of clarifying the broad sequence of events defining Ismaili life, a framework that other scholars can now build upon. This book attempts to do just that, by partially reconstructing Ismaili women's lives in East Africa and East Pakistan as recalled through oral history and archival research.[84]

In doing so, this book joins the more recent effort to examine the lived experience of displaced Ismaili women in the diaspora. Nazira Mawji has filled in details of how intergenerational knowledge transfer operates, looking at three generations of Ismaili women to demonstrate how this shared cultural resource enabled them to navigate patriarchal constraints in both East Africa and in the Canadian diaspora; Parin Dossa studies how racial politics have shaped the lives of displaced Shia women in Canada; and Anjoom Mukadam and Sharmina Mawani outline the settlement patterns of Ismaili women in Britain, emphasizing transformations of their cuisine and language.[85] Alia Paroo, Zayn Kassam, and Rashida Keshavjee, among others, focus on the gender-specific policies as well as colonial engagements of the Imams to consider their impact on women's lives.[86] This book builds on these studies of Ismaili women in the diaspora, examining the activities of a particular cohort to advance our understanding of Ismaili ethics and to note the contribution that women have been making all along in sustaining Ismaili socialities.

A focus on women does not mean a lack of consideration for men. On the contrary, many aspects of community making are shared. At the same time, men and women undertake different forms of gendered care and operate within different domains of religious and social life. David Henig's study of Muslims in Bosnia and Herzegovina in the aftermath of war is an apt illustration of these dynamics.[87] Henig shows that while both men and women engaged in acts of care for the next generation, their practices were influenced by gendered domains of activity: men showed their care by ensuring that inherited property stayed within their families, and women did so through their everyday reproductive work of sustaining life. Recall, while G.V. cooked for, and cleaned up after, Ismaili guests, her husband went to the Council office to draft legal papers for them. Paying attention to Ismaili women's practices of care thus does not mean that men did not perform care; it highlights the often different, undervalued, invisible contributions of women. In addition, while Ismaili men living in Europe and North America have published memoirs—and hence participated in public knowledge production—Ismaili women remember differently. We find their memories in fleeting conversations, food, and stories; we encounter them in the kitchens, in the waiting rooms of clinics, and, more recently, during long hours of oral history interviews. To revise our understanding of recent Ismaili pasts, we must therefore pay careful attention to women's domains of social activity and their modes of remembering. My aspiration here is not to produce a truer or morally superior account of Ismaili lifeworlds. Instead, it is to put women's memories into circulation so that new versions of shared pasts can be created, which will inevitably inform how the present and future are imagined.

In writing a book to archive women's placemaking activities, I hope to contribute to a wider discussion about religious community formation. In this project I have consequently paid less attention to the other side of the story: the kinds of relationalities and intimacies that are not maintained or those that are excluded. As Lauren Berlant reminds us, "Intimacy builds worlds; it creates spaces and usurps places meant for other kinds of relation."[88] While women's care practices maintain, perpetuate, and conserve spiritual intimacies among strangers, they can also—to stay with Berlant—replace and usurp. We will glimpse some of these choices and exclusions in chapter 6 as the second generation looks back on the practices of their mothers' generation, recognizing the presence of anti-Black racism among Ismailis in East Africa, the pressure to act as a "model minority" in the diaspora, and Ismaili participation in settler colonialism. These limitations exist in direct proximity to a generational experience of shared trauma and fear that reinforced connections with coreligionists and similarly affected Ismailis' relations to those outside the *jamat*. In part because this other side of the broader community's story (community exteriority) has been productively pursued by other scholars, it is not explored extensively in this book.[89]

Jamat as an Ethical Relation

Studies of community formation often emphasize boundary making or community exteriority.[90] This focus on the relation between inside and outside has similarly characterized the limited number of studies that examine Ismaili community formation; scholars have analyzed the juridical dimensions of the community that have defined who belongs to the group, as well as the discursive practices—such as education policies, engagement with colonial and postcolonial governments, and construction/building efforts—through which the community marks itself as different from others. I describe a different logic, that of community interiority, concerned with explicating those practices through which group affections, loyalties, and shared ethical imaginaries are produced. Such an exploration, according to religious studies scholars Todne Thomas, Asiya Malik, and Rose Wellman, is crucial if we want to understand the architecture of human societies that are bound together by a shared orientation to the Sacred.[91] The creation of such spiritualized societies is not a given. They rely on a range of voluntary acts of care and support that fashion relationality on an ongoing basis. It is such practices—and particularly those undertaken by women during and against wars and forced migration—that this book highlights. These practices— whether they are performed in times of crisis or not—in turn also produce the Ismaili subject as one who engages in such forms of care for coreligionists.

My approach to the study of religious sociality aligns with Don Seeman's exploration of relatedness in the context of Judaism, where religious kinship is contingent on conduct and commitment, and requires personal agency and voluntarism.[92] Rose Wellman's study of Shia Muslims in Iran similarly reiterates the salience of everyday acts of care in the making of religious community, even as Wellman centers the family as the site of ethical cultivation.[93] I build on these works by elaborating on the making of an Ismaili sociality by highlighting women's ordinary ethics of care and support. A focus on ethics enables us to see din (faith) in domains where it is not usually studied, including in supposedly nonreligious practices such as writing a cookbook or a memoir or helping a widow set up a duka (shop) when her husband passes away. The present Ismaili Imam has insisted that ethics bridge faith and world (din and dunya), and this study accordingly looks at ethics in practice.[94]

While my thinking is shaped by feminist theorizing on ethics of care, I look to the zone of religion for additional morally compelling pathways to care and to the practice of collective social life.[95] When my interlocutors explain the motivations for their actions, the Imam's directives on unity of community and support of its members appear as salient sources of guidance (in addition to ginans on sreva and Quranic notions of tawhid, as we will see). The Ismaili sociality that I describe has a strong collectivist impetus due in part to the central authority of the Shia Imam. It is helpful here to understand that obedience to the Imam is a key tenet of Shia Ismaili spirituality. In the Shia worldview, the Imam is understood to be a manifestation (mazhar) of God on earth and has God-given sanctity (walaya).[96] He has knowledge of both the exoteric/apparent (*zahir*) and the esoteric/hidden (*batin*) dimensions of reality. The Imam complements the Prophet's mission (*nabuwwat*) by teaching initiates the hidden spiritual meaning (*tawil*) of the Revelation. Thus, for Ismailis, the Imam is a focal point of devotion, prayers, and obedience. When the Imam urges his followers to support the weakest member of the *jamat*, to be united, to show generosity, or to engage in mutual support, the statements are understood as directives and not optional practices, as my interlocutor Dilshad Sadruddin repeatedly emphasized to me: "When a *farman* from Imam arrives, that's it, you must follow it."[97] The Constitution of Shia Ismailis, first ordained by the present Imam in 1986, clarifies that the unconditional obedience that we see in Dilshad's comments is due to her spiritual bond with the Imam: "The authority of the Imam in the Ismaili Tariqah is testified by *bayah* (oath) by the *murid* (initiate) to the Imam which is the act of acceptance by the *murid* of the permanent spiritual bond between the Imam and the *murid*. This allegiance unites all Ismaili Muslims worldwide in their loyalty, devotion and obedience to the Imam within the Islamic concept of universal brotherhood."[98] I therefore read my interlocutors' practices as expressing an ethic of care for community that is uniquely Ismaili in its motivations if not necessarily in the service tasks it motivates.

This is not to say that my interlocutors rationalize all their actions by reference to Islam. Indeed, other sources of moral guidance—encounters with other religious traditions and practitioners (like the Lutheran Church members who showed kindness by sponsoring some newly arrived Ismailis in Indiana in the 1970s) or the gifts or sympathetic words received from a non-Ismaili neighbor—also have a place in framing Ismaili women's ethical practices. The idiosyncratic dimensions of everyday living also influence them.[99] It is helpful therefore to understand the Ismaili ethics practiced by my interlocutors not as delinked from everyday life, Indic intellectual traditions, and other moral frameworks, but instead as intersecting with them as sources for reflection and action. We saw an example of this in the beginning of this chapter when Farida mobilized the concept of *seva*, shared by multiple Indic religious traditions, as a heuristic to understand the Imam's *farmans* on voluntary service. Recognizing this dense landscape of moral guidance does not preclude observing that certain pronouncements—such as the Imam's *farmans*—take discursive dominance in many of my interlocutors' lives. What this broader approach offers is a possibility of recognizing Islam as an overwhelming presence in women's lives while not reducing everything they do to a single explanatory framework.

I thus join anthropologists of religion who study the lives of ordinary people as ethical subjects.[100] My approach departs, however, from the direction advanced by anthropologist Webb Keane, who argues that monotheistic religious traditions tend to objectify ethics, that is, produce a set of generalized moral principles to guide practitioners, and in doing so necessarily abstract ethics from everyday life.[101] That interpretation would imply a gap between the abstract moral code and the particularistic everyday life a believer is supposed to live under its guidance. What if, instead of accepting that there exists a gap between everyday living and generalized religious morality, we recognize these as co-constitutive and entangled? Moral codes derived from religious resources such as the Quran or the Imam's *farmans* still require interpretation, judgment, and negotiation, which are all particularistic endeavors that individual Ismailis undertake. Believers form interpretations of these codes in necessary response to the vagaries that shape their daily lives, the specific and varying locales in which they live, and their individual encounters with the ideas or images of other moral frameworks. Lived experience, embodiment, and local enmeshments all inform how moral codes or religious doctrines are (re)interpreted. Rather than assuming a radical break between the domain of morality (as a relatively stable set of norms and codes) and the realm of ethics (the space where morality is practiced), it may thus be more useful to consider them as interlinked. Anthropologist Leela Prasad proposes an approach to religious life that centers everyday practice and oral narratives, because these are the fields where ethics are revealed.[102] Such an approach, she suggests, "would privilege how people engage with precepts and tell us something about the dynamic ways in which individuals not only imagine and live out their ethical worlds, but convey this imagination to others."[103] The lens of ordinary ethics, in other words, allows us to explore how people enact moral codes in relation to the self as well as how they practice (and convey) them in community.

As I have suggested above, scholars of Islam have paid considerable attention to these dimensions of ethics, particularly to the project of ethical self-cultivation. And self-cultivation is not, of course, wholly absent from the practices we will consider in the chapters that follow. When Farida shows up at the DeKalb County clinic to serve as an interpreter for Ramzan but he does not show up, she must "practice *sabr* (patience)," evidently a task of self-cultivation. But I am more interested in the moment when Farida chooses to reschedule, offering her interpretation help the next day, as an action that iterates community. She attends to her Imam's guidance ("Help where help is needed") and chooses an action (interpretation help) that maintains spiritual kinship (her ongoing relation to Ramzan). Community is the field within which Farida cultivates the capacity for ethical action (or in this case, the virtue of patience), but community is also the product of Farida's ethical actions. This book is about uncovering what women's ethical practices *do*. *Jamat* (community) not only is the condition that facilitates the practice of ethics but also names the relation that ethics forge.

Moreover, in paying attention to Ismaili women, we encounter a mode of religiosity where the Divine is both transcendent and immanent, where a subject both acts and is acted upon.[104] The women I spoke with did not see their acts of support for fellow Ismailis as emerging exclusively from their intentions or desires. They interpreted some acts of support as opportunities offered by their Imam (chapter 3, "Imam gives *seva*, we are just instruments") or as the result of prompting by Divine signs (chapter 4, angelic figures or dream-visions). When I asked J.A. why she spent hours on the phone to help a new migrant get a discount on a washer/dryer unit, she responded, "I am just moved to do this work." After a long pause, she added, "*Mawla* makes me do this work."[105] As J.A. points to her Divinely appointed Imam's agency, she makes room for Divine will in everyday life. The Ismaili ethical landscape, then, is more readily charted if we extend our notion of piety so that it encompasses those self-directed deliberate actions that are typically recognized as pious (prayers, rituals, and service, which we will see especially in chapters 2 and 3) and also leave room for Divinely directed action.[106] Here, capacity to act ethically emerges at the nexus of personal intentionality, Divine direction, and material contingencies. I thus join Mittermaier in keeping God in the picture, as "God interferes in, and directs, believers' lives."[107] In Ismaili ethical practice, that Divine direction, or interference, typically—and as we will see in chapter 4, sometimes dramatically—arrives via the Imam.

Because we are specifically observing the lives of *displaced* Ismaili women, we also encounter moments when women struggle with the moral precepts of their faith in new, unfamiliar contexts. They wrestle with the imperative of generosity when they are themselves pressed for time and material resources; they grapple with the obligation to follow the directives of their Imams when those directives seem disadvantageous to their families; they battle with anti-Brown racism while also, as settlers, participating in the displacement and dispossession of Africans, Bangladeshis, and Native Americans. We also see that engaging with the lives of others does not always reinforce bonds or contribute to a sense of belonging. There are moments when care networks are not able to hold each person. At least two of my interlocutors from East Pakistan, for instance, were bullied in jamatkhanas in West Pakistan for dressing differently and being unable to speak the local language. Others struggled with male domination within their families and in Ismaili institutions. Divorced women who had previously served as faith ministers (*mukhianis*) lamented that they would never again have the opportunity to serve in these positions, because women's appointments are typically tied to men's. During my fieldwork, I encountered moments when women engaged in gossip or tried to exclude another woman; on one of the several occasions when I joined other women to clean a jamatkhana, members of the group bickered over who would get to perform which tasks. While the book's central objective is to discover how women recreate *jamat* through care and support, I do not intend to give the impression that they are morally perfect or that they do not face familial and communal constraints. Inconsistencies and ambiguities abound. Ethical living, as Michael Lambek has observed, is both vulnerable to and achieved in the face of rupture, erosion, and skepticism.[108] Ethics then unfold as Ismailis strive to live amid human frailties and social, economic dislocations. Relatedly, religious community emerges as a fragile arrangement, its making and remaking requiring ongoing care.

Faithful Witnessing

When Shamsuddin shared a miracle (*moujza*) story with me—how the Imam rescued him and two dozen other Ismailis trapped in a jamatkhana in Mymensingh (East Pakistan) in 1971—tears flowed down our cheeks. Together we entered the intimate domain of the Sacred. Later, as I wrote about that moment for chapter 4, I re-entered that same spiritual realm. Instead of espousing the viewpoint of the disbelieving academic or writing as a believer, I claim both perspectives. I write as a scholar who is deeply familiar with the religious beliefs of my interlocutors and the rhythms of their religious life. I follow Amy Moran-Thomas, who posits such enmeshments as a hermeneutic that enhances a researcher's understanding of the things she sees.[109] My shared experiences and histories enable me to understand my interlocutors' efforts to build relationships with each other as tied to a spiritual purpose and to read their aesthetic productions and miracle stories as evidencing imbrications of the physical and the spiritual.

My interlocutors brought their own understandings to the research encounters as well; I was welcomed by women into their homes and lives not only as a researcher but also as a younger Ismaili woman, someone who might preserve, convey, and disseminate the stories they shared with me. Thomas has called on researchers to account for how their interlocutors construct research relationships, as those constructions shape the intersubjective spaces of ethnographic interaction.[110] Writing about her fieldwork in a Black evangelical church, Thomas observes that while ethnographers are often described as observers, strangers, or friends, her own relationship with her research participants could be best described as *kin*, characterized by a "closer and longer-lasting form of intersubjectivity" that emerged due to shared socioreligious, ethno-racial, and class solidarities.[111] I shared a similar close relationship with my participants. Telling women's stories and writing this book is my own ethical-spiritual response to the support the community and the Imam have offered to me and my ancestors. I therefore write the book in the tradition of scholars such as Thomas, Alexander, Juliane Hammer, Kirin Narayan, Jodi Eichler-Levine, and Moran-Thomas, who write from within the experiences of their subjects and as their companions on the journey, as their kin, rather than in the disembodied voice of the ostensibly rational outside observer (more on positionality in chapter 4).[112]

Feminist philosopher Maria Lugones calls the effort of transforming invisible and illegible subjects into recognizable ones "faithful witnessing."[113] The ninety-five interviews I conducted in my own endeavor of faithful witnessing included sixty-three Ismaili women born between 1921 and 1965. Of these women, twenty-seven had begun their lives in East Pakistan and the rest as second- or third-generation residents in East Africa. They fled their respective homes as adults, teenagers, or children, and hence each woman offers a glimpse into a different moment of the migration itinerary: growing up in Kampala or Dhaka, fleeing in a steamer or flying alone out of an airport, suspended in a transit camp in Italy, striving to find a job in Toronto, or creating a makeshift jamatkhana in Indiana. Crucially, I inquired not only about women's own life stories but also those of their mothers and grandmothers, who too had been on the move. To glean further insights into the community's experience, I interviewed twenty Ismaili men who had fled East Pakistan and East Africa. And I engaged with twelve second-generation Ismaili women (born between 1978 and 1992) who grew up in North America after their parents were displaced, to examine the transmutation of community making.

Research for this project started with interviews with women in my own family, beginning with Farida and Shakar; they then introduced me to other women in Pakistan, Canada, and the United States, who made additional introductions. In some cases, I met women through their daughters whom I knew through my volunteer work in the community in Pakistan and the United States; some of these second-generation women would later become the subject of chapter 6. I visited women in their homes or met them in jamatkhanas; some interviews were held over Zoom or phone. In certain instances, I met the women I had interviewed over Zoom in jamatkhanas when I visited the city, and those became occasions for follow-up interviews. I interviewed several women, particularly those featured prominently in the book, multiple times. In some cases, I was able to interview three generations of women from the same family, and in others, I interviewed siblings. Throughout the book, therefore, I use the women's first names to avoid confusing them with their daughters or relatives who share last names. I have maintained informal connection with most of my interlocutors through regular home visits, WhatsApp messaging, and email.

Interviews lasted anywhere from one to six hours and were unhurried and unscripted. I tried, as much as possible, to let the women lead the conversations. In one interview, early in my research process, I encountered a situation where a woman's spouse joined our conversation to "correct" the wife's recollections; on another occasion, a woman abruptly concluded the interview when her partner entered the dining room where we were chatting. After these experiences, when possible, I met with my interlocutors in the absence of their male relations. Some women wanted me to use their names to leave a record of their own and their mothers' lives; others were more comfortable with initials or pseudonyms (which I indicate in the notes). Where I have biographical information (such as year of birth and last names), I include those as well. Throughout the book I have chosen to use such information as a gesture against the erasure of women from the historical record that has often characterized the experience of Ismaili women. Interviews were conducted in Urdu, Kuchchhi, Sindhi, and English (often a combination); translations are mine.

While several women began with demurrals like "I don't remember much" or "I don't have anything really to add to your research," when prompted they would go on to remember their personal histories in impressive detail. I treat these memories not as repositories of facts, but as active processes of creating meaning. In the words of Maurice Halbwachs, "[A] remembrance is in very large measure a reconstruction of the past achieved with data borrowed from the present, a reconstruction prepared, furthermore, by reconstructions of earlier periods wherein past images had already been altered."[114] In the spirit of collecting "remembrances," instead of trying to verify the particulars of displaced women's memories in pursuit of "truth" or comprehensiveness, I am more interested in understanding how they chose to share their stories, which episodes and events were meaningful for them, and what memory selections they made as they worked to make sense of the past and their place in it. While the details of women's individual journeys varied, and it would be a mistake to assume that their lived experience represents the totality of experience of Ismailis from East Africa or East Pakistan, certain aspects of community making were shared over and over in the course of my research and collate into a larger collective history.[115]

Archives of cultural memory include not only women's living memories but also images, stories, recipes, and documents of the past through which they construct and transmit shared histories.[116] In addition to interviews, I therefore also examine Ismaili women's memory texts such as unpublished or self-published memoirs, personal journals, photographs, and cookbooks. Some of these texts are translations from Gujarati as family members tried to preserve the lives of their elders. These texts leave an account of the past for future generations and mediate future memory. I also draw on oral histories archived at Khojawiki, Carleton University, Canadian Museum of Immigration at Pier 21, and Cynthia Salvadori's three volumes of We Came in Dhows. Community magazines published during the 1970s and 1980s provide further insight into the experience of the early migrants and refugees in North America and Europe. I studied The American Ismaili (1979–1989); Canadian Ismaili (1976–1989); Ismaili Forum, UK (1976–1986); Roshni (1980–1981, published out of New York and merged with The American Ismaili in 1985); and Hikmat (Vancouver; 1982 and 1985). These magazines, published by Ismaili Councils for the consumption of community members, include news about the work of the Imam and the local jamati institutions, such as the establishment of jamatkhanas and religious education classes; articles on Islamic history; and advice about immigration, emerging careers, setting up new businesses, and applying for loans. Early magazines also contain articles in Gujarati (likely for older members who could not read the English language); list information about marriages, births, and deaths; address health issues from anxiety and heart disease to smoking and drugs; and advertise Ismaili businesses.[117] Written by both representatives of Ismaili

Councils and ordinary Ismailis, the magazines complement my findings from oral history interviews.

Organization of the Book

The second chapter centers on my interlocutors' memories of their mothers and grandmothers' lives as migrants to East Africa and East Pakistan; the third, fourth, and fifth chapters focus on my interlocutors; and the sixth chapter features women from the second generation as they reckon with their parents' experiences and their own position as religious and racial minorities in North America. While women's ethics of care are palpable in each chapter, representing shared norms and ethos of Ismaili community, these ethics are also *of* a given time and place. Ismaili ethics thus emerge as an animate, multiply layered and richly textured domain. This book offers *one* articulation of this ethics, grounded in the memories and experiences of my interlocutors.

In the second chapter I trace the childhoods of my interlocutors and their memories of their foremothers to reconstruct their migration within India and from India to East Africa and East Pakistan. This older story of Ismaili migrations is often told from the perspective of empire, celebrating Ismaili men who thrived in the colonial political economy. I instead home in on the details of women's everyday lives to show their practices of care for self, family, and coreligionists: how Puribai Velji's Ismaili neighbors helped her start a small shop in Zanzibar in the early 1900s to make ends meet after the death of her husband; how reproductive and productive work encircled prayer times for Sherbanu Lalani in Bukoto (Uganda) during the 1930s; and how Ismaili women grappled with the *farmans* of their Imam on education, removal of the face veil, and donning of the Western dress. I join scholars such as Mala Pandurang and Dana Seidenberg, who have tried to piece together the lives of Indian women settlers in East Africa.[118] But instead of searching for "the forgotten pioneers" (to fit into a masculine model of legibility that relies on capitalist and settler alliances) or recovering women by emphasizing their role in the public sphere (as contributors to the entrepreneurial success of Asians in East Africa), I resist the bifurcation of women's lives into private/public, focusing more on what their activities reveal about Ismaili ethical subjectivities. In this chapter my interlocutors also recall the trauma of fleeing the places they had known as home. Both Nargis Somani and Farida Merchant tell tales of memorable childhoods in East Pakistan that were disrupted by war, but they also recollect the generosity of strangers and coreligionists who helped them escape.

The third chapter examines women's efforts to create and sustain Ismaili spaces of worship, the jamatkhana, across generations, first in East Africa and then in North America. We meet Gulzar Kassam and Roshan Pirani, who created makeshift jamatkhanas at their apartments in Atlanta, Georgia, and Fort Wayne, Indiana. In addition to the material practices of laying down bedsheets so congregants could sit on the floor or trimming down the legs of a coffee table to make it resemble a *paat* (a table used during rituals), placemaking had an aesthetic, sensory, and somatic dimension too, and included reciting collective prayers, burning incense, and sharing *juro* (ritual foods consecrated as part of the prayer ceremony). Other women conjured the sacred sensorium of the jamatkhana during flight, on steamboats and at refugee camps, through recitation of *ginans* and sharing food.

The fourth chapter delineates the reproduction of an Ismaili sociality through storytelling in the *moujza* tradition, which include stories of miraculous rescues during the expulsion crises and unexpected aid from strangers during the early years of resettlement. While tales of the supernatural are commonly viewed as sacred narratives, stories of mediated aid can perform the same social function—that is, they can convey belief in Divine help and buttress religious affinities. I thus group stories of unexpected aid within the genre of sacred narratives, for these stories reinforce faith. Their retelling not only memorializes a shared past but also shapes the future moral state of the *jamat*. Placemaking here takes a narrative form. It enables listeners—often younger Ismailis—to emplace themselves in an Ismaili *jamat* that exists beyond the present time and place.

Chapter 5 traces culinary routes to placemaking by examining cookbooks written by three displaced Ismaili women from East Africa—*Mamajee's Kitchen* (2005) by Lella Umedaly, *A Spicy Touch* (1986, 1992, 2007, 2015) by Noorbanu Nimji, and *The Settler's Cookbook* (2009) by Yasmin Alibhai-Brown. In the hands of Ismaili women, the cookbook becomes a memoir, an advice manual, and a testimony. These cookbooks introduce readers to community migration histories, heritage food practices, and the Imam's advice on nutrition; they exemplify the pleasures of belonging through food fusions and experimentations. Using culinary narratives, the authors rewrite displacement as a new form of emplacement, rooting themselves in new environments, discovering and interacting with culinary histories, and creating new ones.

The sixth chapter ponders placemaking in the second generation—the daughters of my primary interlocutors as they now engage with communal pasts, simultaneously interrogating and memorializing a shared history in novels, artwork, and dissertations. Having grown up in the diaspora, this generation articulates an ethics of care that intersects with locally manifest concerns around anti-Brown and anti-Black racism, and engages in critique of settler colonialism and the model minority paradigm. Women in the second generation extend religious symbols such as *seva* to speak to their changing circumstances, including deterritorialization—not, as experienced by their mothers, due to wars and poverty, but in response to the pressures of a neoliberal economy that requires workers to be mobile and flexible. These women thus invent new sites and forms for producing spiritual intimacies, showing us again that the *jamat* is a contingent social formation that is *remade* by each generation.

In the concluding chapter of the book, I reflect on how *Rebuilding Community* draws on the case of a specific cohort of Ismaili women and the context of displacement to tell a broader story about religious community formation. In the process, the book not only writes women into modern Ismaili history but also enhances our understanding of refugee and migrant placemaking, reclaims care work from productivist frames, and illuminates lived Shia Islam.

2

Ismaili Women's Lifeworlds, 1890–1970

Gulzar Kassam (b. 1945) remembers the details of her grandmother's *duka* (shop) in Zanzibar: "[It] was essentially the front portion of her house, with two wooden slabs for a door. She sold spices and maintained that shop even after her children had all grown up and could support her financially. . . . She was very resilient and resourceful."[1] It is November 2020, and the first of my multiple interviews with Gulzar. She tells me that her grandfather Kassam Velji settled in Zanzibar in the late nineteenth century. He returned to Kathiawar a few years later to bring back his new bride, Puribai. The couple went on to have six children, but Kassam passed away at an early age, leaving Puribai to raise their children by herself. Kassam had not amassed much wealth apart from a small farm (*shamba*) and two properties in the lowest-income area of Zanzibar that brought in scant rental income. Unable to make ends meet, Puribai started a *duka* of her own.

While Gulzar uses the terms "resilient" and "resourceful" to describe Puribai, consistent with how many of my interlocutors remember their foremothers, she also stresses the support other Ismailis offered Puribai when her young husband died: "The community was really nice, and she had some relatives [too]. They all, you know, kind of supported each other, supported one other." It is difficult to determine the exact intent behind these long-past offers of aid to a coreligionist; nonetheless, we see in Gulzar's narration one concrete instance of Ismailis extending help to a widow in a context where their Imam had urged unity. In the wake of creedal schisms among nineteenth-century Khojas in Zanzibar, the Imam had instructed his followers not to allow differences in dialect or culture to divide them further, and called on them to work in unison like a *panj* (a palm or fist), whose fingers are weak individually but strong together.[2]

As Puribai's children grew up, she encountered a new challenge. Her daughter Nur wanted to pursue a course in midwifery at the Zanzibar Maternity Association (ZMA), an hour away from their home.[3] ZMA was founded in 1918 to train midwives to assist Asian, Arab, and African women during home births, and to fill the gap in healthcare provision left by the

Rebuilding Community. Shenila Khoja-Moolji, Oxford University Press. © Oxford University Press 2023.
DOI: 10.1093/oso/9780197642023.003.0002

Zanzibari Colonial Medical Service.[4] In 1925, the Mwembeladu Maternity Home was also established to supplement these efforts. Even though a Khoja Ismaili, Tharia Topan, was one of the key funders for both, professional midwifery was unheard of among Ismailis; this work was often undertaken informally by women of one's own community. Puribai, concerned about public perception and the long solo journey to the facility, turned down her daughter's request.

When Sultan Mahomed Shah, the Ismaili Imam at the time, visited Zanzibar shortly thereafter, Puribai decided to seek his guidance. He advised for not only Nur to pursue midwifery but also that two of her female cousins, who were interested in the course, join her. Puribai found this guidance difficult; it pushed her beyond what she considered acceptable for women's education and movement outside the private sphere of the home. However, Puribai's granddaughter (Nur's daughter) Yasmin Hirji tells me that after her encounter with the Imam, she became an "ardent supporter of her daughter's education. So much so that when people would gossip about Nur, she would lash back at them arguing that '*Mawla* had said so.'"[5] At first the three girls walked an hour to the hospital, where they had to report by 6 a.m. After a few months, they sped up the journey by becoming some of the first women in the Zanzibar Khoja community to ride bicycles.

Puribai's story reveals both the adversity and the relations of care that characterized the early Ismaili communities in Zanzibar. It illustrates not only how Ismailis cared for coreligionists but also how the Imam cared for his followers. It also gives us a glimpse into the personal exertion that obedience to a moral code requires: Puribai was uncomfortable with the Imam's guidance at first, but then became an ardent supporter of her daughter's education. Accounts of women like Puribai—their lives, hardships, and ethical practice—have survived only in the memories of their children and grandchildren, or in informal family archives of documents and photos. This chapter endeavors to reconstruct the lifeworlds of some of these early migrants, as their descendants remember them. My substantive engagement with Ismaili women's history begins with the stories of women from the cohort that migrated out of western India to destinations elsewhere in India and to East Africa during the late nineteenth and early twentieth century.

The period under consideration is characterized by creedal schisms as well as efforts by the Ismaili Imams to concretize an Ismaili identity.[6] Even before Imam Hasan Ali Shah Aga Khan I (d. 1881) arrived in India from Persia in the mid-nineteenth century, reformist sentiments were emerging among the

Khojas of Bombay. When Aga Khan I tried to exert control over the community and its property, some elite Khoja leaders challenged him and filed lawsuits in the Bombay High Court. Whereas initially the British judiciary ruled in favor of customary practice and against the Aga Khan, this changed by the second half of the nineteenth century. Now, as Zulfikar Hirji observes, the British were less tolerant of liminal practices and customary laws; they demanded more clarity about who was a Muslim and who was a Hindu.[7] In an 1866 lawsuit, some elite Khojas argued that Khojas were Sunni and not Shia, as the Imam claimed, and therefore he had no authority over them. The High Court, however, ruled in favor of the Imam.[8] The Aga Khan now had legally recognized authority over the communal and religious matters of the Khojas. He could decide on membership criteria for the community and had the ability to excommunicate dissenters. At this point, while the majority of Khojas maintained their allegiance to the Aga Khan, some declared themselves Sunni and others Ithna'ashari (Twelver Shia). In 1908, another dispute arose when certain family members of the then Imam, Aga Khan III, claimed that the religious dues paid to him were due to his status as a *sayyid* (descendant of Prophet Muhammed), and since they shared this distinction with him, they too had a right to the dues. The Bombay High Court again ruled in favor of the Aga Khan, re-establishing his authority over the community.[9]

Against the backdrop of these legal contestations and doctrinal divisions, during the nineteenth and twentieth centuries, the Ismaili Imams introduced numerous reforms to consolidate their followers' identity as Shia Imami Ismailis.[10] They published membership rulebooks (governing who could be a member and furnishing a code of conduct for Ismailis), introduced shared rituals, changed the recitation of the *du'a* from Indic languages to Arabic, canonized *ginanic* literature, established institutions to train itinerant preachers and religious education teachers, demarcated jamatkhanas as the primary and private space of worship for Ismailis, established administrative councils to oversee the religiosocial life of Ismailis, and regularly issued *farmans* (directives). Aga Khan III in particular also set out to reform the community's social values by emphasizing unity, calling for women's education, and stressing health and hygiene. While scholars have written about the juridical dimension of Ismaili identity formation as well as the Imams' efforts to bolster this identity through shared rituals and administrative apparatuses, we still need to know more about how this identity—and its attendant value propositions around spiritual kinship—was understood and

practiced. Said differently, how did Ismailis in general, and women in particular, attend to their Imam's *farmans* on brotherhood? On women's education? Or the setting aside of the face veil? As new migrants to East Africa and
East Pakistan, what challenges and ethical dilemmas did they face? How did
they resolve them? How does this close study of women's lifeworlds complement the standard narrative of modern Ismaili history?

The first part of the chapter, on Ismaili women in East Africa, traverses a
lengthy period, from 1890 to 1970, reflecting the generations-long presence
of Ismailis there. The second part, on East Pakistan, accordingly, addresses a
shorter span—the two decades between partition and civil war, when a significant Ismaili population lived in the region. Instead of providing a comprehensive review of historical events, my aim is to highlight the circumstances
of women's migration and the rhythms of their everyday lives so that we
can understand the choices they made and the tasks they undertook to emplace themselves, their families, and their coreligionists in new contexts.
By focusing here on women's experiences, we can glimpse the nonjuridical
dimensions of Ismaili community formation during the twentieth century.

The narratives included in this chapter are not simply additive, in that
they do not reiterate what we already know about Ismaili history. Rather,
this retracing of the migratory and religious history of Ismailis shows us how
women experienced these movements and how their actions have shaped
present-day Ismaili social formations. In these stories we see less the structural
continuity of the Ismaili community (as represented by forty-nine generations
of Imams) and more the *provisional* nature of that sociality (as portrayed by
the ethical conduct of ordinary Ismailis that help sustain it). Michael Lambek
suggests that an anthropological approach to ethical practice is less interested
in outlining specific master or meta values, and more attuned to illustrating
cultural practices that show people in the continuous effort to find the right
balance across a range of practices.[11] Focusing closely on the particular stories
of individuals (individual women, in this case) and attending to the apparatus
of everyday life (women's hardships, decisions, movements, dilemmas, and
habits) thus works against assumptions of timelessness. It instead highlights
the continuous effort through which Ismaili migrant women reinforced
communal affinities while cultivating ethical sensibilities.

This focus on women's everyday life is not meant to de-emphasize the
salience of the physical infrastructure—such as the jamatkhanas, Ismaili
councils, Aga Khan schools, clinics, and hostels—that facilitated Ismaili emplacement along migratory routes.[12] These sites have been, as will become

clear in this chapter and the next, crucial for Ismaili sociality. What I offer instead is a look into ordinary ethics (acts of care and cultivation of personal virtue) that have sustained the community across generations. This enables us to consider how earlier generations of Khoja Ismaili women experienced geographic dislocation, and also appreciate practices of mutual support as they existed in these prior community geographies, so that we can better recognize them when they are reintroduced in North America. The chapter thus illustrates both tangible and intangible dimensions of an Ismaili infrastructure of care that can be understood to extend through time and space. I begin with Ismaili migration to East Africa and then move on to East Pakistan.

East Africa, 1890–1970

Habib Rahemtulla Lalani's (b. 1910) journal entries give us one glimpse into the circumstances that compelled Khoja Ismailis to leave the Kathiawar region and head to East Africa for a better life, as well as the acts of generosity and care from coreligionists that they encountered along the way.[13] Habib was born in the riverside town of Bilkha, where his father had a small shop selling produce and sundries—handkerchiefs, undershirts, and socks. The town's river location meant its residents lived with the fear of flooding for at least four months a year. Habib's family therefore moved to the larger town of Naagri, hoping to improve their quality of life, but their situation remained precarious. Habib recalls in one entry, "I remember a severe drought. Those were bad times and an infectious disease called *marki*, plague, broke out. Even in the small town of Naagri there were 3-4 deaths every day, later 7-8 per day. Households began to become empty. One day 10 people passed away." When Habib turned fifteen, he moved to Bombay to find ways to contribute to his family's income. He worked in various shops run by Khoja Ismailis until 1929, when his older sister sent him money for a ticket to East Africa. At nineteen, Habib set off for Zanzibar.

There were about four hundred other Ismailis with him on the steamer. When a passenger became ill, the steamer was quarantined for ten days on an island near Zanzibar. The Ismaili passengers looked after each other. Habib writes of those acts of support, particularly noting women's contributions:

All the Ismailis made a joint request for a tent where we could cook for the *Jamat*. We were given a separate camping area. There was [*sic*] good toilet, bathing and cooking facilities. People just lay down their bedding and were comfortable. Whatever rations you needed were supplied. We cooked different foods every day. A group of volunteers was formed. A group of ladies was all set to cook. . . . We enjoyed our meals just as if one were eating at a festival.[14]

Cooking and sharing a meal are the mundane acts through which people identify with kin.[15] By living together, volunteering to cook, and sharing meals, these otherwise strangers reiterated their bonds of spiritual kinship. Habib further notes that members of the Ismaili *jamat* from Zanzibar soon "came by boat to ask how we were doing."[16]

We find similar evidence of community support in the observations of James Christie, a British doctor who spent the years between 1864 and 1870 in Zanzibar, reporting on the cholera epidemic for the Epidemiological Society in London.[17] Christie ultimately extended his investigation through 1874. His findings, published in 1876, illustrate the strong networks of mutual care that he observed among the Khojas and their robust collective life: "On Friday of every week, the several individuals of the Khojah community are expected to meet in a public building [jamatkhana] set apart for the purpose," and the meeting is followed by a communal meal.[18] He goes on:

Rich and prosperous men also frequently entertain the entire community on special occasions. The poorer classes habitually frequent such entertainments, and to them the feast constitutes the principal meal of the day. The community spends a considerable portion of its wealth in this way, and the custom is not without special and important advantages. At the Jumaat they meet on common ground, and a kindly feeling between the individual members is engendered. They take care of their own poor, and exercise a supervision over the conduct of all besides looking after the interests of the whole as a class. . . . [E]very degree of relationship, even the more remote, is recognized, and poverty, or lowness of station, is no reason for anyone being discarded. . . . In no class of society, civilized or uncivilized, Christian or Mohammedan, have I ever seen so much kindness and genuine affection displayed towards each other as I have constantly witnessed among the members of this community.[19]

The "kindly feeling," taking care of the poor, looking after the interests of the community, and genuine affection (albeit within a hierarchal social fabric) that Christie observes are precisely the practices of care that are the focus of this book: this is how Ismaili spiritualized sociality was produced in late nineteenth-century Zanzibar. Christie notes that even during the cholera outbreak Khojas were quick to help each other, visiting homes of sick community members and bringing them food. While he criticizes these visits as a vector for spreading disease, the ethic of community obligation, including tending to the ill, is apparent in these actions. These are the practices of care that Gulzar alluded to when recalling how Puribai was supported by the community after her young husband passed away. Evidence of welfare structures established by wealthy Khojas further suggests strong sentiments of communal support. As early as 1903, a home for poor Khoja Ismaili women was constructed in Zanzibar.[20]

While most of my interlocutors recall the economic hardship experienced by their parents and grandparents, not all Khojas share this history. Some nineteenth-century Khoja merchants in Zanzibar were moneylenders and creditors or acquired wealth in the caravan trade. Tharia Topan arrived in Zanzibar in 1835 and built a large business supplying goods and porters to European explorers, and at one point, secured the position of customs master; Sewa Haji Paroo also furnished supplies, including ivory, to Europeans; Alidina Visram took over Paroo's business after his death and extended its reach further inland. At its peak, Visram's firm employed over five hundred workers of Indian origin, many of them Khojas.[21] Other Ismailis, such as Suleiman Virjee, are also remembered as successful traders who facilitated the settlement of more recently arrived Ismailis. Thus, while the early years of Khojas in East Africa were often marked by poverty, they were by no means a homogenous group. And it is against this background of varied economic experience that wealthy Khojas often stepped in to assist their less well-off religious kin.

Women's Everyday Life

In 1837 there were twenty Khoja women in Zanzibar.[22] By 1874, according to one report, the number of women had increased to 650.[23] They had moved from India with their husbands in the decades before Asian migration increased. Even larger numbers of women began arriving in the 1890s and yet more Khoja women came in the early decades of the twentieth century.[24]

Early women settlers in East Africa tended to continue familiar practices of seclusion, but high mortality rates, limited economic possibilities, and low profit margins pushed some Khoja women out of seclusion. Christie describes an ordinary day in the "Khojah households" of Zanzibar: "Business is commenced early in the morning, generally about six o' clock, and is continued till late in the evening. . . . [T]he outside business is conducted by the husband, who is in the shop only when not otherwise engaged, and the retail, or shop-keeping part of the business, is attended to by the wife and junior members of the family. The wife is thus, not only the domestic partner in life, but also an active and indispensable partner in business."[25] The front portion of the house, facing the street, would typically have been the shop—left open to customers during the day, with goods displayed for sale and the woman of the household often sitting on a stool to keep an eye on her merchandise. Many women found innovative ways to help support their families.[26] Fatma Peera Dewjee (born est. 1903 or earlier), who lived in the Mwembetanga neighborhood of Zanzibar, made and sold *kikuba*—small bouquets that women used to adorn their hair—to supplement her family income.[27] Popular for wedding ceremonies and other celebrations, Fatma's *kikubas* would often sell out during the wedding season. She also sold home-made perfumes and eyeliner. After the death of her second husband, Hirbai Jamal (b. 1896) supported her children by cooking and selling *sev* (deep-fried strings of chickpea flour) and other snack items.[28] Some Khoja women became proficient in the local languages. Bahadur Kassam proudly tells me that his grandmother, Jetbai Dhanji (b. 1886), "only spoke Swahili!"[29] She had arrived in Zanzibar in 1903 when she was seven years old and worked closely with her parents in *dukas*, speaking Swahili with customers all day. Decades later, Bahadur's mother, Nurkhanu Habib Kassam, set out to establish a small *duka* of her own when her husband lost his savings on a failed mining venture. Early each morning she would sell bread, butter, and jam. Growing up in Dar es Salaam, Bahadur remembers seeing many Ismaili women engaged in businesses like these: "They managed the businesses; they sourced materials, figured out what types of products would sell; they sold it all, stitched, non-stitched cloth."

Until World War I, Ismailis who relocated to Africa remained concentrated in the coastal regions. As railway lines were added between the port city of Mombasa and Lake Victoria, and more colonial administrative units established along it, greater numbers of Asians, including Ismailis, moved inland to establish *dukas* at the new railway stations or to farm new lands (although farming remained limited as white settlers controlled most of the fertile lands).[30] In fact, the Imam had advised young Ismaili men to head inland as commercial opportunities decreased in well-established coastal centers.[31] The settlers who moved inland traversed difficult terrain, often on ox carts; their caravans were attacked by animals and they fell sick with novel diseases. Bubonic plague was so endemic in Kisumu that the region was placed in quarantine in 1905. Europeans stayed away, as they deemed it too unhealthy; Ismailis were thus able to purchase land in the area.[32] While Ismailis were participants in the European-driven colonization of Africa, early Ismaili migrants' lives were also complicated by colonial policies that preferred white settlers. Ismailis, for instance, were only able to purchase land in areas where white settlers did not want to live. Prembai and her husband, who moved inland to Moshi around 1900, returned to Tanga four years later because they found it difficult to farm the land that they had purchased from the German officials.[33] The lowland fields sold frequently to Asians often flooded, making it hard to grow crops, whereas Germans retained the rich slopes of Kilimanjaro where coffee plantations thrived.

The move inland brought with it new challenges, particularly for the women.[34] In 1912, when Maniben Rattansi (b. 1886) made her way from India to Nyeri to join her husband, Mohamedally Rattansi (b. 1882), she was one of only a handful of Indian women in the area.[35] When she became pregnant with her first child, she decided to go to Mombasa to give birth among other Ismaili women. She named her Mombasa-born daughter Bachuli, which is simply an endearing term for an infant girl; the baby would receive a proper name at a religious ceremony after she had reunited with her husband. A few months later, Maniben, now accompanied by her husband, headed home to Nyeri. The family traveled by train from Mombasa to Naivasha, then trekked over the Aberdare Mountain range—a journey of three to four days, usually made on foot or in a hand-drawn carriage as there was no train station in Nyeri. Temperatures dropped overnight in the mountains and one morning Maniben and Mohamedally woke up to find that their baby girl had died from the cold.

Maniben went on to have several more children, but the grief of losing her first child haunted her throughout her life. She never forgot the name of the area where she buried her: Kiandongoro. Mohamedally, though he would continue his trading activities for decades, never took that mountain route again. A member of Maniben's family explains why the closest train station was so far from their town:

There were a lot of [white] settlers around Nyeri, growing coffee. The town itself was just a Boma, an administrative centre, with a few Indian *dukas*. Most of the European farms were some distance away. That is why the Railway didn't bother to go to Nyeri. When it was decided to build a branch line up to Nanyuki it was routed so it went through the area of the coffee farms for the convenience of the [white] settlers. The station, which was opened in 1928, was called "Nyeri station" but it was 8 miles away from Nyeri, at Kiganjo.[36]

This scenario illustrates how Ismaili setters often found themselves at the nexus of privilege and subordination: as merchants and traders, they enjoyed favorable access to the region's commerce in comparison to the indigenous African population, but at the same time suffered discrimination from colonial authorities alongside them (more on this below).

The same year that Maniben arrived in Nyeri, Hirbai Jamal reached Kisumu from Kutiyana, India, relocating to Asembo Bay after marriage.[37] Hirbai too went on to suffer stunning losses driven by lack of access to medical care: her first husband passed away from influenza while they were traveling by boat to Kisumu in search of medical help, her second after developing a sore on his back that refused to heal.[38] Women like Hirbai and Maniben navigated these challenging circumstances in part by drawing on their faith and transforming these hardships into occasions for cultivating personal virtue. Hirbai's granddaughter Nimira Shamji reflects on how her grandmother exercised *santosh* (satisfaction) in times of adversity:

It must have been a poor and hard life. . . . [S]he had a strong exterior that perhaps wrapped a wounded and hurting interior—we will never know. I learned a lot from Ma but in particular I learned about strength and the courage to persevere (in spite of your circumstances). Perhaps I was too young to remember but I don't recall Ma ever complaining. She played the hand that life dealt her with a strong upper lip and she left her kids with a legacy of prude[nce], hard work and gratitude. Ma taught me the meaning of the word *Santosh*. She used to say if you have *santosh*, you have everything. Without *santosh* you have nothing. Those words still ring true for me today.[39]

The Sanskrit term *santosh* or *saṃtoṣa* denotes contentment. It appears in the *ginanic* literature and belongs to a universe of ethical dispositions outlined in other Indic intellectual traditions as well that facilitate healthy living and spiritual enlightenment. When a harsh life is assigned meta-meanings through *santosh*, it transforms into a more tolerable one: the believer seeks satisfaction in any destiny and assumes Divine help. Through her ethical practice of *santosh*, Hirbai entwined the cosmological and the material. Concepts like *santosh* were accessible to women within the *satpanth* tradition via the *ginans*, and Hirbai's granddaughter's familiarity with it illustrates that for some contemporary Ismaili women these philosophical concepts persist as sources of ethical guidance.

Women also gleaned models of ideal femininity from Indic epics such as the Mahabharata and Ramayana, which were part of the Indian cultural milieu in which they had been raised. Writing about his mother, Tajbibi Muradali Juma (b. 1926), Mohamed Abualy Alibhai observes that "[For] my mother, these epics were an integral component of her Satpanth *dharam* (way of life enjoined by faith). In particular, two archetypical female personalities in these epics were destined to become very influential in her life: Draupadi in the Mahabharata, and Sita in the Ramayana."[40] Alibhai explains that Draupadi's spiritual power and Sita's patience influenced how his mother interpreted abuse from her in-laws (with silence) and how she treated fellow Ismaili women (with compassion and solidarity). When the Imam visited Dar es Salaam in 1946, for example, Tajbibi and a few of her companions volunteered to breastfeed other mothers' babies over the course of the celebrations to enable these women to take part in the religious gatherings. Alibhai describes this as "*din baheno* (sisterhood grounded in faith)." Women thus drew on a diverse and dense conceptual field of Indic philosophies to make sense of their everyday lives, even as they reworked these messages to the specific world of the Nizari Ismaili spiritual practice.[41] Later generations' recall of the faith practiced by their mothers and grandmothers signals that this philosophical porosity is also broadly sustained in the ethical practice of contemporary Ismailis who tell these stories. Lived religion in this sense synthetizes; it focuses on similarities, instead of divisions and separations.[42]

In recalling the lives of their mothers and grandmothers, my interlocutors also illustrate how religion was not distinct from, but a part of, women's daily lives. A snapshot of Sherbanu Lalani's (b. 1916) typical day in Bukoto (Uganda) during the 1930s, captured by a family biographer, is a case in point:

She would open shop by 8 am sometimes as early as 7:30 am. By this time customers would already have begun to gather outside. A servant would help move the sewing machine out to the veranda. She closed shop at 6:30 pm, cooked a little *khichri* (rice and lentils) to eat with *saag* (curry) left over from lunch. After saying *dua* (Ismaili prayers) she went back to the shop to count the mostly coin cash tying them together by threading a *doro* (thick thread) through the coin holes. She would record in the *chopro* (ledger) the cash count and the amount of coffee bought. Out of it she would take *dasond* (religious dues) money and put it in a box labelled "*khana na*" ("for jamatkhana"). . . . Even household needs she would buy from the shop just like other customers did so that *dasond* was correct. There was another *dabo* (box) containing money for household needs. For example when she needed more blue soap . . . she would take money from the household *dabo* and put it in the shop till.[43]

In this portrait, we see Sherbanu "selling goods to herself" to ensure correct calculation of religious dues (*dasond*) and keeping two separate boxes to prevent it from getting mixed with money available for household expenditure. These mundane actions evidence an ongoing awareness of God, which complement her regular prayers (*dua*).

Even while working through their own difficulties, women extended a helping hand to others. When Habib (whom we have seen above) arrived in Zanzibar, local Ismailis told him to make his way inland to Jinja to see if he might be able to establish a shop there. En route, he accidentally boarded the wrong train and ended up farther north, in Eldoret. Late at night, with the next train to Jinja not due for another two days, Habib wandered anxiously around the station. A local Indian man approached him and, on discovering that Habib was an Ismaili, took him to the home of the *mukhi*. In the Khoja Ismaili communities of India, a *mukhi*—derived from the Sanskrit word *mukhya*, meaning foremost or chief—was often elected to help manage both the social and religious affairs of the community. In time, *mukhis* were appointed by the Imam to oversee the community's religious life and support its members. Their wives, referred to as *mukhiani*, joined them in these tasks. The *mukhi* and *mukhiani* of Eldoret welcomed Habib. The *mukhiani* provided him a room, meals, and a place to wash up. Habib was moved by her generosity: "I stayed in my room when at 10am *mukhiani saheba* came to call me for tea. . . . She arranged laundry for me. . . . We had dinner, *mukhiani saheba* being very hospitable, like I was her brother. . . . *Mawla*'s mercy, I a stranger in this land and getting such good service and help."[44] Shariffa Keshavjee (b. 1945), in our conversation in 2021, recalls similar support to new arrivals offered by her grandmother Shirinbai Jamal (b. 1910), who was the wife of the longtime president of the Kisumu Provincial Ismaili Council. Shirinbai had a busy house full of travelers like Habib: "There were no hotels, so visitors had to stay with relatives and fellow-community members. . . . When they left, Ma always saw they had food for their journey onward—a typical packed lunch would consist of fish and *rotlo*, enclosed between two tin plates, wrapped up in a piece of *amerikani* (unbleached calico) cloth."[45] An early East African jamatkhana, such as the one in Mumias between 1901 and 1912, would often be a single room set aside in the *mukhi's* house,[46] and a traveler would look to find temporary shelter in the local jamatkhana while he was searching for a job. It is therefore not surprising to see *mukhianis* and the wives of council officers, as caretakers of the jamatkhanas and *jamats*, also attending to the needs of Ismaili travelers.

These women, however, offered more than food, lodging, and clean clothes; they also provided Ismaili newcomers with a sense of affiliation. Habib, for instance, emphasized that the *mukhiani* treated him like a "brother." He was so deeply affected by her "hospitality toward a stranger" such as himself that later, when he could afford a house of his own, he made sure to practice similar generosity to what he had encountered in Eldoret. His daughter tells me: "My dad opened our home to any passersby and had an open invitation to whoever needed a place to stay 'for a stopover' or visiting town."[47] In Habib's hospitality we see how the *mukhiani's* care for a lost coreligionist had a long-lasting effect. By redefining the needs of coreligionists as occasions for service, women like the *mukhiani* of Eldoret and Shirinbai bound otherwise strangers as spiritual kin. Such forms of care, repeated unceasingly over many years, held together a community whose members came and went between India, coastal cities, and the African interior.

An Ethical Dilemma: Educating Girls

Puribai's granddaughter Gulzar (whom we met at the beginning of the chapter) credits the Ismaili Imams for stressing girls education and, in doing so, radically transforming the social and economic trajectory of Ismaili women. She explains: "If it was not for Imam Sultan Mohamed Shah [Aga Khan III] and later [the next Imam] Karim Shah's vision, our community would still be suffering in the little fields of Kuchchh and Gujarat. Economically, our people did reasonably well within one generation after migrating to East Africa and by the second generation, their kids had opportunities to get undergraduate and graduate education, either in East Africa or overseas, mainly in UK and some in India."[48] This sentiment was expressed by many of my interlocutors who emphasized to me the importance of education in easing their transition to North America in the 1970s. We now know much about the forty-eighth Ismaili Imam, Aga Khan III's, reforms for Ismaili women's education.[49] I supplement that familiar story by outlining how ordinary Ismailis contributed to the Imam's efforts and women's early experiences of schooling. Indeed, as Puribai's example shows, families often encountered the choice to educate their daughters as a dilemma, given that it led to new roles for women. Further complicating matters was the intense struggle around identity faced by this generation of Khoja Ismailis in early twentieth-century Zanzibar when the community was marked by creedal schisms. Families were split as some members sided with the Aga Khan while others became Sunni or Twelver Shia. In this context of uncertain and changing allegiances, for Puribai to follow the Imam's directives against her own desires and prevailing social norms demonstrates the significant personal exertion that ethical practice requires.

Aga Khan III had begun emphasizing girls' education since the turn of the twentieth century when educating girls was a controversial subject within the Muslim communities of India and East Africa. Early concern centered on whether girls should be educated at all, with the debate eventually shifting to what curriculum and what level of education would be appropriate for them.[50] In a 1913 *farman* to his followers in Bombay, the Imam emphasized that girls should receive an education so that they would "not have to rely on others" nor be forced to support themselves through menial labor, such as "wash[ing] the clothes and utensils of others and earn merely four to six *paisas*."[51] As he explained elsewhere, "I am trying to guide our young women's lives into entirely new channels. I want to see them able to earn their living in trades and professions, so that they are not economically dependent on marriage, nor a burden on their fathers and brothers."[52] In his 1918 text *India in Transition*, Aga Khan III observes that reforms for women's economic and educational progress had been slow not least because they had been motivated by the end purpose of service to men: "The constant argument has been that of the necessity for providing educated and intelligent wives and daughters, sisters and mothers, for the men . . . the time has come for a full recognition that the happiness and welfare of the women themselves, must be the end and purpose of all efforts towards improvement."[53]

He thus directed young girls to say no to their elders if they denied them permission to attend school.[54] He did not want their education to stop at basic literacy or elementary religious knowledge, but instead hoped that "all knowledge in the world should be open to girls."[55] In 1925 in Zanzibar, the Imam admonished any father who denied education to his daughters.[56] And to further encourage his followers to send their daughters to school, he went on establish over two hundred schools (some sex segregated and others coeducational) in India and East Africa during the first half of the twentieth century, with the first school for girls established as early as 1905 in Zanzibar.[57] These "Aga Khan schools" were viewed favorably by the community as an educational option for girls. In communities where Ismaili schools were not available, the Imam encouraged parents to send their children to government schools.[58]

Education in East Africa was segregated along racial lines until the early 1960s.[59] At first the British colonial government was not interested in educating "natives," and consequently Christian missionaries undertook the work of education. Ismailis (like other Asians in Africa) established schools for their own children, relying on private funds and grants from the Imam. From the 1910s, the colonial government founded schools for Africans and also initiated grants-in-aid programs, which would cover some expenses of the Aga Khan schools;[60] it instituted separate schools for the children of white settlers. Many of the earliest Ismaili schools established inland in East Africa were located adjacent to or inside the jamatkhanas and operated as both religious and secular schools. Often these schools hired teachers from India. We learn from Shariffa Keshavjee that Ismailis in Kisumu made a first attempt to set up a primary school for girls in 1919, but the school folded when it could not attract teaching staff.[61] Shariffa's grandfather Hasham Jamal made a new attempt in 1921, but it was not until the 1930s that a school for girls was firmly established (Figure 2.1). This school had three classrooms in the jamatkhana building, and a Parsee teacher was hired from India to teach forty boys and girls, Ismailis and Hindus.[62] Shariffa's mother, Khatija Jamal (b. 1917), studied at this school, which offered a wide range of subjects from Gujarati to mathematics. An Aga Khan school next to the jamatkhana in Kendu Bay employed Hindu teachers and educated children through the sixth grade. Students (both boys and girls) would then head to the school in Kisumu to complete their education.[63]

The education offered to girls at Aga Khan schools varied, however: urban schools offered more subjects than rural schools, and some

Figure 2.1 Students at an Ismaili girls school in Kisumu, est. 1920s. The school, initially established informally, was likely transformed into an Aga Khan Girls School in the 1930s.

Source: Sadruddin Khimani Family Collection, Vancouver, Canada. Reproduced with permission from Malik Merchant.

rural ones struggled to find teachers. For instance, Sakarkhanu Lalji's (b. 1924) schooling at her small Aga Khan school in Migori was less comprehensive than Khatija's:

> There were six or seven other Ismaili families at Migori—just Ismailis, not another Indian community—and there was a jamatkhana there, and next to it there was a small Aga Khan School. The school building was just one room, made of c.i. (galvanized iron or steel) sheets, but it was furnished with proper desks. We were 10 [to] 12 students, and we had one teacher, a Mr. Patel. He was the only non-Ismaili Indian in Migori, and he had come especially to teach. The teaching was all in Gujarati. I went to that school for six or seven years. We learned to read and write in Gujarati and that was really all we learned—we didn't learn any history or science or anything.[64]

Gulab Gudka likewise tells of an Ismaili school that she attended in Kisii in the 1930s, where again all teaching was conducted in Gujarati.[65] Gujarati remained the standard language of instruction in Aga Khan schools until the 1950s, but after that most schools switched to instruction in English and offered new curricular options as well. Zeenat Jamal (b. 1936) shares the changes made at the Aga Khan school in Kisumu: "Much was done to improve the education for girls. One of the changes made w[as] to put up an area for domestic science, taught by Mrs. Fisher. In the new domestic science room there were electric stoves. The women learnt about food and food values. They learnt to cook fat-free food, such as poached fish and fish pies. The girls learnt to sing English and even Swahili songs."[66] Yet changes in curriculum also produced anxiety: Shariffa recalls that her father's efforts to establish a school in Mombasa were met with intense debate around whether it was appropriate to teach girls English customs, including how to prepare English dishes. Community members feared that this kind of instruction could lead to girls losing their Indian heritage. Shariffa explains:

> Because if you teach girls how to do cooking and so they make Shepherd's Pie and fish pie and start to bake cakes, they are going to lose traditional *saak khawo*[67] kind of attitude and then you know trifle was unheard of. Who could bake a cake and then cut it up and then custard on top of it and then serve it? So, it was a very much a debated thing like are we really leading our women astray or is this the wise move? But the education just went on.[68]

Some families were concerned that too much schooling would make their daughters "unmarriageable"; others asked girls to drop out after elementary school because they could not manage the fees.[69] Still others dreaded that sending girls to urban cities to access secondary education might lead them to marry outside the community or could drive them away from the family's mercantile culture.[70] Education for girls was thus encouraged in general terms, but community members continued to deliberate over the what, when, and where.

Nonetheless, many Ismaili women related to me the impact the Imam's *farmans* had on this debate. One *farman* that my interlocutors cited repeatedly was made during the Imam's 1945 visit to Mombasa: "If a man has two children—one boy and the other a girl, and if he can only afford to give education to one, I would say that he must give preference to the girl." On other occasions the Imam emphasized that while boys would manage to make a living through trade, girls would not have such opportunities and therefore should be educated. Such *farmans* provided the impetus for some community members to establish schools (as we have seen above); they inspired others to create boarding facilities or to take in student boarders and thus indirectly support girls' education. Sakarkhanu Datoo (b. 1924) was a resident of one such boarding house.

Sakarkhanu grew up in a household where girls' education was encouraged, but her town of Bungoma had no schools.[71] Her parents therefore sent Sakarkhanu to study in Mombasa, where her education was facilitated by an Ismaili couple, Bhagat Mohamed Premji—also known as "Ada"—and his wife, Mithibai, who had established a boarding house. Popularly known as Ada's Boarding House, this facility accommodated girls so they could attend school; it also hosted male students and other young travelers. Sakarkhanu's daughter explains that Ada and Mithibai "definitely played a vital role in accommodating and facilitating the education needs of the young students from upcountry areas which did not have secondary schools." Looking at the photo reproduced in Figure 2.2, she elaborates, "You can also see how the girls are outnumbered by the boys. In those days, they did not have opportunity to pursue post-secondary education, especially for girls."[72] While several of my interlocutors remembered Ada's name, no one recalled his wife's, suggesting again how women's contributions remain in the

H. S. H. PRINCE ALI S. KHAN'S VISIT TO THE ISMAILIA PRIVATE BOARDING, MOMBASA. 26-2-39.

Figure 2.2 Residents and proprietors of Ada's Boarding House, 1939. Photo taken during a visit from Aga Khan III's son, Prince Aly Khan (seated, in black hat and tie). Mohamed and Mithibai Premji are seated on each side of the prince and Sakarkhanu is seated near Prince Aly's feet.
Courtesy of Gulzar Kassam.

background. I found Mithibai's name among householders listed in a 1935 colonial government gazette.[73]

Mithibai was among numerous Ismaili women who took in boarders from smaller towns. Mohammad Alibhai recalls that his mother, Tajbibi, looked after young Ismailis who came to Dar es Salaam for secondary education or to attend the Ismailia Mission Centre, which trained religious education teachers and itinerant preachers. The tasks of caring for those student boarders fell primarily on Tajbibi:

> She cooked for them, washed their clothes, prepared hot water for their baths, treated them when they fell sick (malaria was common), procured school uniforms, socks and shoes, school supplies, paid the school fees, gave them spending money (including for jamatkhana *dua karavi, niyaz*, etc.), and so on. . . . In the practice of boarders, it was the mother who was at the center of the boarders' lives. In this way, women contributed to the education of children from the interior, and therefore to the growth of the community.[74]

Many of the young women who attended the Ismailia Mission Centre (Figure 2.3) even called Tajbibi "mummy."[75] In doing this often-invisible work and also directing those in their care to perform religious duties

Figure 2.3 Tajbibi (center) with students of the Ismailia Mission Centre.
Courtesy of Mohamed Abualy Alibhai.

regularly, women like Mithibai and Tajbibi participated in the transmission of religious rites and rituals outside the mother-child paradigm.

While education created pathways for women to enter commercial and professional occupations, such work was not easy to undertake because it competed with other social and familial contributions expected of women. Nur, whom we met at the beginning of the chapter, ultimately finished the midwifery course, got married, and moved to Lindi with her husband. She started putting her education to use, but when her husband expanded his business from one shop to two, he expected her to manage one of the shops on top of her work as a midwife. As her daughter recalls:

> He expected her [laughing] to do the [baby] deliveries, stay up all night, all day, and then take care of the shop as well, and the kids and the cooking and everything. So it was really hard on her. . . . [I]f it was the night delivery and she had been up the whole night, he expected her to open the shop at 8am as usual and [have] lunch ready. . . . She kept doing that for many years but in the end, it became too hard for her. There was a lot of friction around that with my parents and my father wouldn't understand why the shop was not open or why she was tired. . . . [I]n the end, she gave it [midwifery] up.[76]

While few women of Nur's generation in East Africa were able to acquire an education, they made sure that their daughters—particularly girls who came of age during the 1950s and 1960s—did so. This generation of Ismaili women attended teacher training schools or secretarial colleges or enrolled in accounting courses. Many launched their teaching careers at the Aga Khan schools. In the 1960s, they also began entering the fields of medicine, architecture, and politics (one of the first female members of the Independence National Assembly in Uganda was an Ismaili woman, Sugra Visram).[77]

Ismaili women's educational achievement and economic activities during the first half of the twentieth century were further enabled by the Imam's measures related to women's mobility and sartorial practices, as well as reforms in communal marriage laws.[78] It is precisely for this reason that Savita Nair cautions against generalizing the experience of Ismaili women to other Indian women in East Africa, and Dana Seidenberg casts Ismaili women as an exception in certain cases.[79] Beginning in the early twentieth century, the Imam discouraged *purdah* among his female followers so they could move more freely in both private and public places, manage shops, and pursue education.[80] This directive applied to women in both India and the

Indian diaspora. During his first visit to Zanzibar and Bagamoyo in 1899, he stated that it was not appropriate for women to cover their faces and encouraged men and women to view each other as brothers and sisters.[81] Speaking in 1905 to an audience of female followers in Zanzibar, he said, "The external *burqa* (veil) is not for you, but [better] for you is the veil of the heart, have modesty (*haya*) in your heart, fill your heart with modesty all the time."[82] That the Imam continued to make these *farmans* into the late 1920s shows that Khoja Ismailis were slow to respond to this directive.[83] In the family biography of Sherbanu Lalani, we learn of an instructive inter-action between the Imam and Sherbanu's sister-in-law Sikina: On her wedding day, sometime in the 1920s, Sikina and her husband met with the Imam in Kampala for blessings. The Imam removed the face covering that Sikina was wearing. Sherbanu recalls, "During those days ladies wore a *bandhani* over the head and an *abochhan* around the neck and they *laaj kadhta* (used the *bandhani* to cover their faces). *Mawlana* Sultan Mahomed Shah removed Sikina's *laaj* and said that it was not important but what was important was *aankh ni sharam* (modesty). Ever since then all Ismaili women stopped covering their faces!"[84] The Imam advised Ismaili men not to beat their wives, quarrel with them, or marry two wives without a good reason—and urged them to treat their wives with love.[85]

By 1945, the Imam was pleased to see that his female followers in Mombasa were no longer veiling.[86] He next called on Ismaili women in East Africa specifically to replace Indian attire with knee-length European dresses to enable better integration into colonial society. Followers again were slow to make the change, and some even considered it scandalous. He reissued the *farman* in 1952—this time promising an autographed photograph of himself and his wife to women who took this further step to change their dress.[87] By the late 1950s, Ismaili women in the region had largely adopted Western dress and were rarely seen in "Asian" clothes in public. Shariffa explains these transformations:

> In India in the 1800s, Ismaili women were wearing typical Gujarati working sarees, known as *sadlo*. Around the turn of the century, as the Aga Khan started to encourage integration, there was a switch to long dresses worn with *pachedi* shawls. By the '30s the transformation was well under way; the young Ismaili women of Kisumu were wearing short frocks (but not too short), spoke English, knew English etiquette, and learned English cookery. . . . Women were encouraged to go out and work, so by 1936 some

Figure 2.4 Ismaili Ladies Volunteer Corps, 1950s, Mbeya, Tanzania.
Courtesy of Dr. Moh'd Manji.

women were running commercial ventures in Kisumu, others took up teaching and sewing for a living . . . this at the time when other communities did not allow their women to work. "Don't lock up your girls within four walls" was what Aga Khan III encouraged.[88]

Figure 2.4 shows a group photo of Ismaili women volunteers from the city of Mbeya during the 1950s; they are all wearing a colonial-style dress without the traditional *pacheri* that we see in photographs from the 1940s (as an example see Figure 3.4 in chapter 3).

Ismailis and Colonial Racial Capitalism

By acquiring the English language, donning the English-style dress, and even adopting English foodways, Ismailis aligned themselves with the colonial regime and its racial hierarchies. Aly Kassam-Remtulla reflects that since achieving parity with Europeans was unlikely, Asians adopted English cultural practices partly to distance themselves from the category of "African."[89] Ismailis, like other Asians in East Africa, tended to marry along communal lines and created their own residential enclaves. The latter followed from colonial policies that organized schooling, housing, and commerce along racial·lines. Umeeda Switlo recalls: "In Uganda, when we were growing up, we had communities that were divided, in that white people went to white schools, black kids went to black schools, and Ismaili kids and Indian kids went to the Ismaili community school."[90] Residential, commercial, and educational segregation meant that Ismailis interacted with Africans primarily as domestic servants, chauffeurs, housekeepers, cooks, waiters, or manual laborers in Ismaili small businesses—or when Africans shopped in Ismaili *dukas*. By the middle of the twentieth century, even less well-off Ismaili families across East Africa employed African staff in their businesses or in their homes as domestic help.[91] Asians and Africans, as Nazira Mawji observes, rarely socialized as equals.[92] Reflecting on her childhood in Uganda in the 1950s and 1960s, Yasmin Alibhai-Brown writes: "Caste and colour-coded ranking dovetailed with colonial race classifications. . . . I never saw a black-Asian couple in public places. Liaisons between Asian men and Black prostitutes or maids were dirty secrets. Their children were foully dubbed "chotaras" (half-caste in Swahili), meaning mongrels."[93] Alibhai-Brown's observations are consistent with a history of widespread anti-Black sentiment among Asians in Africa.

Running in parallel then to the story of Ismaili community interiority is a second narrative of exclusion and competition with out-groups, which was not incidental but an essential feature of British colonial racial capitalism in East Africa. As noted in chapter 1, British colonial regime relied on creating divisions among subject populations; favorable policies toward one group (Asians) ensured that they would view themselves as distinct from (and even superior to) other groups (Africans), setting them up to be in conflict with each other. It is within this system of colonial exploitation that Ismailis tried to broker more opportunities for themselves by structuring their schooling and other social mores along English lines;[94] it is also within this context that they expressed anti-Blackness.

But there are stories of collaboration and collective resistance too. I encountered anecdotal recollections of Ismaili women who tried to establish friendships and partnerships with Africans—relationships that my interlocutors found meaningful though they were undoubtedly shaped by an unequal relation of power. Sherbanu, whom we saw earlier in the chapter, partnered with indigenous Baganda people who farmed land near her husband's shop to grow and sell a range of Indian lentils and herbs.[95] Their partnership evolved into friendship as they began to learn from each other how to use certain herbs to treat ailments. Oral histories collected by Mawji likewise document a number of commercial partnerships between Ismaili and African women.[96] Mohamed Keshavjee's memoirs *Into that Heaven of Freedom* furnishes accounts of many Ismailis who worked alongside African leaders against the apartheid regime in South Africa.[97] And, a Khoja Ismaili, Abdul Rasool, established the "first multi-racial school" in Mombasa in 1921 through a gift of fifty thousand pounds.[98] In a *farman* to his female followers in Nairobi in 1945, the Imam guided women to "not blindly imitate the European women here who get African servants to do their housework."[99] While that *farman* might mean that Ismaili women should remain self-sufficient or that he was urging Ismaili women to see African women in other capacities or both, the Imam directly initiated other efforts to improve race relations: he established the East African Muslim Welfare Society in 1945 to contribute to the welfare of Muslims at large and integrated the Aga Khan schools in the 1950s.[100] Taushif Kara observes in these endeavors a sharp departure from the British colonial project: "Quite unlike the rationale for settler colonialism, which notably sought to exaggerate and harden the space between the 'native' and the 'settler,' while at the same time eliding and even eliminating the former, here it was not distance but rather closeness that the Aga [Khan III] relied upon."[101] Later the next Imam, Aga Khan IV, made material investments in East Africa, establishing insurance companies, investment trusts, schools, clinics, and hospitals that served local populations, and more broadly stressed the importance of racial cooperation. When Tanzania, Kenya, and Uganda gained independence in the 1960s, the Imam advised his followers to obtain citizenship and align their aspirations with those of the new nations.[102]

A vivid illustration of the closeness that Kara refers to above comes to us via Sultan Somjee's two ethnographic-fictional accounts: *Bead Bai* (2012) and *Home between Crossings* (2016).[103] Born in Kenya, Somjee is a fourth-generation Asian-African Ismaili who offers a rare reconstruction of Khoja women's life in colonial and postcolonial Kenya. In *Bead Bai*, we meet Ismaili vendors who sell colorful beads to Maasai and Kikuyu women and become fluent in local vernacular (as we have seen in the case of Jetbai Dhanji above); they influence and are influenced by the aesthetic preferences of their customers (as we saw in the case of Fatma's *kikubas*). The protagonist Sakina learns beadwork from a Maasai elder and draws on techniques of Khoja *zari* embroidery used in *bandhani* shawls to make Maasai *emankeeki* (a beaded necklace). Through these exchanges, Somjee illustrates aesthetic routes of

Asian-African intimacies that existed beside racial, economic, and political segregation (in chapter 5 we will see further evidence of this in Asian-African foodways).

Thus, instead of pitting Ismailis (or Asians more broadly) against Africans, it may be more helpful to examine what Richard Delgado and Jean Stefancic describe as their "differential racialization" within a colonial matrix.[104] Such an approach considers the distinct and overlapping routes through which both Asians and Africans were brought into the orbit of the European colonial project. It identifies conjunctions and indicates, as Kris Manjapra observes, how "different colonial forms nest in each other and fuse with each other."[105] Ismailis, like other Asians, found themselves in a position where they were both victims of anti-Indian racism *and* perpetrators of anti-Black racism; they labored under exploitative conditions set up by the colonizers while also creating exploitative conditions for indigenous people. Paying attention to these dynamics wards off against either romanticizing or disparaging Ismaili settlers. It helps us to recognize the contingency of their actions and to read them as made possible within their specific socioeconomic, racial, and political contexts. It further opens the possibility of appreciating (like Somjee does) the minor gestures, habits, and objects through which Asians and Africans tried to subvert colonial partitions, as well as the political alliances through which they launched a collective resistance to the British (as Keshavjee shows us in the case of South Africa).

It is against this complex nexus of privilege and subordination that I read my interlocutors' insistence that the very practices that would be later critiqued by the second generation as evidence of their ancestors' anti-Blackness and alignment with the colonial regime (see chapter 6)— acquiring British-style schooling, wearing the English dress, adopting English foodways—helped Ismailis rebuild their lives in the aftermath of displacement, when they often settled in English-speaking countries. Women in particular found that because they spoke English and dressed like Western women, when displaced to Canada in the 1970s they were able to find employment in the service industry more quickly than their husbands.[106] Some were eventually able to carve out an independent life in Canada that would have been unavailable to them in East Africa. But Ismailis also experienced xenophobia and anti-Brown racism in North America. The second generation will reckon with these complex histories of settler colonialism, racism, and racialization.

East Pakistan, 1950–1970

Unlike those Ismailis who had made East Africa their home—some of whom for nearly a century—Ismailis who made their way to East Pakistan in the 1940s and 1950s would have only a short two decades in the country before they were forced to flee. Scholars have barely begun to investigate this cohort. To reconstruct their lives I have therefore relied heavily on interviews, unpublished family memoirs, and photographs.

I first met Roshan Kajani (b. 1938) in December 2019 at a jamatkhana in Atlanta and formally interviewed her in November 2020. Her daughter-in-law had arranged the introduction and had explained to Roshan ahead of our meeting that I hoped to ask her about her life in East Pakistan. As she made herself comfortable on her pristine white sofa, the first thing she said to me was: "I don't know what I can tell you."[107] But then she went on to trace her family's journey from Kathiawar to East Pakistan and then onto North America in impressive detail. Born in a small village called Drafa, Roshan recalls a comfortable childhood: "My father had a big shop, which had everything. We were well-to-do." The Imam's directive to Ismailis in the Kathiawar region to move elsewhere to escape poverty and hardship presented her family with a conundrum: if they followed this instruction, they would lose their thriving business. Roshan's family eventually complied. She explains to me the family's deliberations and their final decision: "You see, when a *farman* comes, that is it. We were well-to-do but we left." When I probed further about her family's leap into uncertainty, she responded, "He [the Imam] must have known that things would get bad. It would have gotten bad for us." Expressing faith in their Imam's care and Divinely inspired knowledge, Roshan's family packed up everything and moved. They initially traveled to Hyderabad Deccan, where they sought shelter at a jamatkhana because they had no other accommodations. Later the *mukhi* and *mukhiani* graciously housed them under their own roof until they found a place of their own.

A few years passed and Roshan and her parents had to move again, this time to escape what she refers to as "the police action of 1948," when the newly established state of India annexed Hyderabad: "We packed up and left in such a hurry that we did not even turn off the stove." Roshan eventually got married and had children but continued to struggle with poverty. The family therefore decided to make its way to Khulna in East Pakistan in search of better economic prospects. Life there was difficult too: they lived in a two-room mud house with a leaky roof. "But at least the jamatkhana

was right across," Roshan sighs with relief, signaling the salience of congregational prayer in her daily life. It was her regular practice of faith that kept her
going during hard times: "I went to jamatkhana in the mornings as well as in
the evenings, without fail. I had too many children, but I didn't care [laughs],
I would just leave them with my relatives and go [laughs]. Sometimes my poor
kid would come to get me from jamatkhana when he needed me. *Shukar.*" In
the jamatkhana, Roshan not only prayed but also established relationships
with fellow Ismailis, some of whom ended up sheltering her family in their
homes when violence erupted years later in 1971.

Like Roshan, Karima (b. 1947) headed to East Pakistan with her family in
the early 1950s, also to escape violence.[108] She explains:

I was probably 2 or 3 years old; I don't know my exact age when we moved
to Dhaka, but I know from my parents' stories that they were newlywed and
the partition was affecting their lives. They in fact were looted. Whatever
my mother had received, you know for her wedding dowry, her furniture,
and everything that her parents gave, she lost everything. And my dad was
held up once and they wanted to find out whether he was a Muslim or a
Hindu. So all that scared them, and they made the decision to move, to
move out of India. And then there must have been a *farman*. I am not quite
sure but there was a directive to go and settle you know in different places
from *Mawla*, so they chose to come to East Pakistan.

J.A. remembers this *farman*: the Imam had asked his followers to "keep one
foot in India and one in Pakistan, meaning if there are two brothers then one
should live there and one here."[109]

While most Ismailis in East Pakistan settled in Dhaka and Chittagong,
smaller numbers could be found in Sylhet, Khulna, Mymensingh,
Narayanganj, Rangpur, and nearby villages. Many Ismailis moved from city
to city until they finally found work that could support their families. Saher
Banu (b. 1920) and her husband, much like Roshan and Karima's parents,
journeyed across India—to Gondia and then to Hyderabad—in search of
better prospects until finally, in 1951, they decided to head to East Pakistan,
where they spent a year in Sylhet before moving to Chittagong in 1952.[110]
Although still struggling in Chittagong, the couple gradually began to make
a life for their family of nine. Saher Banu worked as a seamstress, often under
lantern light as their landlord switched off the building's electricity by 9 p.m.
The *jamat* in East Pakistan also included about a thousand refugees from

Burma who had fled after the 1962 military coup. My interlocutors estimate
the overall Ismaili population in the region by the 1970s to be between seven
and ten thousand.[111]

Jamatkhanas, Jobs, and a Positive Outlook

During the 1950s, Ismaili migrants to East Pakistan struggled economically.
Men labored in factories or as petty traders and shopkeepers, and women
worked from home as seamstresses or in restaurants. Mumtaz Noordin
Alibhai, who arrived in Dhaka in 1950, remembers the city as fairly un-
derdeveloped: "There was much poverty. People had no money to do anything, you know. . . . [But] from there we have slowly, slowly progressed."[112]
Others recall lack of basic services such as sewage and running water, and
struggling at first because they did not speak the local language. As in East
Africa, early jamatkhanas in East Pakistan were also makeshift, a room in
someone's house. In Dhaka, for instance, a jamatkhana was organized in a
room provided by Nazarali Chagan; as the number of Ismailis increased, a
structure with three rooms was rented.[113] Later, purpose-built jamatkhanas
and housing societies were established. Ismailis began to enter the jute, tex-
tile, steel, aluminum, leather, construction, and food processing industries—
working as laborers as well as owners—and others made money in trading,
banking, insurance, and the hotel industry. Enayet Jiwani (b. 1954) recalls
that over the years his father launched several businesses, including an ice
cream factory, an ice factory, and a biscuit factory.[114] Hameed Husain's (b.
1945) father started as an executive secretary with the Chittagong Chamber
of Commerce and went on to become a regional manager at a British-owned
pharmaceutical company.[115] Indeed, many of my interlocutors remember
having a positive outlook on life by the 1960s. This was partly because Aga
Khan IV—who had become the forty-ninth Ismaili Imam in 1957—had
taken a keen interest in the economic development of this region.

The Imam visited East Pakistan in 1959 and laid the foundation of a
jamatkhana in Dhaka (Figure 2.5).[116] In 1964, he traveled to East Pakistan
again and visited the newly founded Ismailia Co-operative Housing Society
at Khulna, inaugurated a jamatkhana in Chittagong, and laid the foundation
for an Aga Khan school. He returned in 1970, this time with his wife, and authorized an apartment building in Dhaka and a new jamatkhana at Khulna,
and established the Jessore Jute Industries. During this visit, the Pakistan Jute

THE FOUNDATION STONE OF THIS LUCKY JAMATKHANA BUILDING WAS LAID BY THE DISTRICT MAGISTRATE DACCA, MR. ALI AHMED B. A. ON 7TH. AUGUST, 1959. THE OPENING CEREMONY WAS PERFORMED BY HIS ROYAL HIGHNESS SHAH KARIM AL-HUSEINI, THE AGAKHAN IV ON 11TH. OCT. 1960 AND IT WAS NAMED AS KARIMABAD JAMATKHANA

Figure 2.5 The foundation stone of the Karimabad jamatkhana in Dhaka.
Courtesy of Ayeleen Ajanee Saleh.

Mills Association in Dhaka organized a luncheon in the Imam's honor. His speech on that occasion illustrates his strong desire to advance the economy of East Pakistan so that both his community and others could prosper. The Imam recognized that while his own community was heavily invested in jute mills, this was an industry that impacted the livelihood of nearly one million East Pakistanis.[117] He expressed concern that consumption of jute bags was declining globally in favor of paper bags and urged his audience to explore further applications for jute products. He suggested that research be undertaken on new strains of plants whose barks produce fibers that are softer, more malleable, and thus adaptable to a greater variety of uses. He further recommended to jute mill owners to reinvest their profits to modernize their manufacturing plants. The Imam also gifted fifteen lac takas to the Dacca Municipal Corporation, requesting that the gift "be devoted to the poor and deserving of this city in the social fields of education, health and housing."[118]

Recently transplanted Ismailis were encouraged by the Imam's visits to East Pakistan, his approval for establishing jamatkhanas and housing societies, and his keen interest in the country's economic development. Malek Batada (b. 1942), who had moved to East Pakistan at the age of ten in the early 1950s,

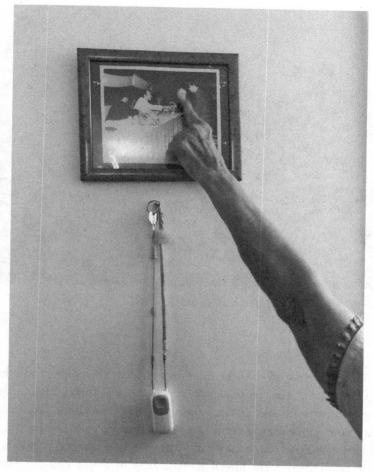

Figure 2.6 Z.H. points to her father, a leader of the local *jamat* in East Pakistan, pictured with Imam Shah Karim Aga Khan IV in the 1960s.
Photo by author, 2019.

shared this positive outlook. While her family struggled initially, by the late 1960s they had moved into a "newly-built housing society around a new Jamatkhana" in the city of Mymensingh and her father had found a stable job at a jute mill.[119] During our meeting in Atlanta, seventy-year-old Z.H. proudly pointed to a photograph that hangs in her living room: it shows her father presenting a gift to the Imam during one of his visits to Chittagong (Figure 2.6)—visits that she explains "brought the *jamat* together and gave us hope."[120] She remembers the *jamat* of Chittagong as gradually becoming more stable,

Figure 2.7 Chittagong jamatkhana in 2000.
Courtesy of Noorallah.

observing that over time "there were four residential colonies and a brand new jamatkhana." That particular "brand new" jamatkhana in Chittagong, Z.H. exclaims, was "bigger and more beautiful than earlier ones" (Figure 2.7).

The new jamatkhanas—and the permanence and prosperity they symbolized—helped reinforce Ismailis' sense of belonging in East Pakistan. At one point there were fifteen jamatkhanas in major cities.[121] Ismailis tended to live around the jamatkhanas, which facilitated their interactions with coreligionists and helped build support networks. Nargis Somani (b. 1953) fondly recalls her teenage years in Dhaka during the 1960s, her days filled with activity centered around the jamatkhana and the Ismaili neighborhood: "We would go to our friends' houses to learn arts and craft. I learned how to make beautiful baskets out of bamboo sticks; another friend's mom used to the teach us *dua*; another's embroidery and there was a teacher who used to come to our house to teach us Arabic. Everyone was so friendly."[122] Zarintaj Sultan (b. 1949) attended *wa'z* courses held at the Dhaka jamatkhana and received a certificate of completion (Figure 2.8) from the Imam himself.

While several of my interlocutors described East Pakistan as "a heaven," "a tropical paradise," and "blissful"—reminiscing about the lush greenery

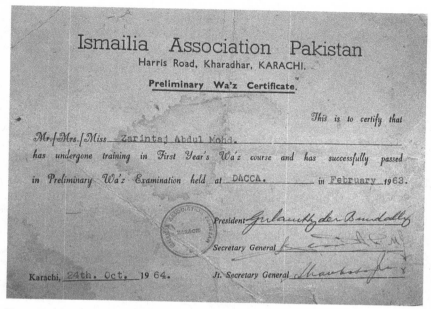

Figure 2.8 Certificate of completion, Zarintaj Sultan (née Abdul Mohammad), 1963.
Photo by author, 2021.

and flowing rivers—the East Pakistan *jamat* also included families who remained impoverished. Roshan Kajani, whom we saw above, recalls many Ismailis dwelling in congested quarters; Dilshad Sadruddin (b. 1955) similarly remembers crowded and poor-quality housing: "Our roofs were always leaking. There were electric wires around and I was worried about getting electrocuted."[123] The small gestures of kindness and aid that we observed in the East African context, though, were also present. A fellow Ismaili paid tuition for Dilshad's younger sister so she could attend school. When Ismailis from smaller villages sought refuge in the Dhaka jamatkhana after their houses flooded due to monsoon rains, Sherbanoo Ajani (b. 1921) cooked meals for them.[124] When a young Dolat Valliani's (b. 1924) husband passed away, leaving her with three children, an Ismaili woman offered to share her kitchen and taught her how to cook snacks that she could sell.[125] Dolat's daughter tells me:

My mother became a widow when she was only 28 years old. At the time, we lived in a small village of Gondia in India. Her brother, who lived in

Dhaka, offered to move us with him and my mother decided that it was the best course of action so we [the children] could have access to education. In Dhaka, the Girls Guide captain suggested to my mom to run the jamatkhana canteen so she could make ends meet, and another woman taught her how to cook snacks, like those that people might buy, *aloo, tili, bhel puri, cholay, chana puri, thepla, samosa*. My mother became famous for her canteen.

When Dolat fled to Karachi in 1971, she continued baking snacks, supplying them to local restaurants. One day, an Ismaili neighbor saw her carrying heavy bags of snacks and offered to help. From then on, he made the deliveries for her. Dolat was eventually hired by an Ismaili woman as a cook, which enabled her to keep her own household running.

Educating Girls

As in East Africa, Ismailis in East Pakistan set out to establish infrastructure to support struggling families, including the institutions and informal systems needed to make girls' education possible. By the late 1960s, Aga Khan education boards had been established that managed schools and hostels in Dhaka, Chittagong, Khulna, and Mymensingh. Farida Khoja and Zarintaj Huda (b. 1950) attended one such facility: Noorani Academy, a hostel for Ismaili girls in Dhaka.[126] The academy accommodated fifteen girls from low-income families, whose room, board, and school tuition expenses were paid by wealthier Ismailis. The residence was maintained by Ismaili volunteers who also provided daily transportation to the nearby Karimabad jamatkhana so girls could participate in evening congregational prayers. The academy then moved to a second location, accommodating about twenty girls. In the mid-1960s, with the sanction of the Imam, it shifted to a larger third location in the Mirpur neighborhood of Dhaka and could now house fifty girls. While girls from low-income backgrounds continued to be supported through aid monies, those who could afford contributed anywhere from 30 to even 100 percent of the boarding fees. Zarintaj and Farida both have fond memories of their time at the hostel (Figure 2.9 shows some students with their parents). Zarintaj recalls, "There were large rooms, 10 beds in each room and four to five attached bathrooms. We lived on the first floor and the entire second floor was a beautiful jamatkhana. We used to get up for

Figure 2.9 Farida (front row, seventh from right) and Zarintaj (second row, eighth from right) at one of the functions at the Noorani Academy in Mirpur during the 1960s.
Courtesy of Farida Khoja.

prayer in the morning, then go to school, have our meals, and then attend jamatkhana in the evenings."[127]

Farida remembers her schooling in East Pakistan as being much more rigorous than her later experience in West Pakistan. In addition to the English language, she studied Bangla as advised by the Imam. In a *farman* made in 1964, he said:

I would like to emphasize again the very great importance for my East Pakistan *jamats* to integrate in all ways possible with the people of East Pakistan. This *farman*, this advice, is not [only] for the men but it is also for the women, and I hope that the women will make a very determined effort to assist local initiative and that the men will do the same thing. I would like that, in the years ahead all our children should be able to speak fluent

Bengali and that the parents who are able to learn the language, should also learn Bengali. I would like that you should mix in as much as possible with local initiative not only in the field of social welfare, but also in the other fields of economic development and other aspects of local self-help programmes.[128]

Although *farmans* like these prompted several of my younger interlocutors to learn Bangla in addition to English, Urdu, and Gujarati, this was not the case for everyone. An Ismaili participant in Ayeleen Saleh's study, for instance, notes that the community maintained its distinction by resisting assimilating into the local Bengali culture:

I went to an English medium school and took Urdu as a second language. Even in Night School our books were in Gujrati, written in Roman English. Ismailis didn't speak proper Bangla. During my school years, around 1963, they started calling me "Mawra"—it's a derogatory word for Indians. Sometimes they would call the Ismaili children "show-offs" since we never mingled with the community and always felt we were superior to the children from the lower class families in the neighborhood in which we lived. Similarly, our parents would not want to integrate in the community.[129]

The Imam's advice to integrate thus was not always attended to by community members as they tried to preserve class and ethnic boundaries (represented by fluency in Urdu and residential societies), which also sometimes yielded favorable treatment from the West Pakistan government.

As in East Africa, girls' education in East Pakistan was a subject of debate. Zarintaj Sultan tells me about how her father opposed her efforts to enroll in a nursing program in the 1960s, although her mother was supportive.[130] Nursing was not considered an acceptable profession for girls from well-to-do backgrounds; in fact, on hearing of Zarintaj's intentions, another patriarch from the family visited her father to caution him against it: "Our women don't work for others." Dejected Zarintaj appealed to her *Mawla* through prayers and received a response:

I was in jamatkhana one day and I said to *Mawla*, "What kind of *Mawla* are you that you can't convince my dad?" And believe me child (*beta*), I still remember that day. It was the eve of the next Islamic month (*chandraat*) and a message (*taliqa*) came from the Imam in which he instructed the *jamat* to send *jamati* girls into the nursing profession. He even created a Nursing School in Pakistan later. I marched up to my dad right after services. I was 15 and a half at that time. I told my dad, "Did you hear what *Mawla* said?" He came home that evening and without hesitation gave me permission. So, you see all is due to *Mawla*. After leaving Dhaka in 1971, I stayed in West Pakistan for some time, but life was so hard there. Then because of my nursing I got [a] green card for the United States. Nursing opened the way for me, *Mawla*'s mercy (*rehmat*). I worked as a nurse for 40 years. (See Figure 2.10.)

Zarintaj's efforts to pursue nursing in the 1960s—and her appeals to *Mawla*—are reminiscent of Nur's endeavors to study midwifery in Zanzibar at the turn of the twentieth century. In both cases, families were persuaded directly or indirectly by the Imam. But, as we have seen, the Imam's guidance requires engagement from followers as well, as they make sense of (and even sometimes reject) the guidance under certain circumstances. The anxiety and ambivalence displayed by Saher Banu is a case in point.

Saher Banu's daughter, Farida Merchant (b. 1948, going forward I use "Merchant" to distinguish her from Farida Khoja, my mother), tells me that although her mother had only studied through fourth grade, she wanted more for her daughters: "She always insisted that we should have an education. . . . She said, 'If I could choose between giving you three meals a day versus two meals and save that one meal and send you to school, I would do that.'"[131] After Merchant completed tenth grade, however, Saher Banu did not see the need for her to continue further, expecting her to get married instead. When Merchant protested, Saher Banu retorted, "You will end up in the kitchen anyway, busy raising your family and looking after your husband. Education will not be of any use."[132] Merchant even mobilized the Imam's *farmans* to convince her mother, but to no effect. What is evident here is that women's ethical decision-making does not unfold in a vacuum; ethical practice is about balancing multiple competing demands, as opposed to following rigid notions of "good" and "bad." In this case, Saher Banu's choices are mediated by her social experience: she weighs the Imam's *farmans* in favor of women's education against other exigencies, including a conventional social expectation that her daughter will have a better choice of marriage partner if she marries by a certain age, and a generational expectation that the choice to marry will then curtail her daughter's career options.

Figure 2.10 Zarintaj Sultan poses with her nursing certificate.
Photo by author, 2021.

Instead of viewing Ismaili women as one-dimensional figures, such examples illuminate how engagement with religious edicts and care for family are weighed in daily life. A different recollection from Merchant about her mother shows us yet another dimension of Saher Banu's ethical practice:

There was another incident involving a young family who lived three houses down from us. Late one afternoon, my mother was passing by their house when she heard children crying. She paused for a few minutes and when the crying did not stop, she knocked. The young mother, who I now know as [name removed to protect anonymity] aunty, opened the door a crack, peeked out, and let my mom in. Her children were crying because they were hungry and there was no food in the house. Mom hurried home, picked up the food she had prepared for us, and fed those children. From that day on, Mom took that family under her wing, always keeping a watchful eye.[133]

Merchant's memories of her mother—generosity to a neighbor, ambitions for her daughter that exceeded her own but not beyond a certain limit—frame Saher Banu as a complex subject and clarify Ismaili ethics as ordinary decisions that individuals make while taking into account social norms, everyday exigencies, and religious edicts.

In 1971 the war between East and West Pakistan reintroduced chaos into the lives of Ismailis, with particularly harsh consequences for the poorer members of the community. Roshan tells me: "People were killing each other. There were not many guns, so they used daggers. Blood, blood everywhere [pauses]. We would grab our children and run to the houses of other Ismailis who lived in gated communities to take shelter there." Merchant explains, "War brings havoc to the the . . . I would say vulnerable. And it's always the poor and the people without means are the ones who have the worst situation." Merchant and her family made their way from East Pakistan to Karachi and then onto North America within a few years, as did many other Ismailis. Their diasporic journeys will be discussed in the following chapters. But at least three thousand Ismailis stayed back and tried to remake life in the newly formed nation of Bangladesh.[134]

"Lessons in *Iman* (Faith)"

My aim in this chapter has been twofold: first, I have tried to bring into presence some Ismaili women's living memory of their foremothers and their own childhoods to complement the standard narrative of modern Ismaili history; second, I have used these memories to illustrate the numerous ways in which women have maintained relations of care and spiritual kinship along migratory routes, emphasizing that we view their actions as dynamic expressions of their faith. I tell the stories of these women not because they are exceptional but because their narratives suggest some common themes: the blending of personal effort and communal aid, the inseparability of *din* and *dunya*, and the expression of piety through both prayers and conduct. We have seen some women's names disappear into the background, buried deep in the colonial archives, even as they are remembered by their contributions to the community; others, while not captured by official archives, continue to inform the ethical development of their Ismaili descendants through their example. Many of the women I interviewed made it plain that when confronted with the horrors of displacement and violence, they had mobilized the memories of their grandmothers and mothers. S.D., who fled East Pakistan in 1971, reminded herself "to have *iman* (belief, faith)" and that she would survive and find her way to a new home just as her mother had:

> I often think of how my mother was always moving and had to build her life, you see, from nothing, from Gujarat to Bombay to Dhaka. So, when the war happened and we had to leave everything one more time and go to Karachi, I was with her. I kept reminding myself that it would be alright, that I should have *iman* like she had *iman* because after all I am her daughter. We are used to moving [laughs and then with a somber expression says] but I was afraid, really. I am sure she was afraid too.[135]

In a moment of personal crisis, it is her mother's faith and determination to survive that become a source of ethical guidance for S.D. She emphasizes her point further by quoting a *ginan* that her mother used to recite and how she now remembers those verses as "lessons in *iman*." *Ginans*, which, as we have seen above, are hymnlike poems of varying lengths transmitted orally for several centuries before being collected and recorded. They are considered texts through which the Ismaili poet-saints (*pirs* and *sayyids*) conveyed the teachings of Islam and thus have a didactic or doctrinal purpose, along with acting as a medium for communication with the Divine (in a parallel spiritual function). S.D. says:

> You know the *ginan* in which *pir* says not to doubt the Imam? *Eji sathi esa kijie, je koi rah batave; Unke sange chalie, man manhe shak na ave* (O brother! Take him your companion who can show you the right path. Go with him and have no doubt in the heart).[136] Ma used to recite it all the time, like even while making *chai*, making *rotlo*, while sweeping the floor

[laughs]. You know, it sticks with you, I mean, these verses stay with you. These are lessons in *iman* and you remember them when you are most scared and alone in life.

We can detect a similar "lesson in *iman*" from Munira Dhanani's recall of her grandmother. During the treacherous bus ride from the city to the Entebbe airport in Kampala under the cover of night, young Munira witnessed her grandmother find strength through constant prayers: "My grandmother was very very supportive in a quiet way because she was praying under her breath and you could feel her breathing just getting heavier and heavier, and yet, you know, her faith in her religion and the spiritual comfort that she just brought into her life through the power of prayer kept her going through all this."[137] S.D. also alludes to the power of prayer, which helped women contend with the ongoing trauma of war. Talking about her mother, she says: "So much moving takes a toll on one's body. For [the] last ten years of her life, Ma went quiet. All she did was say her *tasbih* (invocation of Allah). That's it. Maybe it was all that trauma that finally caught up with her? So she had to rest mentally. But she never complained. She always said, 'Shukar Mawla.' I think prayers kept her going. Her life was so hard, so hard."

It was not only in times of crisis, though, that my interlocutors turned to their ancestors for lessons in faith. Shirin's memory of her mother keeping a separate box for religious dues so it did not get mixed up with the money available for household expenditure, Gulzar's pride in her grandmother establishing a *duka* to support herself and her children, Shariffa's elaboration on how women of her family pursued education in response to the *farmans* of the Imams, Nimira's recall of the ethical value of *santosh* she learned from her grandmother, and Merchant's mobilization of her mother's generosity— each memory displays how an earlier generation of Ismaili women's ordinary ethical practices are imbibed as lessons by later generations. Approaching Ismaili women through the memories of their descendants gives them a fullness and visibility that is not usually accorded to members of this cohort. It restores them as caretakers and as ethical subjects.

A second goal of this chapter has been to draw on women's memories to illuminate the relations of care that permeated Ismaili communities in East Africa and East Pakistan, before the dislocations that are the center of this project. These relations include individual as well as collective forms of care: care for one's own family and care for coreligionists; believers' careful consideration of the Imam's *farmans* and the Imam's caring guidance for his *murids.* Paying attention to such relationalities helps us to recognize that religious community is not given but an effect of ordinary acts that reinforce spiritual affinity. Visiting a sick coreligionist, teaching a widow how to make snacks that she can later sell, advocating for one's daughter's education, cooking food for boarders or for those displaced by floods—all belong to the universe of ordinary ethics. We also see the social impact of collective care efforts as Ismailis established homes for widowed women, schools, and boarding houses, or when they provided festival meals, tuition fees, and subsidized housing to low-income coreligionists. Care for coreligionists then appears as a socially authorized performance through which Ismailis have recognized and enacted their religio-moral obligations. We will see continuities of such practices in the following chapters as well.

While my interlocutors certainly emphasized the more positive aspects of their foremothers' lives, from resilience and hard work to familial and communal harmony, in their stories Ismaili women do not appear as one-dimensional figures. The narratives we have seen demonstrate that the work of living an ethical life can involve difficult judgments, in some cases requiring a woman to balance the *farmans* of the Imam against social conventions that feel familiar and perhaps safer. Puribai, at the turn of the twentieth century in Zanzibar, hesitated to send her daughter to the midwifery course despite guidance from the Imam that women should be educated; six decades later, Zarintaj's father expressed a similar hesitation in Dhaka. Saher Banu insisted that her daughter pursue education but then tried to stop her when she had reached a level Saher deemed suitable for an Ismaili wife and mother; the women of the East African *jamat* were hesitant to remove their face veils and slow to adopt the Western dress encouraged by their Imam, weighing this instruction against, perhaps, their own internalized codes of modesty or a cultural commitment to the Indian dress that asserted their relationship to their homeland; Ismailis in East Pakistan were slow to learn Bangla, preferring Urdu, which aligned them with the more powerful West Pakistan. In these and countless other small daily decisions, Ismaili women appear as multidimensional, complex subjects, which cautions us against romanticizing them.

It can therefore be said that women's practices of care recounted in this chapter are not inevitable. And their significance becomes even more apparent when we situate them against a broader social and economic background. Nazira Mawji records the persistence of male dominance within early settler Ismaili households in East Africa, including the prevalence of domestic violence and sexual abuse.[138] She argues that early settlers held onto gender ideologies and roles that limited women's interaction with the opposite gender and tied familial honor to women's mobility and activities. When women ran their families' *dukas,* their work was often unremunerated. Thus, even those women who were active participants in trade typically remained economically dependent on male members of their family. In these circumstances, women found support in each other; they hid each other's savings and jewelry from husbands or in-laws.[139] Women encountered similar constraints in East Pakistan. One woman shared with me that her mother had considered it taboo to speak ill of her controlling husband; only when her daughter reached adulthood did she openly seek help, and even then she wanted only her daughter to know about her troubles.[140] As noted above, Ismaili women's cultural isolation was further exacerbated by colonial policies and postcolonial politics. Thus, women's ethics of care for community that we have witnessed in this chapter flowed beside hardship, trauma, and precarity; this ethics is best understood as a committed action that required their attention and vigilance.

The next chapter will expand its investigation of Ismaili women's placemaking practices to consider how they created and fostered sacred spaces in the East African and North American diasporas. But it can be hard to understand the commitment to rebuilding without first witnessing the devastation that the women of my primary cohort experienced in the early 1970s. The following interlude will, I hope, help to communicate the trauma that this generation carries. Every person I interviewed shared stories like these, and they show up as well in family histories and journals. It is not possible to recount them all. But I hope readers will keep these flight narratives in mind as we turn in chapter 3 to the care relations that Ismaili women established during flight, in refugee camps, and in the North American diaspora.

Interlude

Fleeing, 1971–1972

Z.H. recalls her journey from Chittagong to Karachi onboard a packed steamer in 1971:

> The entire *jamat* of Chittagong went by the ship. Women and children went first. There were so many people. So many people. There was food shortage. But *jamat* helped each other. We brought *bhel puri*, *thepla*, *puri*, so at least we could eat the dry food if needed. It was very hard. The food and water from the ship was very little. It took us eight days to get to Karachi. I was vomiting all the time. We did not stay on the deck, we were belowdecks so didn't have air circulation. The rich people who bought tickets got to stay in the open deck. 300 to 400 people. It was a lot of rush. But we did go upstairs to sit for a little.[1]

Z.H.'s husband, who had stayed behind to sell their house, had even more difficulty. Unable to find a buyer, he eventually left empty-handed. By that time, however, travel between East and West Pakistan had been suspended. Joining a group of ten other Ismaili men, he journeyed by car, then foot, and then boat, driving, walking, and sailing at night to avoid being caught. They went first to Burma, thinking it would be easier for them to navigate the border there, then headed to Nepal, crossed into India, and eventually arrived at Karachi. Z.H. remarks: "It took them 10 to 12 days. They also suffered a lot of hardship, seeing dead bodies on the way, in the sea."

Z.H.'s account resonates with many of my interlocutors who left East Pakistan and East Africa in the early 1970s. They faced numerous challenges in transit and at refugee camps. Families were separated for months and, in several cases, for two to three years. Many witnessed brutalities, including kidnappings and killings. Some were very young when they fled and, fifty years later, still wake up with nightmares. Others can still "see dead body parts floating in the river" and have an aversion to *kababs* because the roasted

Rebuilding Community. Shenila Khoja-Moolji, Oxford University Press. © Oxford University Press 2023.
DOI: 10.1093/oso/9780197642023.003.0003

meat reminds them of the "smell of burning flesh." Karima's is a particularly heart-wrenching account as her father, then a young man, was killed in Dhaka on the eve of their departure:

> My mother, my dad and my youngest brother, who was nine and a half, they—we—all were coming to Karachi on the 15th of May or something. They had the tickets. And on the 12th of May—my my dad was in the store and my brother was there [long pause] and my my my dad knew these people.... [H]e must have sensed something, so he ran out of the shop and whatever the conversation was. My brother doesn't know. Or something to the effect that, you know, "your people weren't supposed to go, how come so many of them have left?" and stuff like that. Because my dad was also, if I can go back, was also on the Academy, Noorani Academy for girls, he was a volunteer. So, he was helping girls, you know, if they needed a ride to the airport, if they needed some financial help to get on the plane and he was helping. And they may have gotten a whiff of that, you know, that he is helping people to get out [of East Pakistan]. So they, one of them—but then the siren for the curfew went off because there was curfew they would have from 6 o clock or whatever 5 o clock or whatever and the curfew siren went on and one of the guys, you know—shot my dad [pause, sobbing].[2]

Karima's father died at the hospital later that day. Her mother was unable to cope for several years: "My mother was totally devastated. All I remember is her eyes had, you know, they had become bloodshot from crying. All she was doing was, you know, she got in the corner, and she was just crying, clutching dad's shirt."

Munira Dhanani recalls the fear that gripped her family when they first heard that they had to leave Kampala.[3] In my interview with her in January 2020, she explains the events of those few days in such detail that it seems as if they had happened yesterday. I share a rather extended quote from her because it shows the remarkable clarity and hour-by-hour detail seared into her memory. Her mother has just received a phone call from her husband asking her to pack a light bag and be ready to get picked up by a driver. "We've got to get out," he had said:

> So here she is running around getting every can of baby formula out of the covers that we had into a bag. Whatever clothes, diapers she could get her hands on were going in a bag. My grandmother was just racing

all over the place trying to get a few clothes put together and then just so we would be able to leave with clothing on our back. . . . So this is what happened Shenila. By Monday late afternoon we, and when I say we so grandmom, mom, my sisters and I were picked up by the driver. We were driven down to my uncle's home in the city and even that again had to be very discrete in the sense that our bags had to be left in the car and we couldn't leave the car and walk up to his flat with our possessions in our hand but the driver had been given instructions when he left the office to come pick us [up] by dad, [and to] keep all the belongings in the car.

So, we, you know, went upstairs, everybody was very sad. You could feel the tension, but nobody could say anything. You didn't know whether we were being followed, whether you were being recorded, you know, code by eye contact and body language, and within a half hour of getting to my uncle's flat we were downstairs again getting into another car and dad kept saying, "it's okay, you know, we are just heading up to the bus terminal." In the meantime, here is my uncle just sobbing away. Dad had to give him a little bit of an update or two on what's going on and, you know, having to say goodbye and yet pretend not to be saying goodbye, it was just beyond description.

We made it to the bus terminal heading to Entebbe and of course, the transit was never going to be simple. Like curfew was setting in by 6 pm and this is already 4:35 pm, and I remember everything so clearly, my God. Like, you know, you are traumatize[d] by all this and yet it's hard to forget, even though you just adjust and you move on.

We got on the bus and started driving and traffic of course that time in the afternoon. And spot checks every little while, but luckily, we didn't have as many so just as we left the boundary of Kampala and entering the roads leading to Entebbe taking us to the airport there, the first spot check wasn't so bad. It was pretty tense. It was starting to get a little hazy, not so dark yet. And this military man walked into the bus with his machine gun, which starts dangling. And then he talked to the driver and he is counting all of the passengers that are on the bus. And for some odd reason all of us sat by the door there, none of us went and sat on the back of the bus. I don't know why [laughing]. But it was extremely scary because my grandmother is now praying with her voice, loud, not just under her breath and heavy breathing. And, you know, she is thinking "Oh my God, my son is sitting right there at the edge of the step by the door and the military man with his gun just dangling all over the place. What are we in for?"

Luckily, you know what, that conversation between the military and the driver was quite short but it seemed like the longest. The military man stepped out of the bus and off we went.

Not less than 15 minutes heading into a highway still there's another spot check and by this time it started to get dark so now you've got headlights going back and forth with all the traffic just passing you and another military person climbed on. And this time this guy's eyes were like red, and he smelled awful and his breath. . . . He too had his gun just dangling on the side of his shoulders, he is trying to speak to the bus driver and here even the bus driver you could tell was fearful because this military person was not in [the] right frame of mind. That too again, scarier it was, he got off very quickly and off we went.

Now just as we were entering the borderline of the airport strip off Entebbe Highway and getting there, there was another spot check. This one wasn't so bad. He just, he stood on the foot of the door of the bus, said a few words to the driver, it was alright and moved on because it was almost the curfew time so didn't stop anywhere so luckily, we, we didn't have to go through any palpitations I would say [laughs] at this third and last stop. But the first two were definitely scary.

Umeeda Switlo's experience at the Entebbe airport was similarly frightening.[4] She was fourteen years old at the time and had to leave Uganda alone, as her parents could not arrange tickets for the entire family at once. She tells me her harrowing story, including being strip-searched at the airport, having her jewelry (the one or two pieces she was allowed to carry under the expulsion decree) snatched by the security guard, witnessing a killing after having confronted one just the night before, and yet mustering up the courage to swipe back her jewelry while the guards were distracted before boarding her flight:

So, the day that I'm leaving Uganda, a few days before, Idi Amin had said, given some kind of edict about how much gold and currency that we were allowed to take. So, it would be something like one bracelet, one necklace, one ring, one pair of earrings, okay? So, as you know, with Ismaili and Indian families, gold is really important to us and goes back to ancestry.

For example, a bracelet my mum got at her wedding, to pass down. Or, that Gandhi brought to South Africa that was my mum's mother's *dhagina* they call it. So, we have to think of ways to get some of this jewelry out. A day before I left Uganda, we were sitting at the house, and heard about this edict and started to glue back bracelets, bangles, and necklaces so they could pass as one.

So, okay, so then I am only 14 years old and, I'm leaving for the first time.... For the first time, I'm leaving Africa by myself. And, I get dropped off at the airport. They begin their search. So, I have one suitcase, a stuffed animal like a toy, and this *dhagina* on me. So the first thing they do is they cut open the toy animal and look for currency or something in that toy. And then, I get taken to a room where a male soldier tells me to undress till I'm naked and he's watching [pauses], and then he grabs the jewelry off my body. So now the jewelry is taken away, it's at the table outside. And then, there's, I don't know whether I'm going into too much detail, but then there's a screaming and a yelling at the airport and this English girl is being held because she won't let them take away a little stone that she has. And, in those days, we would submit, and they [the English] would not. So the screaming and yelling, and then her father rushes through the airport into the restricted area and they shoot him. And all of a sudden, they realize, "oh damn we've just shot a white, a British person," so this is a problem. They all, the army guys, all go to that area and I come out of the room and realize that I'm alone and I don't know, I see my jewelry on the desk but there is nobody there so I decided to just go in there and take it. I took it and put it on real quick, and then they called our flight and now we're leaving to board the plane by the steps, the old way. And, my mother is on the balcony looking at me and I'm saying goodbye and I'm saying "Look! I got the necklace! I got everything" and she [is] saying "Quiet. Stop it." So we brought the *dhagina* back and each one of my sisters brought them in those ways.

Umeeda has saved the suitcase she carried with her when she left Uganda (Figure 2.11):

It's got a bit rusty at the handles, and it's really of no use but why I kept it after this long period of time was that once I met refugees from [Burma]—this is about 20 years ago—and I showed it to them. And while most Canadians

Figure 2.11 Umeeda with her suitcase.
Still image from oral history interview with Umeeda Switlo and Lella Umedaly. Canadian Museum of Immigration at Pier 21 (14.02.21USLU).

would just be "Oh my god! That's all you have?" the response from these other refugees was tears. They told me that I was lucky that I had a suitcase, they came to this country with plastic bags. So I continued to keep it because it was part of my story. It was how much that meant to me.

3

Fostering Sacred Spaces

Sakarkhanu Hassanali Bandali belongs to the generation of Ismailis who lived most of their lives in East Africa before being displaced in the 1970s. Born in 1921 in Dar es Salaam, she attended school through the seventh grade and then worked as a teacher at the Aga Khan Primary Boys School.[1] She lost her job in the mid-1950s when the school changed its language of instruction to English, prompting her to start a catering business serving schools, private parties, and weddings. On festival days, including during the Imam's visits to Dar es Salaam, she volunteered to serve as the main chef for community-wide meals. These *sagari dham jamans* (communal feasts) brought together thousands of Ismailis; Sakarkhanu, together with other women volunteers, prepared *biryani, lapsi, gundpaak,* and *ladoo* to feed the crowds who gathered to see the Imam. For two decades, she was also involved with the Ladies Volunteer Corps, who were responsible for the daily cleaning and upkeep of the jamatkhana (Figure 3.1).

In the early 1970s, when the Tanzanian government nationalized commercial property, Sakarkhanu lost the meager savings that she had invested in real estate. Educational and economic prospects for the younger generation of Ismailis seemed bleak, and her children started to make their way to Canada. In 1974 she too headed to Toronto, carrying with her a bulky book of handwritten recipes. Sakarkhanu's son-in-law, Mohammad Manji, remembers that when the first *sagari dham jaman* activities were planned in Toronto in 1975, Sakarkhanu "was called back by the [Ismaili] Regional Council to get involved again. . . . With her recipe book at hand, she again became one of the main persons for cooking at yearly July and December *khushalis* (religious festivals)." Mohammad's use of "back" and "again" points to the continuity that women like Sakarkhanu have fashioned for the *jamat* through their care work.

Scholars have observed that resuming religious festivals and establishing religious facilities can be salient placemaking activities for new migrants.[2] Particularly for refugees, who suffer the trauma of displacement at the same time as they confront the demands of settling in a new country, a connection

Rebuilding Community. Shenila Khoja-Moolji, Oxford University Press. © Oxford University Press 2023.
DOI: 10.1093/oso/9780197642023.003.0004

Figure 3.1 Sakarkhanu Hassanali Bandali (front row, fourth from left) with other Ismaili volunteers outside the Dar es Salaam jamatkhana.
Courtesy of Dr Moh'd Manji.

to a sacred place can help introduce them to resources, offer stability and security, and foster a sense of belonging.[3] In the diaspora, religious institutions therefore take on new functions: under their auspices, leaders and members transmit not only religious doctrines but also cultural traditions and social services.[4] Scholars who study the Ismaili jamatkhana have similarly described it as a site that facilitates the cohesiveness of Ismailis, enabling individuals to form their religious identity by reference to others.[5] These findings are not surprising. Yet they tell us little about the precise practices through which this sense of belonging and spiritual kinship is produced. What types of routine activities enable strangers to connect with each other and the Divine? What practices contribute to a sense of, and a desire for, community? If we accept Claudia Moser and Cecelia Feldman's proposition that a "sacred space does not exist *a priori* but is the outcome of actions, intentions, and recollections," then we must also ask what are the actions, recollections, and intentions that produce jamatkhanas as a sacred space?[6]

Nigel Thrift emphasizes that it is often an "infrastructure of mundane activities" that transforms physical locations into affective sites that engender familiarity and foster common moods.[7] The actions of women like Sakarkhanu constituted those mundane activities that transformed makeshift sites into places of belonging and prayer (the jamatkhana). Yi-Fu Tuan refers to such bonds between people and places as "fields of care."[8] This chapter contemplates the fields of care that women generated through their mundane activities. In joining the cleaning committees, women cared for the physical space of the jamatkhana; as part of the Ladies Volunteer Corps, they assisted in the orderly operation of prayer services; as faith ministers (*mukhiani* and *kamadiani*) and educators, they engaged in pastoral care; and as members of cooking committees, they prepared meals to serve at religious festivals. We learn that from India and East Africa to North America, Ismaili women have sustained fledgling congregations through such work.

Several of my interlocutors labelled this work as "*seva.*" Sherbano Ajani (b. 1921) explains the broad range of tasks she used to perform at a jamatkhana in Dhaka: "I was a [Ladies Volunteer Corps] volunteer in the jamatkhana and then I served in the health center. Then I used to make *sukrit* (consecrated food) and also used to do *nandi* (food offering) in jamatkhana. I did everything a volunteer does. Make *sukrit*, fill the *thala* (plate), take it upstairs, collect donation . . . whatever big or small *seva* I got, I did it all."[9] An act of *seva* is simultaneously social and spiritual: through these acts, women like Sherbano have contributed to fostering Ismaili spaces of worship and deepened bonds of congregational life over decades. In Figure 3.2, we see Sherbano, aged ninety-eight, who now serves as a volunteer in a jamatkhana in Chicago. Women's *seva* has emplaced Ismailis in new environments as well as within the symbolic Ismaili sociality. In the chapter, we discover two distinct yet entwined sets of such placemaking activities: a first set geared toward maintaining the jamatkhana as an existing permanent structure and a second set of activities that work to conjure the *sensorium* of the jamatkhana among community members in circumstances where no fixed facility exists.

The Ismaili Jamatkhana

J.A. and I often meet in a jamatkhana in Atlanta. One day after services, while we were enjoying *sherbat* on the veranda, our conversation veered toward the importance of jamatkhana in the lives of Ismailis. J.A. explained: "Jamatkhana is the place where we learn how to become a true Ismaili."[10] When I asked her to elaborate further, she recited the following verses of a *ginan*:

> *Eji Gat maanhe aavine viraa bhai kar joddine rahie,*
> *Gur-naa vachan apnna sir par dharie*

Figure 3.2 Sherbano Ajani in her Ismaili Volunteer Corps uniform, 2019.
Courtesy of Aziz Ajani.

O brother! Having come to Jamatkhana, sit with respect,
Accept the teachings of the spiritual guide whole-heartedly
Eji Gat maanhe aavine viraa bhai sanmukh rahie,
nindaa thaae tiyaan thi utthine jaaie
O brother! Having come to Jamatkhana, engage in remembrance
   (of your Lord)
When you encounter backbiting, get up and walk away[11]

J.A. then added, "In *khane* we learn about the true guide, how to behave with each other, what is good, what is bad, our purpose. It is also a place of fun, like us having *sherbat* and cake and [playing] *dandiya* [laughs]."

Introduced to Khojas in the fifteenth century by a *pir* named Sadr al-Din, jamatkhanas became a central place of worship and gathering for Khoja Ismailis over the course of the nineteenth and twentieth centuries.[12] In the past, they had operated as caste halls and their use was locally negotiated. From the late nineteenth century onward, coinciding with the efforts of the Imam to concretize the Shia Ismaili identity of Khojas, jamatkhanas were re-served only for those who expressed allegiance to the Aga Khan. The rituals performed in these spaces came under the sole purview of the Imam, with certain practices, such as mourning rituals during Muharram, discouraged in order to distinguish Khoja Ismailis from Khoja Ithna'ashris. Similarly, home-based religious gatherings (often facilitated by and for women) too were discouraged to increase the use of jamatkhanas as the main space of worship and gathering for Ismailis. Whereas in the past male leaders—*mukhi* and *kamadia*—were elected by other elite men to manage the affairs of the Khojas, these positions were incorporated into the religious infrastructure to be appointed by the Imam. The jamatkhana's female leaders, referred to as *mukhiani* and *kamadiani*, are usually the wives of the *mukhi* and *kamadia* and are appointed concurrently with their husbands.[13] In 1905, Aga Khan III established an administrative body (Council) in Zanzibar that was respon-sible for governing the community's local affairs; a similar Council was es-tablished in Bombay in 1906.[14] Over the next three decades, the bureaucracy was strengthened as additional territorial and provincial Councils, respon-sible for the education, trade, and social welfare of community members, were added.[15] In 1937 the Imam added the Supreme Council for Africa to oversee the work of the numerous provincial Councils. As these new admin-istrative structures were established, the role of the *mukhi* and *kamadia* be-came restricted; these local leaders now oversee only the jamatkhana and its religious life.

The central rituals performed daily in contemporary Ismaili jamatkhanas include observing *du'a* (a supplication composed of Quranic verses) at sun-rise and sundown, reciting *ginans* and *qasidas* (devotional poetry), reading *farmans* (edicts of the Imams), and sharing *juro* (consecrated food).[16] Men and women sit side by side but in separate sections; while physical partitions (latticed screens, curtains, and in some cases separate rooms) were used to segregate men and women in early jamatkhanas, no such divisions exist today.[17] The *paats* (small tables used for after-service rituals and where *juro* is placed) are arranged in front of the congregants, and behind the *paats* sit the faith ministers: women on the women's side, men on the men's side. Regular attendance in jamatkhana for congregational prayers has been encouraged by the Imams.

Because jamatkhanas provide spiritual sustenance, information, and fellowship to Ismailis, it is not surprising that community members strive to set one up as soon as possible after arriving in a new location. One of my interlocutors from Kenya remembers a *farman* where the Imam had instructed that if there was even one household in a town, then the members of the household should establish a jamatkhana by setting aside a room. Early jamatkhanas in East Africa, therefore, were often rooms in someone's house or a separate small structure purchased for this purpose. They evolved rapidly, however, during the twentieth century. The mud and chalk huts of early years—in some cases a single room in a *mukhi*'s house—were replaced by baked brick compounds. By the 1930s, Ismaili jamatkhanas were some of the most prominent structures in the East African landscape.[18] In East Pakistan too, as noted in the previous chapter, several jamatkhanas were established during the 1960s, representing stability and belonging to Ismailis.

Fields of Care around the Jamatkhana

The jamatkhana and its associated administrative infrastructure have provided women numerous avenues to participate in Ismaili religious life. We saw in the previous chapter how *mukhianis* and *kamadianis* offered support to newcomers. Shariffa Keshavjee, who grew up in Mombasa and Kisumu during the 1950s, reflects on another service *mukhianis* and *kamadianis* performed—representing the community's values through their behavior and appearance:

> Education for that generation of Ismaili girls consisted of far more than just the classroom curriculum. In the jamatkhana the mukhi and kamadia were the leaders but by their sides were their wives, the mukhiani and kamadiani. They had special tasks relating to rites of passage for children and giving advice on health and social issues. . . . [M]y grandmother . . . as mukhiani ma had great responsibility in leading the women of the community. She would get the women together, welcome every newborn baby in the community, attend all weddings and funerals, and visit the sick.[19]

Sometimes the Imam sent messages praising *mukhianis* and *kamadianis* for being role models. One such message, in 1952, went out to those *mukhianis* and *kamadianis* in East Africa who, acting on the Imam's guidance, wore Western dress in jamatkhana; the Imam encouraged other women to follow their example.[20]

As jamatkhanas were established across India and East Africa, so were myriad volunteer committees created to look after the sites and manage the congregations. These committees offered additional opportunities for women to perform voluntary service—on top of the informal care activities, such as hospitality for travelers, asking after the sick, or taking in female boarders, chronicled in the last chapter. Many women I spoke with—especially women in their sixties—remember their mothers' efforts through the Ladies Volunteer Corps, welfare societies, and ladies committees, as they were variously named. The origins of the Ismaili Volunteer Corps can be traced to a group of young Khoja men who in 1912 formed a literary society in Bombay, which they called the Young Ismaili Vidhya Vinod Club. In 1919, the group added a volunteer corps based on a model encouraged by the British colonial state to bolster local security by recruiting volunteers. The corps engaged in crowd control during the Imam's visits and attended to other community safety needs.[21] In 1920, impressed by their accomplishments, the Imam changed the name of the organization's volunteer branch from the Young Ismaili Vidhya Vinod Corps to H.H. the Aga Khan's Young Volunteer Corps.[22] Ismailis outside Bombay also adopted the volunteer corps model and soon new volunteer organizations were established: in Karachi in 1920 and in Kisumu in 1923.[23] Also during the 1920s, independent Ladies Volunteer Corps appeared, first in Bombay's neighborhoods and then in other Indian and East African cities. Figure 3.3 shows a group of women volunteers from Mombasa; they are pictured with a framed photograph of the Imam, symbolically articulating themselves as his deputies.

Such ladies committees proliferated in the ensuing decades. In an interview with me, Shirin Sondhi explained her mother Maniben's active involvement in the Aga Khan Ladies Committee in the 1940s (Figure 3.4). The committee provided social and economic support to struggling community members: "There were many poor Ismailis in Nairobi at the time, and I remember my mother was a very active member [of the ladies committee]. We remember her getting ready soon after lunch, grabbing a cup of tea and running out of the door to meet another member to visit needy families in Pangani and Eastleigh."[24] Shirin recalls a particular Ismaili household with

Figure 3.3 The Mombasa Ismaili Ladies Emergency Committee, 1920s.
Photo: Sadruddin Khimani Family Collection, Vancouver, Canada. Reproduced with permission from Malik Merchant.

such limited resources that the "children slept sideways on the bed because there was no space in the house." Maniben, in collaboration with other Ismaili women, provided food and money to ease this family's transition to Nairobi.

Even in smaller towns, women organized themselves into volunteer corps responsible for the upkeep of the jamatkhana. Laila Bandali's (b. 1959) mother, Gulshanbai Badrudin Lila, and her grandmother Sakarbai Kassamali Lila were part of the volunteer corps in Soroti, where they tidied the physical space of the jamatkhana and washed the objects used during

Figure 3.4 Maniben Rattansi (seated, second from the right) with other members of the Ladies Committee, 1942–1943. The grandsons of the then Imam, Sultan Mahomed Shah, are seated in the center of the front row.
Courtesy of Shirin Sondhi.

rituals (Figure 3.5).[25] Laila herself was a Brownie in a Girl Scout troop that was open to young Ismaili girls and in this role served water to congregants and helped adult volunteers with cleaning tasks. Later in life, Laila would follow in the footsteps of her mother and grandmother, serving as a volunteer corps member in Kitchener and Edmonton jamatkhanas in Canada from 1975 to 1981.

Nazira Mawji (b. 1946) and Shaida Adatia (b. 1954), both of whom grew up in Kampala during the 1960s, recall two distinct types of women's committees—one that tended to the upkeep of the jamatkhana and the other that engaged in social service outside the jamatkhana. Nazira's mother, Nurbano Jetha, was a member of the latter kind of ladies committee: "They did all kinds of things, like they would look after the Ismaili girls who lived in the hostel in Kampala. They would look after things like baby shows, where babies were brought in once a month to be weighed at our local dispensary, which used to be attached to jamatkhanas. The ladies committee

Figure 3.5 Soroti Ladies Volunteer and Jamatkhana Safai (cleaning) Committee, ca. 1962. Gulshanbai Badrudin Lila is standing on the far right and Sakarbai Kassamali Lila is seated second from left. The jamat included 300 to 350 Ismaili families.

Courtesy of Laila Bandali.

ran these kinds of things."[26] Shaida remembers women volunteers at her school inquiring about students from low-income families, looking for ways they could support them.[27] These volunteers also ran a canteen during the lunch hour so that students who lived too far away to return home for lunch and those from low-income families would have access to meals. In Tanga, members of the Welfare Society provided groceries to the less well-off members of the community.[28]

During the first half of the twentieth century the Ismaili institutions authorized certain individuals, typically men, as itinerant preachers (*waezin*).[29] In time, as women accessed formal education, they too were able to participate in this form of community religious education. One woman whose name came up repeatedly during my interviews was Bachibai Tejpar (b. 1891), who was known for her spiritual teachings. Bachibai was born in India but moved to Zanzibar with her parents when she was five years old. The family later relocated to Mombasa. Salma Tejpar, Bachibai's granddaughter, tells me that Bachibai's parents taught her to read and write at home and she started reading all the books in her father's well-stocked library—on theosophy,

religion, philosophy, and Ayurveda.[30] In 1953, she became a member of the
Ismailia Mission Association, which was responsible for training itinerant
preachers, and Salma conjectures that "she was most likely the first woman
al-waeza."[31] Salma explains further, "*Maji* (an honorific for an older woman)
was an extraordinarily well-read and broad-minded woman, who was at least
50 years ahead of her time. I would describe her as a trailblazer."[32] Bachibai
delivered talks in jamatkhanas not only in East Africa but also in India,
Pakistan, Burma (Figure 3.6), and Europe. A review of notes from Bachibai's
1965 lectures compiled by her disciple Sadru Pradhan shows deep knowledge of the *ginans*, Muslim history, and the Imam's *farmans*.[33] Recordings of
her sessions still circulate among older women of the community.

While few women exercised religious authority publicly like Bachibai,
many more were engaged in the study of religion. Evidence from oral
histories suggests that women organized religious study groups at homes
called *satsang*, where they came together to discuss esoteric interpretations
of the faith.[34] Nazira recalls her grandmother Qamarbai Jetha taking part in

Figure 3.6 Bachibai Tejpar (seated) visited Burma in 1962 in her capacity as an
itinerant preacher (*al-waez*a).
Courtesy of Salma Tejpar-Dang.

such groups: "These women belonged to this kind of a society, where they got together and they prayed in secret in different women's homes, or maybe even in one woman's home. And they discussed faith and things to do with faith and a lot of the issues were esoteric. They weren't to do with the physical life, they were to do with afterlife, or with spiritual life. And they were very very secret."[35] Some of my interlocutors speculate that in addition to studying together, the women of the *satsang* groups may have engaged in certain hushed forms of volunteer service, including an effort to run a home for girls who had children out of wedlock and find Ismaili adoptive parents for them.[36] In fact, Bachibai, who had established a maternity home in Mombasa, reserved an area within it as a "foundling home." Her granddaughter recalls: "She gave refuge to unmarried pregnant women. *Maji* and her daughters-in-law cared for these women until they delivered their babies, who would be adopted by pre-approved families."[37] It was not just Ismaili women who found refuge at this home; it was open to all.

As Ismaili Councils consolidated their jurisdiction by the mid-twentieth century, such private efforts and home-based study gatherings were discouraged in favor of religious gatherings (*majalis*) held at jamatkhanas. Mawji conjectures: "I think at some point, it is my theory, that these kind of home societies, in order to remove them, that these *majalis* were created so that these women could be moved into that, rather than these private little communities, societies, that were carrying on with their own interpretation of the faith."[38] The diffused nature of institutional authority had de facto allowed women to work behind the scenes to meet the needs of other women, especially those needs that they could not publicly articulate in a male-dominated society.[39] Now welfare work would be largely directed by the Councils.

More recently, women's-only *majalis* in jamatkhanas—which became mainstream from 1930s onward—have also been largely discontinued. In the intervening decades, they provided women with much-needed private space for prayers and socialization. As an Ismaili woman who grew up in Mozambique during the 1950s shares with Susan Trovao:

There was a ceremony exclusively for women and girls. At the *farman*'s time, even male children had to leave. But for us, it wasn't a mere prayer. Rather, it was an opportunity to meet with our relatives and friends later, to pour out our worries and secrets, or even to cry with someone we trusted absolutely. We shared what to do, what could work or fail. Sometimes, we were quite vocal in criticizing mothers and older sisters-in-law, gossiping behind their backs.[40]

The formalization of service through jamatkhana-based committees or the restriction on at-home religious gatherings did not mean that personalized forms of care and devotion were eliminated. Shariffa's mother, Khatija Jamal (b. 1917), continued to organize meals for Ismaili orphans every week at her home in Mombasa. While in Kisumu, she shared extra produce from her family's gardens with a poor Ismaili woman who would then sell that surplus. That said, institutionalization directed women's labors toward particular kinds of service or committee work; the impetus to come together outside the jamatkhana or to informally organize large-scale efforts such as homes for unwed girls declined as such activities increasingly came to be viewed as belonging to the purview of the Ismaili institutions.

Jamatkhanas and the committees, an arrangement that we have referred to as fields of care, were thus important sites for women to engage in voluntary service to please their Imam and to contribute to the welfare of coreligionists. The 1970s diaspora—bringing with it new demands for spaces of worship and new care obligations for displaced members of the community—would create new opportunities and public roles for women such as Gulzar Kassam and Roshan Pirani, whom we will meet below. These women threw themselves into the work of community making, creating makeshift jamatkhanas at their apartments in Atlanta and Fort Wayne, and providing support to newcomers from East Africa and East Pakistan. Even during flight, women such as Laila Datoo and J.A. imbued sacrality to the otherwise perilous sites of steamboats and refugee camps by reciting *ginans*, sharing food, waking up fellow Ismailis for prayers, and observing *majalis*. I begin with the community's efforts in North America—as we can see here most clearly the continuity achieved when Ismailis were able to reproduce familiar sights, sounds, and aromas in a space they used week after week—before turning to the more tenuous sacrality that they were able to sustain in flight, when they had no physical space to claim as their own.

Makeshift Jamatkhanas in North America

Fariyal Ross-Sheriff (b. 1940) reminisces that when she arrived in the United States in the mid-1960s on an African scholarship program for American universities, there were less than ten Ismaili students in the country.[41] They were soon joined by coreligionists fleeing political turmoil in East Africa and East Pakistan. These early migrants and refugees had no formal places of worship, and gathered in each other's homes to pray and eat together.[42] As their numbers increased, they rented office spaces or transformed church basements, gymnasiums, or private homes into makeshift jamatkhanas. At these gatherings, Ismailis not only prayed together but also found respite away from the everyday anxieties of economic precarity, uncertain futures, and racism. My interlocutors tell me of their early struggles in North America, when they could not find jobs, were underemployed, or were teased in schools and on the streets. Shirin Karsan, the daughter of Sherbanu and Habib Lalani, whom we met in chapter 2, remembers racist encounters at school: "We would all like literally be thrown things at, we would be called 'Pakis' and you know just like a lot of name-calling, a lot of things literally being thrown at us."[43] Sumera shares her own struggles in Chicago, feeling crushed emotionally by the cold weather and heavy snow. Since she could not drive and did not have proper work documentation, her only choice was to work at a bakery near her house, where the employer took advantage of her situation:

> You know how people say, everyone takes advantage of you when you are down? And when one is in difficulty, one decides to do any job offered. So at the bakery they would give me all odd jobs, sometimes at the counter or slicing bread at other times. But every Saturday they would give me like big huge pans, you know large, large pans that bakers use. They were heavy, heavy. Every Saturday, they would give me to wash the pans. 100 pans.[44]

Other women remember saving ketchup and mustard packets from restaurants so they could have it with bread, sharing one bed for a family of six, and getting "beaten up more" as frustrated husbands struggled to find jobs. The editorial board of the *Canadian Ismaili* published on July 11, 1976, describes the new migrant experience in this way: "The new immigrant finds himself in a place where yes may mean no, where what was taboo back home may be an accepted way of life here, where religion is simply shrugged off when it was literally a way of life where we came from. All this results in frustration, bewilderment and disorientation, more so when we find ourselves in a society with incessantly changing values."[45] Against this backdrop, makeshift jamatkhanas offered rare moments of repose, joy, and affinity.

Dozens of informal jamatkhanas were established in Canada and the United States during the 1970s. In the United States alone, by 1979 jamats could be found in twenty-four locations and had established some form of gathering space to pray together.[46] Below I tell the story of two such jamatkhanas, focusing on the wide-ranging activities that the *mukhianis* and *kamadianis* performed in creating and sustaining these places of worship and gathering.[47] My interlocutors tried to reproduce the interior design and affective atmospheres of the jamatkhanas they had known in East Africa or East Pakistan, using familiar material objects as well as participatory rituals and commensal eating. They also engaged in other forms of care work—cooking and packing food for young community members, waking up interested congregants for morning prayers, and checking in on those who were sick. As in the past, so too in the North American context, women's care practices traversed both material and affective domains and spilled beyond the physical boundaries of the jamatkhana into more general community support.

Mukhianis and *kamadianis* did not, of course, single-handedly sustain the makeshift jamatkhanas or early congregations; they often worked alongside male faith ministers and had the support of their spouses and other male and female congregants. But studying the recollections of these women leaders, as well as accounts offered by those who congregated in their living room jamatkhanas, gives us insight into the extensive and expansive *seva* that they performed during the early years of the community's settlement in the region.

Atlanta, 1972–1974

In the late 1960s, as anti-Asian sentiments were on the rise in Tanzania, Gulzar Kassam saw her chances of progressing in her career as a gynecologist diminish rapidly. She therefore considered leaving. With a couple of other Ismaili women doctors, she decided to take a test that could lead to medical residency in the United States. She passed and was accepted into a program at Emory University. In 1972, together with her husband, Bahadur Kassam, Gulzar made her way to Atlanta.

Through a contact at the Emory library, Gulzar connected with two other Ismailis in the area, and they decided to get together at her apartment. Gulzar recalls in an interview with me: "We thought maybe we should meet every week, and maybe we should probably do *dua* together. And we all got excited about it, and we said fine. R.K. was a great cook so she would cook, and I would be her helper. And then every weekend we would meet."[48] While initially this gathering only included Gulzar's immediate family and a couple of other Ismailis, they were soon joined by another four students who had moved to Atlanta. Gulzar describes this "first congregation" of twelve people: "We all said *dua* and *tasbih,* and then we would have our dinner. And mind you, we were not all very religious or anything, we have evolved a lot [laughs]. But at least we knew about getting together and having food and doing, you know, saying our prayers together." Here Gulzar mobilizes a different meaning of being religious—one that conjoins performing prayers with commensality and community, positioning this practice of religion against understandings that might limit it to the domain of formal prayers or exclude social life from its ambit. Iqbal Paroo, then a student at Georgia State University and a member of this small congregation, remembers looking forward to those gatherings as a chance to enjoy Indian food: "She [Gulzar] would cook *biryani* and *samosa,* so I would say, I am coming! [laughs] . . . and she even used to pack food for me to take home, so I always had food for the next day [laughs]. It was the only good food that I got. They [Gulzar and Bahadur] really took me under their wings."[49] Another participant in this gathering, R.K., recollects how "tight knit and important" this group was for her during those early years in the United States.[50]

As more Ismailis arrived from East Africa, the makeshift jamatkhana moved to another congregant's apartment, and Iqbal Paroo and Gulzar Kassam were officially appointed as its *mukhi* and *kamadiani* by the Ismaili Council. The congregation remained rather small and close-knit. Seventeen-year-old Naila Jamal arrived in Atlanta from Kenya in 1973 to study at Spelman College.[51] She tells me of how this makeshift jamatkhana literally became her "home." During that December winter break, she did not have money to go back to Kenya and so "became homeless!" With Gulzar's help, she moved into the apartment where the jamatkhana was established and served as "the unofficial *jamat bhai!*" *Jamat bhai* is a vernacular term used by members of the Khoja community to name the men who are tasked with the upkeep and safety of the jamatkhana and who tend to live near or inside the jamatkhana compound. While numerous volunteers participate in maintaining the jamatkhana, *jamat bhai* denotes those men who do so full time and command both respect and awe for their service. After moving into the jamatkhana, Naila performed such tasks and appropriated the traditionally masculine *seva* of *jamat bhai*. She set up the apartment, readied it for services every day, and cleaned up afterward: "I would do everything morning and in the evening."

Naila remained separated from her family for the following ten years due to financial constraints. During this entire time, it was the Ismaili jamat—in particular, Gulzar and Bahadur—that became her family. She explains, "I would ask them [Gulzar and Bahadur] for everything . . . *hi ghapay, hu ghapay* (I want this, I want that)." For a young student, alone in Atlanta with limited financial means, the 1970s makeshift jamatkhana and the community became an anchor, a place that made her feel safe and nurtured. In Naila, then, we find one example of how such jamatkhanas—and their faith ministers—supported newcomers, and how these newcomers in turn labored to sustain those very spaces and congregations.

In 1973 several refugees from Uganda joined the small congregation. The members began to want more for their jamatkhana—a larger space and daily services. Gulzar and her husband, Bahadur, were now appointed as *mukhiani* and *mukhi*, along with Rehmat Nanji and her husband, Haider, who served as *kamadiani* and *kamadia*. The jamatkhana moved to yet another location, a house on Lisbon Street. Gulzar recalls that while the request for daily morning and evening services came from the patriarchs of the Ugandan refugee families, it was their wives who actually did the work that kept the jamatkhana running:

> One person would be in charge of clean up and do everything. We vacuumed every time after khane, they would vacuum. . . . [I]t was mainly done by women, like *mehmani* (preparation of food offerings) and all that stuff. So that really created the environment that we were used to traditionally. And in fact, whoever came early did the *agarbatti* (incense), we always had *agarbatti*. . . . So we ran the jamatkhana as a very formal place, and the women basically kept it clean and went on with the traditions.

Gulzar's vivid recollection shows how seemingly quotidian activities—preparing food offerings, vacuuming, cleaning, and burning incense just as they had in East Africa—evoked imaginings associated with jamatkhana, reminding the participants of its rituals and sensorium. As geographer Phil Hubbard has suggested, "Place emerges as a particular form of space . . . through acts of naming as well as through the distinctive activities and imaginings associated with particular social spaces."[52] And Lefebvre notes that both materials and *matériel* are involved in the making of make-shift spaces; whereas the former involves brick and mortar, the latter denotes "tools and directions for their use."[53] The body's behaviors and patterns are shaped by the environment around it and linked to both materials and *matériel*. Burning incense as the service begins turns a repurposed house or storefront into a spiritual place and directs individuals toward a certain protocol of prayers. Women thus participated in the community's continuity not only by establishing physical sites for prayer but also by maintaining traditions (as Gulzar's words remind us) that included reproducing the jamatkhana's sensorium and the practice of commensal eating. During our meeting, Rehmat used "*jamat*" and "family" interchangeably to describe this early Atlanta congregation, revealing the kinship feelings that this place engendered: "Every Sunday we cooked food at jamatkhana. We [ate] together. It was a good family. Good family, um, *jamat*."[54] In Figure 3.7, we see Rehmat with her *jamati* family.

Figure 3.7 A young Ismaili *jamat* gathered for a festival at the jamatkhana building on Lisbon Street. Rehmat is standing in the last row (third from right) and Naila is to the left (fourth from the left).
Courtesy of Gulzar Kassam.

Fort Wayne, 1973–1975

Kulsum and Daulat, born in the 1930s in Rajkot, had been good friends while growing up in India.[55] They played in each other's homes and attended jamatkhana together. Over the years, however, they lost touch. One married a man from Uganda and headed to Kampala; the other married and then, seeking to escape poverty, traveled across India, first to Bombay and subsequently to Chittagong in East Pakistan. Both women went on to have children and supported their husbands in making ends meet. Between 1971 and 1972, both were compelled to flee their homes. Each spent some time at transit camps and in the homes of relatives before eventually finding her way to Fort Wayne, Indiana. On a drafty midwestern evening, Kulsum and Daulat met again at a makeshift jamatkhana in Fort Wayne. The two women embraced each other and rekindled their friendship. I learned about this reunion from their daughters, who also became friends.

The makeshift jamatkhana where Kulsum and Daulat met was organized by Roshan Pirani (b. 1950), who too had been displaced from Chittagong.[56] After fleeing in 1971, Roshan spent two years in Karachi working at a hospital while trying to enter medical school. However, she was denied admission because she was not considered local. She then convinced her older brother, who had left for the United States, to arrange a visa for her. In the United States, she was still unable to pursue a medical degree due to visa restrictions, so she pivoted to a career in radiology and headed to Fort Wayne. In 1973, Fort Wayne had a few Ismaili families who had been displaced from Uganda and East Pakistan, as well as several young Ismaili men studying at local colleges like the Indiana Institute of Technology. For the first six months, Roshan organized an informal jamatkhana in her apartment; the following year, the Ismaili Council officially appointed her as *mukhiani* of that jamatkhana. She remained either a *mukhiani* or *kamadiani* for the next nine years. In these positions, she was appointed on her own accord (rather than as the wife of a male faith minister) since the small number of congregants did not warrant the usual four faith ministers and only two (one man and one woman) were appointed. During the 1970s, the jamatkhana was organized in the homes of congregants and later at the Keenan Hotel in downtown Fort Wayne.[57] My interview with Roshan reveals not only how she transformed her living and dining room into a sacred space but also how she kept the community together through feminized forms of care.

Roshan remembers the specific changes she made to her apartment every Sunday to convert it into a jamatkhana: "So in the living room I would put all my furniture aside, vacuum, place white bedsheets (*chaddars*) down on the floor, and use curtains to separate the area." Two members of the congregation purchased center tables and "cut the legs [a] little shorter and that was our *paat* (a table used during rituals), so we would lower the *paat* and then that's how we made the jamatkhana." Like Gulzar, Roshan explains how she carefully replicated every ritual that is performed in formally established jamatkhanas: "I really tried to make the environment as jamatkhana, when it's *dua* time it's *dua* time. We literally had all the ceremonies." Roshan recalls that they even recited the specific *ginan,* called *anant akhado,* that signals to the congregants that *dua* is about to commence, acting as a transition from common to sacred time.[58]

On festival days, Roshan cooked for dozens of congregants: "For everybody, whatever the number was. So, I had to make *haleem,* I had to make *biryani,* I have made *muttiya.* You name it. And plus, on top of that I would make *sufras* (extended assortment of food offerings) and *gulab jaman* and *ras malai* and things like that for dessert." Other members of the congregation helped her prepare desserts and appetizers, and everyone sat and ate together at the conclusion of the services (Figure 3.8). Like Gulzar, Roshan froze some food to send home with the young men who attended services. The chance to eat home-cooked Indian food would make these young men "so happy they would literally come to jamatkhana just so that they could have *nandi* (food offering) [laughs]. I cook[ed] all this good stuff, you know." Although, as we have seen above, young single men received these gifts of food at least partly in secular terms—"It was the only good food that I got"—the re-encounter at home with the aromas and tastes recently shared in connection with prayer services also extended the sensory experience of jamatkhana and the care labor that women like Roshan dedicated to it.

Establishing makeshift sacred spaces, according to cultural geographer Rhys Dafydd Jones, entails a "negotiation between sacred acts and profane settings, challenging the established notion of sacred space as absolute space, and bring[s] considerations on adapting sacred conventions."[59] We see Roshan and Gulzar challenging the idea that space is absolutely sacred or profane, asserting through their actions that by adapting sacred conventions they can temporarily, and repeatedly, make their living rooms a place where the sacred can transpire. Moving furniture, vacuuming, demarcating space through temporary barriers and white sheets, modifying material objects

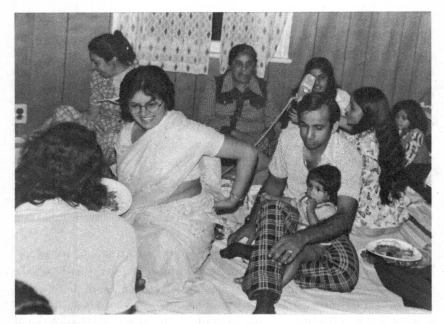

Figure 3.8 Ismailis of Fort Wayne sharing a meal after prayer services in a makeshift jamatkhana, 1970s.
Courtesy of Gulabeh Pirani.

(reducing the height of a coffee table to mimic a *paat*), using sensory markers such as the *ginan*, *agarbatti*, and Indian food—all constitute the placemaking activities through which women transformed otherwise profane sites into sacred ones. These adaptations elicited the practitioners' adherence to norms and enabled them to worship in accordance with authoritative conventions.[60] Women's labor fashioned Ismaili newcomers into "a family, a *jamat*," as Rehmat framed it; it benefited the women too—Roshan's daughter, Rozina Jivraj, emphasizes this reciprocity: "I am happy my mom had a community to rely upon and felt like a brotherhood. They each had each other."[61]

It would be naive to imagine that all displaced Ismailis encountered jamatkhanas—makeshift or otherwise, whether in Pakistan, East Africa, or North America—as welcoming spaces. Indeed, a key finding that underlies the more specific conclusions of this project is that the *jamat* is a delicate social formation, one that requires consistent, ongoing effort for its reproduction. This formation can be—and indeed is—threatened by actions that may fray these connections. I close this section by considering one such example.

Sumera was seventeen years old when she fled East Pakistan and arrived in Karachi.[62] She recalls that the early years were tough for her family: her parents did not have enough money, so she had to leave school and look for work. She was introduced to a man in the jamatkhana who needed help at his home office. Excited at the prospect of having a job and being able to support her family, she went there the following day. Sumera explains what happened next: "The office was an Ismaili's so I went, but you know, you cannot believe people. He was looking at me so lustfully. Once he even tried to touch me and so I said I cannot [chokes up, long pause]. I quit right then and left." Sumera further explains that she experienced the jamatkhana as a less-than-friendly place:

> When we would go to jamatkhana there, people were so, they were so, mean to us. They would push us. Allah! They would say that "because of the people from Bangladesh now, our *jura* (consecrated food) runs out. They eat all our *jura*." God knows what all they used to say. And my sister, she used to have long hair that she used to braid. Kids would pull on her braids so much. We had such a hard time there. We used to come home and cry.

Some of my younger interlocutors report being bullied in jamatkhanas in North America as well (more in chapter 6); others report conflicts in volunteer committee work, which caused them to avoid attending jamatkhana for months on end. The jamatkhana can thus be a site of deep belonging but also estrangement, a place where one can experience affinity but that can also, when some community members take advantage of proximity to exploit or bully others, for instance, exacerbate the sense that one is unwelcome. The salience of the care practices I have traced thus far becomes all the more vivid when viewed against this context of potential risk.

Sacred Sensorium during Flight

As we have seen above, Ismailis view the jamatkhana as a distinct and distinctive space. Sociologist Parin Mawani argues that "the experience shared in the jamatkhana, the atmosphere created therein, cannot be reconstructed in any other place."[63] Even as a temporary construction, the Ismaili jamatkhana is a material site ensconced within a boundary. In this sense, as Mawani suggests, the jamatkhana is a physically distinct Ismaili structure of worship. But because God is omnipresent, any space carries the potential to be transformed into a threshold between transient and eternal worlds. Specifically, the *sensorium* of the jamatkhana can be conjured, shared, and transmitted by and through a collective of Ismaili practitioners. Thus, while I agree with Mawani that the jamatkhana carries a distinct quality as a physical site, I also suggest that we recognize the potential for its sensorium to exist separate from fixed, dedicated structures—as we have seen in the makeshift jamatkhanas of Atlanta or Fort Wayne—and, indeed, to exist separately from any physical structure at all. The soothing fragrance of incense, communal recitation of *ginans*, bodies collectively falling in prostration or swaying in *dhikr*, and commensal eating are the olfactory, auditory, visual, and embodied practices—and rituals—through which practitioners can summon the sensory structure of the jamatkhana even outside its material boundaries. Lauren Berlant argues that "the drive toward [intimacy] is a kind of wild thing. . . . It can be portable, unattached to a concrete space: a drive that creates spaces around it through practices. The kinds of connections that *impact* on people, and on which they depend for living, do not always respect the predictable forms."[64] The drive toward spiritual intimacy, then, can be portable, and the sensorium of the jamatkhana can be activated even without the usual physical forms (buildings or ritual objects). I will share two such efforts: first, onboard a ship leaving Chittagong for Karachi, and second, at a refugee camp in Italy. Examining women's practices during transit/flight not only expands our understanding of their contributions but also extends our conceptualization of jamatkhana as a sacred space that is both material and sensory.

Shams Steamer, Chittagong to Karachi, 1971

Several of my interlocutors from East Pakistan remember scrambling to pack their bags in April and May of 1971 and making their way to the dock to escape the riots that had broken out in Chittagong. They were headed for the Shams steamer.[65] As expected, ships leaving the city were packed. Roshan recalls: "That day we had about 300 or 400 people in a vessel that usually carries around 100." Food and water ran short, exacerbated by a journey that was longer than usual—twelve days, instead of the usual eight—because the steamer was not allowed to cross Indian waters and ended up briefly lost at sea. Passengers were seasick and vomiting.[66] Adding to the inevitable anxiety about heading into an uncertain future, women were further distressed because their spouses and adult male children had remained behind in Chittagong, either hoping to sell family possessions before leaving or simply because there were so few seats available on the steamers. In these tumultuous moments, the predominantly Ismaili—and predominantly female—passengers of the ship invoked the Divine through collective prayers and through expressions of care for each other.

Roshan remembers, "Every day we would do our *dua, tasbih, ginan*." *Ginans,* as we have seen above, have a central role in the religious life of Ismailis. They are often recited during formal congregational services, either as memorized texts or read from printed sources. Ismaili children of South Asian descent learn *ginans* as part of their formal religious education as well as informally from their parents and elders at home. When Ismailis found themselves in limbo, languishing on overcrowded ships or waiting months at refugee camps for permission to move on, they often recited *ginans,* which reinforced their belief in Divine aid. Roshan recalls seeing women crying and often reciting the *ginans* to soothe themselves. J.A., who fled Chittagong on the same steamer as Roshan, explains, "The chanting of *ginans* created an atmosphere that comforted us, like a jamatkhana."

Among the passengers were two Ismaili itinerant preachers. They not only provided pastoral care to those on the steamer but also continued the religious classes they had offered back at the Chittagong jamatkhana. Roshan had been their student and the onboard classes provided her an unexpected sense of continuity: "Kamalu missionary and his wife would sing *ginans* all the time, and they would actually teach us *ginans* on the ship too. All of us were his students in Chittagong because he came there as a missionary, and we used to go to *waez* class. So, he would teach us *waez,* he would teach us *ginans*." Women further reinvigorated familiar forms of commensal eating. J.A. recalls that she had received news from community members who had left on an earlier ship that food would run short, so she and four of her friends cooked dry snacks to share—*thepla, puri, chevra:* "We were told that everyone should bring a little bit [of] food, so we all shared." J.A. says traveling with friends was a source of relief for her, "but we faced a lot of hardship."

The sensory and somatic dimensions of religious experience have long been recognized in the study of religion in South Asia.[67] Smriti Srinivas posits religion as "also an experience of the senses" and argues that while there is no single sensorium of the sacred, it is possible to identify elements of experience that are historically shared by a group of practitioners.[68] Such a sensorium, tied to memories of places and bodies, can connect practitioners of a shared tradition to each other and to a collective past. On board the Shams steamer, singing the *anant akhado ginan* under the stars on a wet and crowded deck, paying attention to a *waez*, performing collective *tasbih*, and sharing *chevra* unified the passengers in their memories of jamatkhanas in Chittagong, reinforced their bonds to each other, and harnessed their faith. These activities temporarily imprinted the steamer with the sacrality usually associated with jamatkhanas.

Refugee Camp, Italy, 1972–1973

When the expulsion decree was announced in Uganda in August of 1972, Laila Datoo (b. 1946) was away from home visiting friends in Nairobi.[69] Her friends urged her not to return to Uganda, but Laila also remembers struggling to obtain permission to stay in Kenya as her Ugandan citizenship had been revoked. Without a passport, she could not travel elsewhere either. In the end, the United Nations High Commissioner for Refugees (UNHCR) came to rescue the few thousand Ugandans who remained in the region after Idi Amin's deadline. Laila and other "stateless" Asians boarded United Nations planes that transported them to refugee camps across Europe. She arrived at the Colonia Trieste camp in Italy in November 1972 and remained there for six months.

Over 90 percent of the camp residents were Ismaili, and Laila describes the routine acts of care that she and others performed to forge a community. On their first morning, they were served something "soup-like," which turned out to be octopus: "Nobody drank it probably [laughing] but then we are Ismailis, and we are volunteers, and we have worked, and we know, so we told them [the camp staff] 'we will cook,' and started cooking *biryani* and everything." After an Ismaili woman died during childbirth, Laila and other women cared for the baby while the father tended to the two older children. She recalls, "Everybody took care of the baby, the whole camp. We helped each other. We were Ismailis." Laila also assisted the elderly residents who needed help with their personal hygiene: "These old ladies who they brought into the camp. They came a month before us or 15 days, I don't know how long, but nobody was there to take care of them. Nobody gave them [a] shower. Completely old ladies you know like in the wheelchairs." She remembers walking the women to the bathroom, cleaning their bed pans, and waking them up for morning prayers. These concrete acts of care reinforced religious bonds, palpable in Laila's repeated assertion: "We were Ismailis."

A hallway at the camp was sectioned off and labeled as the jamatkhana, with regular performance of rituals in the mornings, afternoons, and evenings. "Even in there," Laila recalls, "we opened up *khana* and we said all *tasbih*, you know long long prayers for relief of our difficulties (*mushkil asan ji lambi lambi tasbih*), because [we] didn't have anything but . . . every day, even 12 o'clock, we had nothing to do, so we said *tasbih*." Just as onboard the Shams steamer, at the camp, residents had none of the distinct physical markers or objects that Gulzar and Roshan employed in their living room jamatkhanas—it was, instead, the rituals themselves that imprinted the space with a sacred quality. Laila further contributed to the spiritual suste-nance of this transient congregation by recreating the rhythm of daily life around prayers. Since she regularly awoke around 4:00 a.m. for medita-tion (*ibadat*), the camp's residents nominated her for the task of waking up other worshippers: "I was used to going to morning prayers so [in the camp] I would just get up and everybody select[ed] me. Then every morning I go, wake everybody up, and there was a paralyzed lady and give her a bedpan."

Religious festivals added another dimension to the making of an Ismaili sociality in transit. Laila and the residents found themselves at the camp on December 13, the birthday of their Imam, celebrated by Ismailis globally as *khushali* or a day of happiness. Laila remembers dressing up for the occa-sion and trying to replicate the program of festivities—prayer, then dinner, then *dandiya* (traditional stick-dancing) and music—that they knew from Uganda: "On *khushali* we met. We wore saris and we had *dandiyas*. We had so much fun [laughs], and there was a musician with me, so we had a music party. I think my camp wasn't like a refugee. I think other camps might be different, but I think I heard from [name removed] that they had fun, too" (Figure 3.9). Getting together for the religious festival and sharing food and music enabled the residents to find joy—a sentiment not normally associ-ated with the refugee camp experience. Such activities transformed the oth-erwise drab and dull site of the camp into a space of spiritual rejuvenation. Celebrating their Imam's birthday was a reminder of his presence and benev-olent grace.

With support from the UNHCR, Laila eventually settled in Ontario, where, for the past three decades, she has been responsible for maintaining the garden that encircles the Oshawa jamatkhana. She recalls that when the jamatkhana was first moved to this location, in 1989, its exterior was

Figure 3.9 Laila Datoo (second from the right, in white sari) along with other Ismailis celebrating *Khushali* at the Colonia Trieste resettlement camp in 1973.
Courtesy of Laila Datoo.

barren. She asked the *mukhiani* if she could cultivate it. She tells me that she prayed, " 'Oh *Mowla bapa* make me your gardener.' And he did, he did. He listened; he listens to me." When I last spoke with Laila, the jamatkhana had been closed for several months due to COVID-related restrictions, and she had been asked to suspend her garden work. She mentioned how dearly she missed caring for the garden. Figure 3.10, an image taken before the pandemic, shows Laila standing beside the flower beds she tends.

Seva and the Ismaili Subjectivity

Gulzar and Roshan described their activities as "*seva*," a term that, as noted above, is used by contemporary Ismaili Muslims of South Asian descent to denote service to the Imam as well as to individuals and institutions in the Ismaili community and beyond. Given how frequently the term appeared in interviews, it is useful to examine *seva* in some detail.

When I asked J.A. about her work on the *safai* (cleaning) committee, she explained it as "*seva*." When I probed her further, she said: "*Seva* is good

Figure 3.10 Laila Datoo outside the Oshawa jamatkhana.
Courtesy of Laila Datoo.

works that are a form of prayer. *Seva* is *sreva*." She then proceeded to explain this wordplay to me by reciting the following verses from a *ginan*, in which the term *sreva* (which means to worship) is used:

> *Eji kahore jiv tame kis karan ayaji,*
> *Na kidhi sahebjini srevaji*
> O man! If you did not worship the Lord then say,
> why have you come?[70]

J.A. appears to understand *seva* as broadly equivalent to "ethical conduct," which in turn is recognized as a form of worship (*sreva*) because it is anchored in a consciousness of the Lord. But many Ismailis also understand *seva* as opportunities given by the Imam to elevate their souls. In doing so, they evince a mode of religiosity where good actions are directed not just by personal intentions (*niyat*) but also made possible by the Imam; we thus observe the limits of human intentionality as space is made for Divine agency, which arrives via the Imam. Consider my interview with Khurshid Bhimani.

Khurshid arrived in New York City from Tanzania in August 1971 and joined forty other Ismailis who were meeting weekly for prayers in the apartment of another Ismaili woman.[71] In the months that followed, she built a secure position for herself at her new job, helped fellow Ismailis obtain legal documentation, and organized outings to give members of the community a chance to get to know each other. When the first Regional Ismaili Council for the Northeastern and Midwestern United States was formed the following year, Khurshid was appointed as the "Member for Women." She describes Ismaili women at the time as being focused on finding employment and adequate healthcare facilities, assimilating into their new environment, and integrating their children into the new culture and school system. She therefore organized programs that taught women how to navigate the vast array of social services available to them in the United States. Khurshid went on to serve on numerous Ismaili institutions over the next several decades. During our meeting, Khurshid described her expansive and extensive work as "*seva*." When asked about what *seva* has meant to her, she says: "a blessing." She then mentions a *farman* from the previous Imam, Sultan Mahomed Shah, in which he had said, "When I am happy with somebody, I give *seva*. And when I am happier, I give them more *seva*." Even though a believer's intent (*niyat*) is considered a defining element of *seva*, Khurshid's reference to this *farman* shows that she received the *seva* also as a favor from the Imam.[72] Agency for pious effort, or *seva* in this case, then does not rest solely with the individual but emerges in a relationship with the Divine.

Because *seva* is offered by the Imam, women tell me of moments when the Imam eased the difficulties they encountered during their volunteer work. At the time Gulzar was serving as a *mukhiani* in Atlanta, she was also a full-time hospital resident; she would rush to the jamatkhana, still in her work clothes, to perform her duties with no time in between to rest, change, or eat. Another woman who served as a *mukhiani* tells me of being so tired at the end of the day that she would "fall onto a pile of clothes and sleep right there." And then there was the anxiety. Leila Hirji, who was a *mukhiani* of a jamatkhana in New York in the 2010s, remembers worrying that she would be unable to manage a full-time job and a long commute along with her *seva* responsibilities: "I would come home and I would be in tears that I can't do this. I can't go to jamatkhana. I am so tired. All I want[ed] to do was to sit and cry."[73] But she would experience a burst of vitality when she entered the jamatkhana: "The moment I sat behind the *paat* it was like [a] shot of energy, completely. It was like, you know, how you change clothes? My tiredness just

dropped. It was just so amazing." Other women expressed the same transformation to me using phrases such as "the *barakah* (blessings) of *seva*"
or "feeling *Mawla*'s hand on my shoulders" or "an invisible bubble around
me." These phrases point to a metaphysical source intervening and guiding
women through the difficulties of their *seva*. Roshan reminisces about her
time as Fort Wayne's *mukhiani*: "I didn't realize how fortunate I was to be
doing these things at my house. It was one of the biggest blessings I have had."
Seva brought happiness and *barakah* to these women's lives. That potential
for Divine reward explains in part why *seva* is not viewed as entirely determined by the devotee.

Seva has worldmaking capacities. Khurshid explains: "In a community,
what is *seva*? You help the community. I find that anywhere in the world
where I go, I can relate to people because they are Ismaili. Community is
an anchor. It is a safe haven; you *will* be helped. We are a brotherhood and a
sisterhood." There is a sense of simultaneity in Khurshid's statements; while
she gives, she also receives. The latter includes not only potential help from
others but also a feeling of embeddedness and emplacement around the
world. She can move about convinced that she will find an Ismaili who will
come to her aid if needed. She is confident that she will be able to enter an
Ismaili jamatkhana in India or Canada and fall into the rhythms of their care.
Such certainty indicates how *seva* by women, such as Khurshid and others
considered in this book, has provided Ismailis with a sense of ongoing intimacy within experiences characterized by hardship. This intimacy is not
of the emotionally intensive kind, but one that subsists through low-key
affirmations and the deep knowledge that, when called upon, the distant
Ismaili-stranger will leap into supportive action. Khurshid elaborates that
she frequently extended help to those she did not know and would likely not
meet again. Yet she did so because "one of the common elements was that we
belong to the same community. I may come to you, and you may not know
me, but I can be of your *seva*. You will still help me because we both belong to
the same community." The relationality that Khurshid describes extends beyond shared doctrines to a domain of deep spiritual connection.[74]

But not all women used the emic term "*seva*" to describe their care
practices. For instance, when I asked Laila about her care activities at the
camp, she insisted that she undertook this work "because we were Ismailis"
and added, "Yeah, I mean, you know when you have to do, you start doing
it." Mol, Moser, and Pols argue that "in care . . . 'qualification' does not pre-
cede practices, but forms a part of them."[75] In this sense, Laila's care for

fellow Ismailis was the means through which she simultaneously discovered, expressed, and practiced her Ismaili subjectivity. Anthropologist Zahra Jamal, in her study of Ismaili volunteers in Houston, found that her informants had a similar attitude toward community care: "[Volunteering is] something that one 'just does'—volunteering becomes a natural thing, a matter of common-sense action."[76] Ismaili moral codes in these instances become manifest through mundane care activities in the flow of everyday life where qualification is not deemed crucial; cooking *biryani*, cleaning an elder's bedpan, and looking after a baby become tasks that one does as a matter of religious identity anchored in an ethos of care: "We helped each other. We were Ismailis," as Laila insisted. It is the repetition of these activities, over a period of many months, that produced community as a feeling and as a care infrastructure in transit.

The Gendered Dimensions of *Seva*

At first glance, many of the activities that appear in this chapter—cooking and cleaning, for instance—seem to reinforce women's gendered participation in Ismaili religious life. But we can acknowledge that women performed different services than men in Ismaili settings and at the same time recognize that the women's services were meaningful ways through which they enacted devotion to the Imam and the community. As one of my interlocutors commented (after we had finished vacuuming the jamatkhana and were exhausted): "Women like us who clean the jamatkhana are a means (*zarya*) for the spiritual development of others. Our hard work facilitates everyone's prayers so in a way we get the *barakah* of all those who pray in the jamatkhana."[77] Another woman explained that she cleans jamatkhana toilets because "it is Imam's house."[78] Writing about Hindu women's religious labor in the kitchen, Anindita Ghosh argues that while such spaces may indeed be gendered and the associated division of labor can bolster male privilege, women can "also subvert and create their own socially specific meanings of that space."[79] Through such work women may acquire "a very private space," be relieved temporarily from the burdens of their everyday lives, and be "in direct and private communion with God."[80] Such private spaces and personal meanings emerged among Ismaili women too.

Nazira Mawji tells us about a widow in Kampala who joined a jamatkhana volunteer committee after the death of her husband, gained valuable skills through it, and used those skills to start her own café at a cinema.[81] Another woman found personal autonomy, away from the watchful eye of her husband, by joining a committee responsible for organizing religious festivals.[82] Numerous women speak of the jamatkhana and *seva* opportunities as affording them religiously permissible social opportunities. A woman might, for example, meet female relatives from her extended family at a meeting for the cleaning committee when seeing those relatives was otherwise prohibited by a domineering mother-in-law or husband.[83] The voluntary services rendered by Ismaili women in East Africa were, according to Rashida Keshavjee, "their acts of service to the community, sacrifice and charity."[84] But Keshavjee also sees these as "occasions to build strong bonds among women who needed each other's assistance, guidance, friendship and camaraderie."[85] Women's support for each other was of course mediated by Ismaili administrative and organizational structures (the ladies corps, the cooking committees, the welfare societies) that we have seen in this chapter, but it relied on women's initiative too and, as we have seen, predated these institutions.

Paying attention to the fields of care created by women does not, of course, deny the efforts by men in these early years of settlement. While women did most of the cooking, men set up tables, took out the trash, and lifted heavy pots. Roshan notes that while she prepared *biryani* or *haleem* in her Fort Wayne apartment, her husband would often be unfolding the *chaddars* and moving the tables around to set up the jamatkhana. Men's tasks, as Gulzar recalls them, included leading ceremonies, delivering sermons, driving congregants to and from services if no public transit was available, and engaging with the Ismaili Council officials. Highlighting in particular the contributions of one male congregant, Mansoor, Gulzar explains: "I have to say that the men of the *jamat* really helped out. . . . Mansoor *bhai* (brother) was excellent at *ginans*. He was an itinerant preacher by training in the past. So, he was pretty knowledgeable." Once the jamatkhana moved to a dedicated facility, Mansoor was also responsible for opening the facility each morning before services: "One day when Mansoor *bhai* opened the jamatkhana, he saw that all the lights were on. He still went in and there was this guy—there was a thief—inside! He had a knife in his hand. And he came to hit him. Mansoor *bhai*, with his hand, held the knife and the guy got so scared because, he got so scared because—he got so scared, he ran away. And then we had to take Mansoor *bhai* to hospital and [he] had stitches and all that." Rehmat remembers Bahadur Kassam giving her family rides to the jamatkhana since they lived some distance away. Likewise, as a *mukhi*, Iqbal Paroo was tasked with figuring out housing and furniture for families arriving from Uganda, as well as getting their young children into schools. The acts of care that Mansoor, Bahadur, and Iqbal performed to emplace Ismailis in Atlanta thus looked different from those performed by women, mediated perhaps by prevailing and historical gender roles and norms. But men too have been integral to the fields of care described in this chapter.

At the same time, men have had access to a much wider range of service activities. Men could hold leadership and decision-making positions, first as *mukhis* of jamatkhanas and then, as the Ismaili community institutionalized its social welfare work in the first half of the twentieth century, in the Councils and other administrative bodies that took on this oversight. Until recently, these administrative bodies were heavily dominated by elite Khoja men. Women's participation has been comparatively circumscribed, with certain leadership positions available to them contingent solely on their relationship to men. Commenting on whether she might serve as a *mukhiani* or *kamadiani* again, Roshan sadly reflects on these limitations: "I am not married anymore, so they won't give it to me." Roshan lives in an area with a large *jamat*, and except in very small congregations, women normally can access these roles only through their husbands, co-serving when their spouses are officially appointed to leadership. Despite these constraints, women have always found a way to serve the *jamat*.

Continuities: Atlanta, 2019

Atlanta jamatkhana, November 2019, 5:45 a.m.[86] Formal prayers have ended but instead of heading home, Farida stops by the kitchen near the exit of the jamatkhana. It is already bustling with activity as six women are crammed into a fifteen-by-eight-square-foot space. Two are leaning over the sink washing ritual objects like *kumb* and *pyalis* used to distribute *ab-e-shifa* (healing water or water of purity), another wrestles with a large percolator in which *chai* was served to the congregants, a few hover over a cart meticulously drying the objects as they come out of the rinse water, and farther down is another woman repacking them for the next prayer service.[87] There is a particular order for stacking the *kumb* and *pyalis*, and as Farida enters, the lead volunteer points her toward this final task: "*mukhiani ma*, this one is ready."[88]

Most Ismaili jamatkhanas have a kitchen where food offerings are organized, trays of *juro* are prepared, and utensils used during rituals are cleaned and stored. This space is often maintained by women volunteers and is delineated as feminine. While some women are officially assigned kitchen responsibilities as members of the jamatkhana's cleaning committee, it is understood that anyone can enter the kitchen area and offer services when time permits. There is always something to do. I was one such volunteer on this crisp November morning, joining my mother in her daily routine.

The women in the kitchen chatted nonstop with each other. They shared news of events in other jamatkhanas, discussed thought-provoking articles and *waezes* (which they promised to forward to each other on WhatsApp), and asked about the health of each other's family members. In one corner of the kitchen, two women talked about their ailing mothers and how important it was to make sure they felt comfortable in old age: "Ma has done so much, so much." A commotion began when the lead volunteer switched the lights on and off to signal that the *mukhi* had arrived to offer *dua*: "Let's go, let's go." Every morning, before he departs the building, the *mukhi* of the congregation conveys blessings upon the volunteers who have stayed behind. Everyone is expected to drop what they are doing and rush out into the hallway where he, along with the women faith ministers, offers effusive *duas*: "May your faith remain strong. May you have more opportunity to serve the Imam. May your difficulties ease. May all your good wishes come true. May your children thrive." The hallway echoes with "Ameen, Ameen." The *mukhi* leaves and the women return to the kitchen. We now sense an urgency to finish up and head to work or home. One woman tells me, "I have to cook breakfast for my daughter-in-law." Another explains, "I go straight to work from here. You see, I can only come to jamatkhana in the mornings due to work, *shukar*."

As the tasks are checked off, a volunteer urges everyone out the door; it is time to mop the kitchen. Munniben points to me: "She can do it. She is young." Another woman whom I had not seen before (perhaps because she was cleaning the *paats* inside the prayer hall) calls out to Munniben: "Can you drop me to Carriage Place, please?" Munniben nods.

I finish mopping and get ready to leave when Shahbano takes my mother aside and asks if she can help a non-Ismaili woman (who had moved in next door to her) get into the county's free medical assistance program. My mother promises to stop by her apartment later that afternoon.

The jamatkhana in Atlanta where this exchange took place is the current incarnation of the one that began when a handful of Ismailis from Tanzania came together at Gulzar Kassam's apartment in 1972. It now hosts not only those who fled East Africa and East Pakistan but also more recent arrivals from India, Pakistan, Iran, Tajikistan, and Afghanistan, as well as second- and third-generation Ismailis born in the United States. And yet the rhythms of women's care work that I observed in 2019 still resonate with the activities that Gulzar, Naila, and R.K. performed nearly fifty years ago, some fifteen miles away. In a matter of thirty minutes, women cleaned up the physical site of the jamatkhana and prepared objects to be used again in the next service. They washed incense holders that were much more elaborate than the ones used in 1972 and yet carried in their fragrance the same placemaking effect of transforming the ordinary into sacred, fashioning olfactory continuity between Ismailis past and present. The well-established nature of the activities (ritual objects stacked in a specific order, *sukrit* prepared from a familiar recipe, the entire sequence of washing, drying, and mopping) allowed volunteers to work from habit, leaving plenty of room for chitchat and a chance to relate more closely to each other. While washing and drying ritual objects, women expressed care by inquiring after each other's health, provided material support by offering rides, contributed to each other's intellectual development ("I will send the *waez* recording to you"), acknowledged the intentionality it takes to balance *din* with *duniya* ("I can only come to jamatkhana in the mornings due to work"), expressed gratitude ("*shukar*"), and invoked Divine presence ("*dua*"). In Farida's offer to help a non-Ismaili migrant, we witness the seamless transition of *seva* within jamatkhana to the community outside. These acts, though seemingly minor, all reinforce non-kin spiritual intimacy and form a tradition of placemaking that extends through time and space.

4

Storying Divine Intervention

I met eighty-eight-year-old Shamsuddin in his first-floor apartment in Karimabad, Karachi. He looked frail in his wheelchair and did not, at first, feel able to talk with me. But his caretaker insisted that I just sit in the corner and wait: "He will open up eventually."[1] And so I did. After some initial inquiries—which helped Shamsuddin establish that I was in fact related to his sister—he seemed more comfortable and warmed to the conversation.

Shamsuddin spoke in short sentences, primarily in Urdu and Gujarati. I was all set to work through the oral history protocol I usually followed, asking questions about childhood and seeking information about the Ismaili community and then experiences of fleeing from East Pakistan. However, as soon as I mentioned interest in his life in Mymensingh, Shamsuddin went straight to the trauma of 1971. "It was a massacre," he said, and began to weep. I was caught off-guard by the sudden shift in mood but followed his lead.

In late 1971, as tensions between East and West Pakistani forces intensified, Shamsuddin decided it was time to flee. He wanted first to sell his meager belongings so he would have some capital to start over in the new city. But riots broke out in his neighborhood and he found himself trapped along with a few dozen other Ismailis. They decided it would be safer if they moved into the jamatkhana, rather than remain isolated in their homes. They camped in the jamatkhana for twenty-nine days—eating, sleeping, and praying together. They were so certain of impending death that the *mukhi* performed final rites for each person: "We received *madan ka chanta*. None of us could speak [during the ritual ceremony]. The *mukhi* was weeping and we were weeping."

As one of the few men left behind, Shamsuddin was tasked with safety and security: he was to stand by the gates of the jamatkhana and keep the rioters out. One day some locals arrived at the entrance to warn him: "You are next." Shamsuddin remembers community members sheltering in fear that night, "but nothing happened." The next morning, the men returned to report that

Rebuilding Community. Shenila Khoja-Moolji, Oxford University Press. © Oxford University Press 2023. DOI: 10.1093/oso/9780197642023.003.0005

they had in fact been prevented from attacking. "Your Imam was holding a wooden staff (*danda*) and guarding the gates of the jamatkhana," they said. "Your Imam was riding a white horse and circling the jamatkhana."

As Shamsuddin shared this episode, tears trickled down his deeply wrinkled cheeks. Then suddenly, I saw his chest swell up like a young man's. He sat up straight in his battered wheelchair. In a loud voice that belied his frail frame, he announced the presence of the Imam: "You see, he is standing in our midst! He is standing in our midst! He is standing in our midst!" Shamsuddin repeated the refrain aloud as if it were a declaration to people passing on the streets outside his building—as if, decades later, he was finally revealing the secret details of an intimate meeting with the Beloved. "They ran away. Not a child was hurt. We all passed with ease. We went in the Shams steamer. It was the last steamer to leave Chittagong."

I sensed that Shamsuddin wanted to say more, but twice he pushed his wheelchair away from me. "I have said too much already," he said, hinting again that this was a story he felt he needed to safeguard. For ten minutes we sat in silence as I ate the biscuits and slowly sipped the *chai* Shamsuddin's caretaker had brought me. Suddenly Shamsuddin lifted up his *tasbih* (prayer beads) and said, "*Tasbih* does not lie. He takes care of us like a mother takes care of a small child. This is the *moujza* (miracle) of my life."

Shamsuddin pushed back his wheelchair one final time, wiping his tears away with a ragged, stained handkerchief. I knew that the interview was over. Brushing away my own tears, I agreed: "Yes, this is the *moujza*."

* * *

Trauma, violence, and narrow escapes are inextricable from the experience of forced migration. Yet, only a few of these experiences metamorphose into stories that are repeated in the company of fellow migrants or shared with Ismailis belonging to a younger generation. Why these memory-stories? What function do they perform? What norms do they affirm?

Memories are rarely rehearsed for their own sake, as Astrl Erll has argued; they are occasions of self-description and function as models of future conduct for others.[2] In this chapter we see the normative and formative work of memory-stories that Erll describes, specifically in relation to stories of miracles or *moujza*. The Urdu term *moujza* (or *mu'jiza* in Arabic) derives from a root meaning "that which overwhelms" or "that which disables." In Muslim theological discourses, *moujza* points to those occasions when God and saintly figures overpower. Religious studies scholar Amira Mittermaier explains that miracles "gesture toward a larger Divine order that evades causality and human reason. They rupture the surface reality (*zahir*) and bring to light an underlying dimension of hidden reality (*batin*)."[3] In Shamsuddin's *moujza* narrative, the Imam saves his *murids* and reveals his true nature to the community of believers (and to the unbelievers who reported being frightened away when they saw him on his white horse). The believer's subsequent exclamation—"He is standing in our midst!"—alludes to this space-time-defying power of the Imam. Shamsuddin thus affirms key Shia Ismaili beliefs related to Imamah: namely the Imam's Divinely designated appointment, his Divinely inspired knowledge (*ilm*) of both the exoteric/apparent and the esoteric/hidden dimensions of reality, and his God-given sanctity (*walaya*), which includes the belief that the Imam can intercede (*shafaʿa*) with God.[4] Shamsuddin accordingly believes that the Imam can alter the situation of his followers in the material world through intercession with God. By storying his experience, Shamsuddin simultaneously seeks to make sense of a traumatic moment in his own life *and* recruit me (the listener) as a believer. When he shouts, "The *tasbih* does not lie," he gives me a lesson in daily spiritual life: that prayers are not left unanswered, and that the Imam will always protect his followers.

Moujza stories have an emplacing effect. For the storyteller, the story is a chance to structure an accessible narrative from an extraordinary experience and to revisit past intimacies with the (ever-present) Imam. For the believing listener, the story mediates a connection to the narrator's past and establishes an expectant intimacy with the Imam—if the listener is ever in need, the Imam will intervene. I thus view the scene of *moujza* storytelling as one where both the narrator and listener become aware of God's presence via the Imam and the *moujza* story itself as a device for harnessing *iman* (faith). These scenarios bring different generations of Ismailis into closer relation with each other. Because these are stories that can recall the past as well as shape the *jamat*'s future spiritual state, their narration is an ethical act of community making, both in the here and now and in a broader symbolic sense.

It was not just one or two Ismailis that shared these miracle stories with me; I heard them from as many as three dozen people, over a third of the first-generation cohort I interviewed. The obvious value my interlocutors attached to the stories and the secret-sharing mode of their transmission were constants, even as the details differed. I heard the same *moujza* story that Shamsuddin shared with me from another interlocutor, who reported the miraculous turning away of a rioting crowd and the sparing of trapped Ismailis at a jamatkhana in Chittagong. The specifics of the event were less important than the work of spiritual renewal and moral attunement the story was to perform.

Whereas in the previous chapter we saw how Ismaili women created material and sensory environments to enable individuals to connect with the Divine, this chapter shows how the Divine via the Imam *acts upon* (to use Mittermaier's phrasing) the material world and the believers who inhabit it. In studying such interventions from the Elsewhere—the otherworldly, the spiritual—I am guided by methodological orientations articulated by Annalisa Butticci and Amira Mittermaier, who call for close attention to the interlocutors' terms (including familiarity with the textual traditions that shape their interpretations) and for a willingness to bracket one's own ontological convictions.[5] They urge researchers to suspend disbelief and the usual primacy of sight and human rationality. Similarly, writing about religious stories that circulate in western India, anthropologist Kirin Narayan positions herself somewhere between participant and observer, arguing that this in-between positionality led her to more nuanced insights during her fieldwork.[6] This chapter and my embodied, visceral responses to the *moujza* stories—tears, awe, and wonderment—vividly illustrate these dynamics. In fact, it is likely that I gained access to many of these stories only as an insider—for their disclosure, as I will explain more below, hinges on an ethical transaction between the narrator and the listener. This transaction assumes shared hermeneutics and an implicit recognition that there exists a realm beyond the *zahir* (apparent/exoteric).

Indeed, my interlocutors often shared stories of miracles only after establishing trust with me and ascertaining my spiritual disposition. Sharing these stories was akin to passing on a secret, telling a tale of the Beloved rupturing material reality to save the devotee. A disbelieving listener could dismiss them as fantasies or delusions and not recognize their otherworldly origins. Since the narrators believed the latter, they often wanted to ensure that I too would recognize them as such. Shamsuddin, for example, was reluctant to speak at first and needed to confirm a distant family relationship to me before he felt comfortable speaking at all. Most of my interlocutors showed a similar need to establish trust before they would tell me about a *moujza*. These stories were typically whispered only at the end of hours-long interviews, and only when the interviews were conducted in intimate settings—such as a participant's home or in the corner of a jamatkhana. Even those women and men who had initially started speaking with me in English or Urdu would switch to the vernacular, Gujarati, Sindhi, or Kuchchhi, likely the language that they used in their most intimate conversations with God. While some storytellers emphasized the Imam breaching the *zahir* to save his *murids* or changing the course of events, others sensed Divine intervention when they received unexpected aid from strangers. It was at the moment when his followers were filled with fear, anxiety, and uncertainty that the Imam made his appearance through *moujza*.

While I was trusted with many stories, some were shared with me on the condition that I would not write about them but would only draw on them for my personal spiritual growth. Those stories therefore do not appear in the chapter but shaped my interpretation of the stories whose tellers allowed me to share them. By the conclusion of my research, I too had become a keeper of secrets.

Moujza Stories in the Ismaili Tradition

Stories of miracles circulate in many religious traditions as testimonies of the power of God and saintly figures, interweaving the physical with the spiritual realm.[7] When miraculous healing stories are shared in Pentecostal Christian circles, writes Andrew Singleton, they encourage believers to keep praying for miracles.[8] In Simon Dein's examination of storytelling among Chabad Hasidim, the stories of a Lubavitcher Rebbe's miraculous feats create a sense of his continuing presence among believers.[9] Miracle stories are widespread among Muslims as well. The Quran cites numerous examples of God's intervention to protect Prophet Muhammad and the nascent Muslim community. During an invasion of Mecca in 570 CE, God sent flights of birds to drop baked clay on the Abyssinian governor's army—saving Mecca, the birthplace of the Prophet, from the attack. During the battle of Badr in 624 CE, when soldiers of the Muslim army were outnumbered three to one by their opponents, God sent angels to fight beside the Muslim troops. These interventions are viewed by Muslims as *moujza* and understood as testifying to the presence and power of a transcendental being as well as evidence of the Prophet's authenticity. When Ibrahim was thrown into fire, it became cool and safe; when Musa threw his staff, it transformed into a snake.[10] Isa cured the sick and Sulaiman could comprehend the language of birds.[11] While it was

the prophets who performed the miracles, God's will was the agent behind them. Muhammad's miracle is understood to be his mediation of the
Divine word of God, the Quran; since he was an "unlettered" man, the revelation points to God's agency.[12] In popular lore, however, Muhammad is
said to have performed numerous other *moujza,* from speaking to animals
to splitting the moon.[13] Nonprophetic miracles (i.e., those performed by
saints) are called *karama* (marvels), and Muslim theologians have tried to
maintain a careful distinction between *moujza* and *karama* to reinforce a
gradation in power, signaling the higher status of the prophets.[14] Matthew
Pierce, however, argues that this distinction is not as useful when considering the miracles of Shia Imams because the Imams are understood to be
Divinely appointed and so their miracles function as prophetic miracles.[15]

Moujza stories belong to a corpus of narratives (colloquially referred to
as *dakhlas*) well known to Khoja Ismailis. Such stories trouble the often-
assumed primacy of the human subject as the only actant in this world and
direct attention to Divine agency, which often arrives via the Imam. In popular Khoja Ismaili traditions, *moujza* stories reaffirm the Imam's Divine appointment and his Divinely inspired knowledge. They indicate a cosmology
in which the Imam is at once physical and metaphysical. A *moujza* might
occur when a believer is struggling with a question or experiencing hardship. It may happen when members of the community are threatened, as
in Shamsuddin's case. During moments like these, the Imam might make
an appearance—in a waking vision, in a dream, or through a person or an
object—to deliver the answer or facilitate a resolution. For Ismailis, then, the
Imam is an active spiritual force; they beseech his intercession with God and
rely on it, particularly during tumultuous times.

Ismailis come across *moujza* stories at numerous sites: at dinner tables
where elders pass on these narratives to the next generation, in jamatkhanas
where accounts of miracles are retold by itinerant preachers, and at youth
camps where these stories are shared by Ismaili teachers. Growing up, my
father told me these stories, reiterating how the Imam protects his followers.
One story has stayed with me. This *moujza* took place in Pakistan, sometime
during the 1940s. At that time, Ismailis who lived in villages deep in the interior of the province of Sindh routinely sent their religious dues (*karsazi*) to
the Ismaili Council located in the city of Hyderabad. The journeys were dangerous. Robbers often preyed on the Ismailis who carried the monies over
the dirt roads through barren lands. My father tells me about the time when
robbers attacked the father of a friend:

You know Feroz Uncle's dad, Rai Juma Khuwaja, he was responsible for transporting *karsazi* from Sultanabad [Number One] to Hyderabad. To get to the bus from his village, he had to walk two miles, and on one such occasion, he was accosted by two robbers. Rai Juma, he was a rather large man, you see, and he had tied the money in a knot and placed it under the belt of his *shalwar* to hide it. He told the robbers he didn't have anything. But they refused to let him go, perhaps fearing he would alert others. Meanwhile they continued to rob people passing by. The old man pleaded, "I have been here for so long. I am so hungry. Let me go." They wouldn't. Ultimately, he bothered them enough with "I am so hungry, I am so hungry" that the robbers got frustrated and gave *him* 10 rupees to go get food and leave them alone [laughs]! When Rai Juma reached Hyderabad, he told everyone, "Instead of robbing me, I robbed the robbers! The *karsazi* is safe!" So you see we have seen many *moujza*. The Imam takes care of his *karsazi*, his *murids*. Oh, I have witnessed so many *moujza*.[16]

For my father, it took nothing less than a *moujza* for a man carrying *karsazi* to be held for hours by notorious robbers just to be released unscathed. That the memory of this event from the 1940s survived into the 1990s—when I first heard this story—relies on numerous factors. Ansgar Nünning notes that the transformation of an event into a story requires that a certain temporal section be singled out and given meaning.[17] Each story, then, is "already interpreted in a certain way."[18] My father's story, like the one Shamsuddin shared, depicts a discrete moment of peril, its resolution interpreted always as an instance of Divine intervention. If we were reading this account within a different story tradition—such as the trickster tale—the narrator might interpret the resolution as a reflection of the protagonist's cleverness or personal magical powers. But as the narrator of a *moujza* story, my father looks past Juma's clever trick to see instead the miraculous intervention that caused the robbers to spare the *karsazi*. Through these interpretive moves, and by sharing these stories with me, my father participated in my religious formation.

Moujza stories are not usually found in formal Ismaili curricular texts; they are transmitted orally. Their telling is a form of cultural reproductive work aimed at cultivating religious sensibilities, and in that sense they are similar to the care work we have seen thus far in the book. This specific kind of cultural reproduction, however, is undertaken by both men and women, even though there are subtle differences in the content of the stories that each share. Accounts of the Imam's supernatural intervention were told to me primarily by men who were tasked with gatekeeping responsibilities for the Ismaili jamatkhanas or residential societies in Dhaka, Mymensingh, and Chittagong. These stories have circulated widely and were known to many of my interlocutors. In contrast, women shared stories of Divine help that were more personal and intimate—describing, for example, when they sensed "Imam's hand" in unexpected forms of aid. Such stories often have limited circulation given their personal quality. Yet stories of this latter variety belong to the same universe of sacred narratives as the more readily recognizable *moujza* stories, for both perform a similar function in relation to the listener: they bolster faith in the Imam and convey a moral imagination where a metaphysical, otherworldly force acts upon believers. It is also interesting to note that while my male interlocutors shied away from sharing the specific traumas of flight, perhaps since such wartime experiences expose vulnerability, they readily shared *moujza* stories. One reason for this, I suspect, is that in *moujza* narratives masculinity is shifted onto the Imam, as opposed to other men (such as the rioters or the robbers) or women. Men can thus participate in their telling without loss of honor.

Moujza narrations are often dramatized through gestures and voice modulation and contain details from the Islamic tradition to tie the particular story to the genre of miracles. The teller's imagery, repetition, tone, and posture work together to initiate a spiritual stirring in the listener. The white horse in Shamsuddin's narrative, for instance, recalls Duldul, Imam Ali's mule that is referenced in the *ginans* and is popularly depicted as white in color,[19] or the Buraq, a horselike winged creature that carried Prophet Muhammad to the heavens and back in the traditional stories of the Night Journey (*isra*) and the Ascent (*miraj*). It is said that other prophets also rode the Buraq. Depictions of this creature, referencing the Prophet's mystical powers, abound in Islamic art. Thus, when the Imam appears on a white horse in stories of Ismailis sheltering from violence in Dhaka and Mymensingh, the image connects him to his biological and spiritual ancestor, Prophet Muhammad. When Shamsuddin loudly, and with great emotion, repeats three times the refrain "He is standing in our midst!," his tone and posture evoke the experience of a sermon (*waez*) in the jamatkhana. As religion and affect studies scholar Donovan Schaefer has argued, religion is not exclusively cognitive: it is also the field of sensations that emerges from affectively driven, embodied practices.[20] The aesthetic repertoire of *moujza* storytellers is then not incidental to, but a constitutive element of, the genre's faith-inspiring capacities.

And its delivery is a cultivated practice; not everyone is a charismatic teller of *moujza* stories. Beyond the ethical transaction (centered on belief) is the narrator's hope to convey affect to the listeners—and, in so doing, transform their experience of time and space, and intensify their faith.

Consider my interaction with Shamsuddin's caretaker—an Ismaili woman in her fifties. As I spoke with him, she hovered nearby. She kept finding reasons to come into the room where we were sitting: to make the bed, bring a jug of water, separate Shamsuddin's medicines into neat piles. She would sometimes pause and listen with keen interest to Shamsuddin, repeating "*Subhan Allah* (Glory be to God)" under her breath, suggesting that she too was imbibing the lessons being imparted. When I was leaving, she looked at me expectantly and asked, "When will you return?" I explained that I was heading back to the United States. She sighed, "*Kitna mazaa aaya na? Mawla kay moujazay sun kar iman taiz ho jata hai. Chalo wapas aana tau aur sunnay milay ga, mujh ko bhi* (Wasn't that delightful? Listening to our *Mawla's* miracles really sharpens the faith. Come again when you are here next time so you get to listen to more, and me as well)."

The caretaker chose the word "*mazaa*" to describe her experience. In Urdu, *mazaa* conveys wide-ranging feelings from fun and delight to relish and pleasure. It is often linked with enjoying delicious, savory, flavorful food; to be *be-mazaa* (without *mazaa*) is to be bland, flavorless, vapid. In the story-event, the listener savors a story (experiences *mazaa*) that reiterates what she already knows of her Beloved (if she ever needs rescue, her *Mawla* will be there). She thus becomes *mauji* (emotional) and feels *mauzuu* (emplaced, situated, established) in a world marked by uncertainty and precarity. This feeling of emplacement is perhaps what the caretaker indicated when she declared, "*iman taiz ho jata hai* (one's faith is sharpened or reinvigorated)." The intimacy with the Imam experienced by Shamsuddin, transformed into a story, makes the Imam's charismatic reserve available to the listeners—the caretaker and me—and transmits shared Ismaili beliefs about the Imam's Divine appointment, his *shafa'a* (intercessory power) and his care for his *murids*.

Beseeching the Imam

Believers hope to invite the Imam's intercession via an utterance or an object. Numerous Ismailis from East Pakistan related episodes of men and women who were kidnapped by local militia but then released after they showed their kidnappers a photo of the Imam or spoke his name. I met Shams, a sixty-five-year-old Ismaili man, by sheer coincidence.[21] He worked as a driver for a Karachi-based nonprofit I was consulting with in 2019 and learned about my research as I was explaining it to a colleague in the car. When he told me he also hailed from East Pakistan, I arranged to interview him. He related a *moujza* tale where he was captured by militia. In desperation he yelled, "Ya Ali Madad (O' Ali help me!)," only to see one captor's facial expression suddenly change. When Shams explained he was a Shia Ismaili, his captor left him waiting alone for some time. When he returned, he set Shams free: "He just let me go. He did not say another word." The believer's utterance of "Ya Ali" is a call to the Imam for intercession—"Ali" in these formulations refers not only to the first Shia Imam, Ali ibn Abi Talib, who lived in the seventh century, but also to the cosmic, ever-living, Imam. Ismailis, like other Shia Muslims, call upon Imam Ali when facing hardships. He is known as *Mushkil Kusha*, the one who alleviates difficulties. This belief is captured in the Shia prayer of *Nad-e-Ali*, which many of my interlocutors remember reciting nonstop:

Call upon Ali, the manifestation of wonders
You will find him a helper in all adversity
Every worry and sorrow shall surely be removed through his protection
O Ali, O Ali, O Ali

Hameed Husain, similarly, describes an experience of a thwarted kidnapping in his unpublished memoir.[22] He was visiting Khulna for business with an Ismaili friend when unexpectedly curfew was called. They decided to stay at a boarding house. Gunfire erupted in the middle of the night, likely because someone had broken curfew. When the shots receded, Hameed and his friend stepped out into the street to inquire what had happened and found themselves in a crowd of locals gathered around two injured men. Distrustful of Urdu speakers, the locals soon turned their attention to them, probing them about their business in Khulna: Were Hameed and his friend in any way connected to the West Pakistani military? Did they have anything to do with the gunshots in the street? Unsatisfied with their responses, the leader of the Khulna men escorted the two Ismailis to an old building for further interrogation. There Hameed explained that they were followers of the Aga Khan, which "soften[ed] their stances."[23] He writes, "The

Aga Khan had established the Jubilee and the Crescent jute mills in Khulna sub-division, which had resulted not only in thousands of new jobs, but laid the pathway for increased industrialization of East Pakistan."[24] Hameed and his friend were released unharmed.

Such instances of Ismailis calling on the Imam or showing his photo were commonplace and often led to deliverance. Z.H. recalls that the protective power of the Imam was so widely known that "even non-Ismailis started keeping a photo of him [the Aga Khan] for protection."[25] As she explains, "Memons saw this, and they looked like us in terms of looks and language, so they used to show Hazar Imam's photo too." We might compare this use of photos in moments of crisis to the broader use of objects in a Shia context. Sana Chavoshian, in a study of women visitors to a martyrs' cemetery in Iran, describes believers routinely inviting spiritual encounters through objects, photographs, and gravestones.[26] I noticed that while Z.H. does not have many keepsakes from her time in East Pakistan, she prominently displays a photo of the Imam's visit to Chittagong in the late 1960s in her living room (see Figure 2.6 in chapter 2). She often gazed at it during our interview, as if wishing for his presence again. Anthropologist Zahra Jamal observes that the Ismaili Imams' charisma extends to the objects that they touch (holy water, coins, the carpet they walk on, the chair they sit on) as well as to the objects associated with them (photographs, *tasbih*, even buildings).[27] Such objects are viewed as containing blessings and therefore bring good tidings. For Z.H., then, the photo was a material, tangible means through which she not only accessed the memory of the *moujza* (when she was saved by the Imam) but also invited blessings in the here and now; it was a portal for both memory and *barakah*.

Stories of the Imam's miraculous intercessions are supplemented by stories of aid he offered in his role as a global leader of the Nizari Ismaili people. Ugandan refugees in Canada never tire of reminding me that it was their Imam who convinced his friend Pierre Trudeau, then prime minister of Canada, to give asylum to his followers. Between September 28 and November 9, 1972, 4,450 Asians flew into Canada on chartered flights from East Africa; many of these were Ismailis. Even before Idi Amin's decree, in 1960, the Imam approached the Commonwealth Relations Office to express concern about his followers in Uganda and to seek guidance from the British about their future.[28] In 1969, he again approached the British to discuss the possibility of providing United Kingdom passports for four hundred Ismaili children from Zanzibar who had become stateless due to conflicts there, and to consider similar measures for members of the Ismaili community from Kuwait, Rwanda, Burundi, and the Malagasy Republic.[29] My interlocutors who fled East Pakistan on Red Cross flights explain that their flights were arranged under the auspices of the United Nations High Commissioner, who at the time was the Imam's uncle, Sadruddin Aga Khan. The High Commissioner's office became a focal point for coordinating aid to millions of refugees who crossed the border from East Pakistan into India. Later, after the founding of Bangladesh, the same office was also responsible for the repatriation of three hundred thousand people. Meanwhile, in Uganda, Sadruddin Aga Khan intervened in the final weeks to fly out 3,600 Asians under UN auspices to transit accommodations in Austria, Belgium, Italy, Malta, and Spain; these refugees were permanently settled over the following several months.[30]

Many times during the interview Laila Datoo (whom we met in the previous chapter and who spent six months at the Colonia Trieste transit camp in Italy) mentioned the fortunate coincidence that the Imam's uncle was the High Commissioner at the time: "We were lucky that Prince Sadruddin was High Commissioner. Yeah, that was the best thing. During that time, our luck that Prince Sadruddin was High Commissioner—that's why we had fun. Otherwise, we would have had one bowl of rice once a day."[31] My interlocutors did not interpret these more political forms of aid as miraculous per se, but they saw in them a continuity that reinforced the Imam's spiritual status.

Moujza in the Quotidian

In addition to stories of supernatural interventions, I encountered narratives of more quotidian ways through which my interlocutors sensed Divine aid— in particular, when aid arrived *unexpectedly* from strangers or from fellow Ismailis. In a fortuitous meeting, a timely introduction, or the offer of a discounted price on a used car, believers sensed the "hand of God," as one of my interlocutors described these *moujza*, alluding to a verse in the Quran. As Michael Gilsenan observes, "The miracle is in the eye of the believer"[32]— and Ismaili believers see the miraculous when an ordinary moment turns extraordinary. In almost every interview I conducted, I heard at least one personal experience of receiving unexpected aid, and often many more. The transcendental, in this genre, is not indescribable or residing elsewhere beyond the world; it materializes and exerts power through human (and even nonhuman) mediating figures. In that sense, these stories advance the perception that the Imam can deliver the miraculous not only directly—appearing on a white horse—but also via a human intermediary. This notion intersects with the work of *seva* that we have seen in prior chapters, binding Ismailis not only to the Imam in their experience of the miraculous but also to each other as both deliverers and recipients of the miraculous.

I met N.A. at a noisy restaurant in Atlanta in 2019.[33] It was definitely not the best location for an interview, but our meeting was scheduled after a morning *majlis* and the restaurant was close by. N.A. spoke softly and I often found myself asking him to repeat his comments. He recalled sending his wife to Karachi early in 1971, but he postponed his own departure until the very last minute since he was the *mukhi* of one of the jamatkhanas in Dhaka: "You see, I was the *mukhi*, the caretaker, so I could not leave the *jamat* by themselves." But N.A. was also a well-known banking official and had heard that his name was "on the target list of Mukti Bahini": the Bengali resistance forces "had a list of all high-profile people." When most of the *jamat* had migrated, N.A. decided to head to Karachi. By then, however, transportation via commercial ships and flights had been halted. A well-wisher suggested he try and join the Pakistan navy officers who had recently been captured by the Mukti Bahini as prisoners of war: "You see, the Mukti Bahini treated the navy officers well, and the officers were to be transported to Burma for trial so that was a potential way out." N.A. did not know anyone in the navy, but his friend insisted that they at least visit the camp where the officers were being held. N.A. tells me what happened when they approached the camp: "One of the officers there saw me and recognized me and told the captors that I worked under him. By God *beta* (child)! I did not know that person. That was a *moujza*. I did not know him. He just recognized me." N.A. was transported to Burma along with the naval officers and held in custody for forty days. They were then loaded onto a plane bound for West Pakistan, and he eventually reunited with his family in Karachi. N.A. proceeded to remind me that "in Surah Yusuf, Allah is called the 'Protecting Friend' so He protects us all the time." The Quran furnished N.A. with a hermeneutical frame through which he interpreted the kindness of the navy officer as a *moujza*, as a moment when the Protecting Friend intervened.[34]

Farida Merchant's is another narrative that finds the miraculous in the quotidian. Merchant (whom we met in chapter 2) fled Chittagong at a young age and is one of the few women I encountered from this generation who has left a written record of her life—in this case, an unpublished family memoir she titled *Mountains before Me*. When I met Merchant, we talked mostly about her childhood and the horrific events that unfolded in 1971 as she and her mother fled on the Shams steamer. After an interview that ran for several hours, she felt comfortable enough to share a copy of her memoir. The memoir recounts in fascinating detail a number of instances when Merchant senses Divine intervention. "God's helpers" and "angels," as she calls them, appear throughout the text, always stepping in when she is at her most vulnerable. *Mountains before Me* thus discloses both the suffering that wars unleash—the hardships of finding housing and employment in West Pakistan—and the Divine mediation that shields believers. In reading it we see how unexpected forms of aid from strangers are interpreted as Divine help.

For many weeks during the political clashes of 1971, it was too dangerous for Merchant and her family to leave their home. The militia had cut off their water and electricity, and local vendors refused to sell groceries to non-Bengalis. They were trapped and worried they would run out of food. Merchant recalls that in those moments of desperation their Bengali housekeeper, at great personal risk, came "under [the] cover of darkness, dropped bags of rice, beans, and vegetables over the fence in [their] backyard."[35] In April 1971, Merchant and her family were finally able to flee to Karachi, but life remained very difficult. Her mother, Saherbanu, struggled to find clients for her work as a seamstress. As the Eid festival approached later that year, Merchant's younger brother asked Saherbanu to make the traditional elaborate meal. She had no money to buy the meat, rice, and *mithai* she would ordinarily have purchased ahead of an important festival. And yet, Merchant recalls, her mother "believed in the power of prayers." On the eve of Eid, a rush order arrived: a family urgently needed holiday outfits. Saherbanu worked all night to get the clothes ready and with the money she earned was able to prepare the *biryani* and *zarda* that only the day before had seemed out of reach. Merchant reflects: "My mother had never met the lady who ordered the clothes before. How did she know our situation? Who can say? God had sent an angel in answer to my mom's prayers."[36] The Bengali maid and the last-minute Eid customer are both mediating figures through whom Merchant senses Divine intervention. She interprets these forms of unexpected aid as a response to prayers, emphasizing a dynamic relationship between the believer and God.

When Merchant was struggling to find a school for her son who had been diagnosed with acute hearing difficulties, a stranger gave her an admissions form for a school for deaf children in the United States, where she eventually moved and enrolled her son. When her husband was having a difficult time finding work in Atlanta, a stranger she had met through her volunteer work offered to hire him. As she struggled to raise her son while working full time, her friends stepped in to babysit. Merchant wonders, "Was this just a coincidence or God sending angels our way once again? . . . It is said that God sends angels in human form. I truly believe that having experienced it myself."[37] She ponders further: "Every time our family runs into a brick wall, some strangers come to our aid. . . . Are they really strangers? I smile to myself as I write this. God—You are All-Knowing, All-Seeing. You just test us each time to see how much faith we have in YOU."[38] In Merchant's reflection, angels appear as mediating beings through whom God interacts with humans. Indeed, in Muslim cultures angels are often revered as facilitating the relationship between God and his prophets. Jibrail communicated with Prophet Muhammad and accompanied him on his journey of ascent. Other angels include Maalik, the guardian of hell; Izrail, the angel of death; and Israfil, who will blow the trumpet on Judgment Day. Angels are said to engage in constant praise of Allah and dwell in the heavens. They are also tasked with recording the good and bad deeds of humans, and may even intervene to guide human actions and choices, sometimes by taking human form. Thus, when Merchant understands strangers as angels, she invokes this commonplace belief.

N.A. and Merchant's accounts give a transcendental quality to mundane encounters with strangers. The narration of such stories furnishes a call for ethical behavior from readers/listeners if similar interventions are to be invited in the future. Merchant explains that she wrote the book "to instill in [her] family the core values of compassion, integrity, kindness, and ethical behavior."[39] The book clarifies the interpersonal traits of believers—loyalty, sacrifice, self-reflexivity, service to others, and perseverance in hardship—that prepare the way for Divine grace.

And stories like these were common: many of my interlocutors experienced Divine grace in their everyday lives, in their children, in their good health, and even in the rupture caused by their displacement. In the storytelling process, the anxiety they felt in the 1970s is replaced by calm, confidence, and a narrative register in which the Imam's influence is powerfully experienced. On the advice of the Imam, most of my interlocutors from Uganda had given up their British citizenship and become Ugandan citizens. When Idi Amin stripped Asians of Ugandan citizenship, they became

stateless and were terrified: had they kept their British passports, they would
have been more secure. Looking back, however, many of the migrant generation emphasize that moving to North America was the best outcome.
Almas Lalji, who fled to Toronto with her husband in the early 1970s,
explains: "Everybody, I think, is doing very well with Allah's blessing, and
hopefully all children will do better."[40] Rossbina Nathoo concurs: "When we
came to Canada, we received material wealth in tenfolds, right?"[41] Women
recognize this outcome as a product of the Imam's *ilm*: because their Imam
knows all dimensions of reality, he guided them appropriately during their
time in Uganda. Zarintaj Huda, while saddened to leave Dhaka and all her
friends, echoes this understanding: "Imam opened the doors for us, because
he *knows*."[42]

An Ethical Transaction

I heard Shamsuddin's *moujza* again from Madad Ali, who was about eighty
years old when we met in the Aliabad residential society in Karachi.[43]
We began by talking about his childhood in India and his adulthood in
Mymensingh. Surprised that someone was interested in these details, he
probed me about my family history too: "Where is your *nani* from? Which
jamatkhana did she go to? Where is she now?" After an hour of conversation,
as I sensed that the interview was coming to an end, he leaned forward and
whispered: "You know, we were trapped in the jamatkhana but we heard that
at night a man in a white horse circles the colony [pauses, tears start flowing].
He protected us. No one could touch us [wipes away his tears]." The man
on the white horse remained unnamed. Since I had heard this story before
from Shamsuddin, I nodded. Madad Ali went on to share other details of his
life after fleeing Mymensingh but returned to this tale, this time ending on
the ineffable "We don't know"—perhaps dreading that I might view him as
delusional.

In Madad Ali's hesitancy we can see how a *moujza* tale moves between the
realms of the spiritual and a world constrained by observable facts. He simultaneously acknowledges Divine aid that arrived via the Imam—palpable in
his tears and clasped hands as if in prayer—and is guarded in his explanations
("We don't know"), for believing in such tales requires an ethical transaction between the teller and the listener, one he was unsure I was willing to
participate in. Mittermaier argues that engagement with *moujza* discourse

demands an "attunedness to the invisible" because unlike other phenomena, *moujza* and dream-visions evade the power of the gaze.[44] Miracles are by definition disruptive and subversive: they confound our expectations and point instead to a nonhuman, transcendental source at work.[45] Attuned to the invisible, participants recognize that humans are not the only actants in this world, and the apparent (*zahir*) and hidden (*batin*) are not antithetical to each other but coexist in a complementary relationship. The ethical transaction between the narrator and listener of the *moujza* story, then, demands that each acknowledges this textured relationship between the seen and unseen. A receptive listener is thus crucial to the successful telling of a *moujza* story. Anthony Shenoda has argued that miracles rely on "interpretation and one's willingness . . . to be impressed by such gestures or accounts of them."[46] And where the story transaction's success depends in part on the listener's willing participation, narrators may begin by asking questions. We have seen in the conversations above a pattern where interlocutors would take care to establish a connection before beginning to narrate a *moujza* tale.

Noorallah, like Madad Ali, also experienced a *moujza*, but it was a few years earlier in 1966 when some people attacked the jamatkhana in Chittagong after mistaking Ismailis with a different group of Gujarati/Kuchchhi speakers.[47] A young man at the time, Noorallah was put in charge of protecting those taking shelter in the jamatkhana. He and his friends had no weapons, so they decided to display toy guns, hoping these might scare away anyone who contemplated harm to the congregation. One night, as they were guarding the compound, they heard that an attack on them was imminent. All the young men, carrying their toy guns, went up to the roof so they could have a better view of the area. Noorallah explains, "We saw a group of thugs coming toward the jamatkhana. They were able to break the main gate and get right to where the steps were, beyond which lay the jamatkhana hall and the women and children. But as they climbed the steps, the steps would not end; the staircase had become an escalator. It was a *moujza*. Believe me *beta* (child), I saw it with my own eyes!" Noorallah recognized that what he was saying was unbelievable by the ordinary standard of observable facts; that is precisely why he kept insisting to me that what he was sharing was not a dream or a hallucination, that he was not "making it up" but had "seen it," and that his rational faculties—especially his vision—were fully engaged. Because the work of the *moujza* narrative is not to convey facts but rather to create an aesthetic encounter that affirms belief in Divine agency for both the narrator and the listener, we might perhaps instead read these asides by

Noorallah as an invitation for the listener to confirm participation in the *moujza* transaction: does the listener agree to the reality that lies beyond consciousness? Thus, as he spoke, I nodded vigorously: yes, I was a believing participant.

Furthermore, in the *moujza* story's apparatus of comprehension, the narrator and listener may agree to meanings or facts that are beyond external verification. For example, numerous women I interviewed assumed that the Shams steamer that carried them away from an increasingly dangerous Chittagong was sent by the Imam. Roshan Pirani called it "a chartered ship that Hazar Imam sent for the Ismailis." In her version of the story, the Imam is involved in both warning his followers of danger and providing the means to escape it: "Hazar Imam sent us a message that all the women and children need to get out of this country right now and the next morning he has also sent us Shams ship. . . . [I]t was piloted by an Ismaili, you know sailor or whatever you want to call captain of the ship, was Ismaili, so Hazar Imam sent him to Chittagong." I am unable to verify if the Imam communicated directly with the owner of MV Shams, though I did discover through archival research that the ship was not owned by an Ismaili.[48] It was a passenger-cum-cargo ship of the Crescent Shipping Lines Limited and was put into service between East and West Pakistan in 1960. The ship made an average of thirteen round-trip voyages per year on the Chittagong-to-Karachi route, until the fall of 1971. These details, however, are not important—not for my interlocutors nor for me. What is significant is Roshan's interpretation of the event and the meaning she assigns to it: her Imam did not abandon her; he sent a ship to transport her and other Ismailis to safety.

As we have seen above, *moujza* stories were reserved for private settings and were shared only after the narrator and I had established rapport. Once during a rushed interview, I inopportunely asked an elderly woman to "please share a *moujza* from your life." She rebuffed me, saying, "I don't remember." A year later, I found myself spending an entire day with her at her home, and over *chai* she shared numerous *moujza* (or *dakhla*, as she called them) with me. By this time, we had been trading WhatsApp messages for over a year and had shared several phone conversations. She had had the time to get to know me and to assess my ethical disposition. The environment was suitable: it was the end of the day, we were having *chai* and biscuits, and we were getting ready to say our *dua* shortly thereafter. Narrators of *moujza* stories thus are keenly aware of the moral and emotional work of such oral transmissions and they decide when and with whom to share these stories.

The narrative cannot be rushed, and the listener cannot force the process by asking or seeking.

Moujza Stories and the Second Generation

When I met Farhana Esmail (b. 1989) in 2021 to discuss the miracle-stories her family members had shared with her, she echoed the spiritual reverberations of these stories—the renewal and intergenerational connection—that Shamsuddin's caretaker had communicated to me in Pakistan two years earlier. Farhana's father and his siblings had sought refuge in the Chittagong jamatkhana for about two weeks in 1971, as violence between East and West Pakistani forces intensified. Farhana had heard the stories I now knew well—the Imam on a white horse, the staircase that became an escalator, the toy guns that appeared as real guns to those charging at the jamatkhana. Reflecting on these stories, Farhana uses phrases such as "not rational but also not implausible" and "made up but also not made up," demonstrating how *moujza* stories blur the edges of the material and spiritual for listeners in the second generation:

> Somebody standing on the roof protecting seems so weird and not like rational but also not implausible. It's interesting because they [the *moujza* stories]—they are made up, but they are also not made up, you know. I mean, I think at the core they showed that people trust the Imam and they think that he can get them out of any situation. I think part of that is like, okay there is some diplomacy happening that's working in the background to protect the community, but at the same time there is also some type of spiritual energy that also serves as a protection.[49]

What Farhana sees as "spiritual energy," Shamsuddin calls the Imam. Both articulate themselves and other Ismailis as being accompanied by this spiritual force. The story then becomes a means through which a second-generation listener (Farhana) is instructed into an awareness of Divine omnipresence experienced via the Imam.

As second-generation Ismailis reflect on *moujza* narratives, they bring to bear their own evaluative frameworks; they do not simply consume and retransmit them without analysis.[50] Farhana elaborates, "I do think people like to tell these stories to give meaning to that experience or to remove the trauma but to think that, okay, there is some empowering narrative there or that like we were protected because of belief or faith or like we are part of this group that is *special*." We see in Farhana's comments how she considers the different meanings a listener could derive from the story and then chooses one for herself. It is possible, then, that second-generation listener-narrators might modify some *moujza* stories and ascribe new meanings to them as the stories are refracted through their own experience. Anthropologist Kirin Narayan found this to be the case in her study with second-generation South Asians, particularly for those stories that proffered gendered behaviors that her interlocutors found to be repressive.[51] Listeners thus have agency in deciding where to take the story next, as narrators. In my most recent interaction with Farhana I learned that she has launched a podcast (for mostly Ismaili subscribers) where she may retell some of these stories, indicating a new direction for *moujza* storytelling that shifts this ethical transaction from a personal exchange of secrets between coreligionists to a more open and public medium. In that sense, this book too participates in this shift from private to public—as a 1.5-generation Ismaili in North America, I am now, with the blessing of my storytellers, introducing some of these stories to a scholarly audience.

Extending Ansgar Nünning's observation that stories and storytelling "are not only the most important means of making autobiographical selves, but an equally important means of worldmaking," I have suggested in this chapter that displaced Ismailis retell *moujza* stories both autobiographically—to better understand the traumatic events they experienced in the 1970s—and as part of the project of remaking the *jamat* in the diaspora.[52] The *moujza* accounts connect the younger generation to the places inhabited by earlier generations of Ismailis and to shared sensations of the Divine. The story becomes a medium, a pathway, for conveying spiritual beliefs. And in telling the story the narrator not only cultivates a personal consciousness of God but also assists other practitioners in this endeavor.

* * *

Shamsuddin passed away on August 11, 2021, in Karachi. His caretaker and I will not be able to partake in the *mazaa* of his stories again, but the ones I am able to capture in this book will hopefully continue to "sharpen faith"— to borrow the caretaker's words—with every reading.

5

Culinary Placemaking

When I visited my nani in Karachi during summer vacations, she made me *bhel puri*.[1] Ten-year-old me did not particularly like *bhel puri* because I was not allowed to have the tangy and spicy tamarind and cilantro-based chutneys that usually go with it. But even at that age I knew that there was something about cooking and eating with my grandmother that deserved respect. So when she told me to sift chickpea flour for the *sev*, I sifted. When she said to wash the potatoes, I washed. When it was time to measure and mix the puffed rice with onions, I mixed. I would say her *bhel puri* was delicious, unparalleled, like nothing I could eat at home in Hyderabad. She would smile—not a full beaming smile but a half-clouded, coy one. She insisted, "Write it down, *beta*." For nani, cooking was an everyday practice, its knowledge passed down orally. She did not have any formal schooling. "Write it down" was not something she could do, but something she asked of me, "so that you don't forget."

Nani passed away as I was drafting this chapter in the spring of 2021. COVID travel restrictions meant I could not attend her funeral services. I ate *bhel puri* every day for months afterward. I wasn't actually planning to eat it; I just ate it, every evening, as if following a Divine plan. Weeks later, as I rewrote the chapter, I could intellectualize my actions. Perhaps this was my way of mourning her? But my body did not await such intellection before plunging into action, before remembering her, before aligning with her through *bhel puri*. My body has its own memory; it knew how to honor the passing of an ancestor thousands of miles away, how to conjure her into being again through the sensory memory of food, and how to keep returning to her by making and eating again the dishes we had once prepared together.

Bhel puri was first prepared in Gujarat in India but traveled with Khoja Ismailis as they migrated within India and on to East Africa, fleeing famines and wars. It fed my nani and her family through multiple displacements and a life of poverty. When her husband died young, she supported her five

Rebuilding Community. Shenila Khoja-Moolji, Oxford University Press. © Oxford University Press 2023.
DOI: 10.1093/oso/9780197642023.003.0006

children by preparing *bhel puri* at a restaurant in Dhaka. *Bhel puri*—typically eaten as a snack by the middle-class customers of the restaurants where she worked—was often the only meal that she and her children could afford for days on end. When the 1971 war between East and West Pakistan uprooted her family, she began making *bhel puri* in Karachi for a small canteen at the local jamatkhana, run by and for Ismaili Muslims. When nani and I made *bhel puri* together, she would tell me stories of her past work as a cook, her tin-roofed home in Dhaka, and how she had sneaked her way into Karachi in the early 1970s.

I knew that there was something different about nani, about *bhel puri*. *Bhel puri* is still a popular street food in India, but street vendors did not sell it in Hyderabad, Pakistan, where I grew up. I could only eat it in nani's kitchen or at the jamatkhana canteen in Karachi where many migrant and refugee women from Gujarat (like nani) worked. As a child, I did not understand why nani spoke Gujarati and not Sindhi, my "mother tongue"—or, in this case, my father's tongue. I did not recognize all the ways that her life was marked by displacement and dispossession, or how her body and her care practices carried remnants of other places. But I took in some of that knowledge along with the *bhel puri* that back then I was only pretending to like. Much later, as I remembered her life, I remembered it through this dish.

Food, of course, is not only about nourishment. It tells a tale about where, how, and when it was created and about the people who consumed it. It is tied to political economy and social class. Its modifications and fusions reveal encounters between people and places in the diaspora. Its preparation is both an expression of care and subject to exploitation. When I look back on the hours I spent with nani making and consuming *bhel puri* and writing down recipes of the foods she prepared, I understand those moments as drawing me closer to her then and bringing me closer to her memory now. My recent *bhel puri* craving, and the time I spent ransacking my suitcases to see if I could find her recipe, are evidence of how food memories get embedded into one's body at a cellular level. My nani's *bhel puri* showed me that food is an archive: it records individual and communal pasts; it transfers memories of women past.

Food and cooking are recurring motifs in the lives of displaced people and migrants.[2] Sometimes it is the scarcity of food—during flight or in the wake of recent displacement—that reminds them of the comparative abundance in their past lives; sometimes reproducing food cultures permits migrants to keep alive memories of their homes. And yet at other times, sharing food enables recent arrivals to establish relations with host communities in the diaspora. If, as David Howe proposes, emplacement is a "sensuous interrelationship of body-mind-environment," then increasing familiarity with local tastes and smells can lead migrants toward a sense of emplacement and belonging.[3] Food in the diaspora, then, as Anna Maria Tomczak observes, is an "identity builder" and a "crystallizing force of collective remembrance."[4] It provokes memories, harnesses desires, and binds people together. At the same time, the otherness of immigrants is also portrayed through their food.[5] Food, then, has a complicated presence.

In this chapter, I consider cookbooks written by three displaced Ismaili women to discover how certain foods crystalize the memory of diasporic encounters and how through food fusions women created bridges with new communities as well as future generations of Ismailis. I am also attentive to how food—its aroma in particular—has been used to mark ethnic and racial differences. Specifically, I examine Lella Umedaly's *Mamajee's Kitchen* (2005), Noorbanu Nimji's *A Spicy Touch* (editions published in 1986, 1992, 2007, and 2020), and Yasmin Alibhai-Brown's *The Settler's Cookbook* (2009).[6] In the hands of Ismaili women, the cookbook becomes a memoir, an advice manual, a testimony, and a wish. Through it, they introduce readers to histories of community encounters from East Africa to Canada, memorialize their past lives, pass on heritage food practices, share their Imam's advice on nutrition, and imagine familial and communal futures. They reframe the trauma of displacement by crafting new forms of emplacement through food: food enables them to return "home" but also to recreate home in the diaspora through fusions and interactions with other foodways. The cookbook, then, is simultaneously mnemonic and aspirational. Like the *moujza* stories in the previous chapter, it is at once didactic (how to cook) and narrative (cookbooks often tell stories about their authors' journeys), acting to emplace the younger members within the community's historic and geographical experience through the habits of cooking and flavors of heritage foods.

In fact, heritage foods can play a salient role in the reproduction of religious life in the diaspora. Sakarkhanu, whom we saw in chapter 3, passed on her cooking skills to younger Ismailis. Figure 5.1 shows her working alongside other women, preparing food for the *jamat* in Toronto in the 1970s. After praying together in their makeshift jamatkhana, congregants came together to share these meals. During such meals, to draw on an observation Daniel Sack made in relation to American Protestants, "religious identity is shaped, community is built, and memories are created. They may not be religious

Figure 5.1 An Ismaili women's cooking group in Toronto, 1970s.
Courtesy of Dr Moh'd Manji and Khojawiki.

but they're not just another meal."[7] Since kitchen work is heavily feminized in Ismaili religious life as in many other religious groups, it is women who have facilitated these forms of communal commensality—and the community building and memory creation it generates—across generations. The cookbooks considered in this chapter, then, operate as an additional mode through which women induct younger Ismailis into the preparation of foods that can be shared during religious festivals and rituals. Indeed, the cookbooks include recipes of *seero* (which is also distributed as a ritual food in jamatkhanas), as well as *biryani* and *lapsi* (foods that Sakarkhanu made in the image shown in Figure 5.1).[8] When Yasmin, Noorbanu, and Lella teach these heritage dishes to their readers, they are also contributing to the reproduction of rituals and traditions of *sagari dham jamans* (communal feasts, chapter 3) long practiced by Khoja Ismailis of India and East Africa.

Archival Marginalia: Cookbooks

Cookbooks were often the earliest texts penned by Ismaili women in the diaspora, yet these collections remain an understudied source. This is an unfortunate oversight, as people, and women in particular, use cookbooks and cooking to care for community, share spiritual values, and recruit new generations to heritage practices.[9] While cookbooks have often been dismissed as ephemera, lacking in serious historical value, feminist scholars have recently turned to cookbooks to seek evidence of minoritized and quotidian labor—work often undertaken by women.[10] Janet Theophano suggests that the cookbook, "like the diary and journal, evokes a universe inhabited by women both in harmony and in tension with their families, their communities, and the larger social world."[11] Rosalyn Eves therefore views cookbooks as "memory-texts" that commemorate female domestic traditions and "provide a space for vernacular and countercultural memory to flourish."[12] As objects that memorialize and circulate food cultures, cookbooks both archive women's experiences and show their effort of establishing intergenerational connections.

If the cookbook can be considered an aesthetic artifact of displaced Ismaili women's placemaking, then we can look to these memory-texts as not only preserving Ismaili foodways but also instructing their readers to view cooking as an occasion for practicing spirituality. My nani often said, "I don't use red chilis (lal mirch) in my food because Imam Sultan Mahomed Shah advised against it." My mother learned in turn to avoid red chilis "because it burns the stomach, and we must care for our body. Our body allows us to pray." Food practices can thus affirm certain spiritual values (caring for the body that in turn performs prayer), and a person who avoids certain foods or ingredients can thus embody the *farmans* of the Imam, whose influence on the nutrition of Khoja Ismailis is unmistakable. This does not mean that all Ismailis make food selections or renunciations by reference to the *farmans* of Imams or that food prohibitions are universally shared by Ismailis; it does, however, show that for some individuals the practice of cooking is not delinked from the practice of faith (*din*).

The choice to study cookbooks is not without controversy. While cooking is a paradigmatic care activity, it also naturalizes women's place within the home and kitchen. Cooking can exploit women, as the labor of food preparation is often unremunerated and undervalued. But, as we will see, by engaging in care through food preparation and later by documenting (and publishing) their activities in cookbooks, displaced women seized subjectivity. The Ismaili women authors whose cookbooks I examine in this chapter explain that they wrote them to leave a record of their lives, to help their own and the next generation of Ismailis build bridges in the diaspora, and to engage an audience that is beyond their own community. Each cookbook does different work. In *The Settler's Cookbook,* Yasmin looks at how people from different racial groups encounter each other through the idiom of food. She explains what those encounters mean in relation to the search for emplacement. Noorbanu's *A Spicy Touch,* published in four editions between 1986 and 2015, illumines the trajectory of one woman's care for her community: we see Noorbanu attending *to* the needs of the nascent Ismaili refugee community in Calgary (preparing heritage foods) and later in life work *for* Ismailis to build bridges toward other communities (through culinary experimentation or by sharing Ismaili food cultures with others). Lella's *Mamajee's Kitchen* shows how food furnishes sensory connections across generations of Ismailis. Without denying that kitchen work can be a means of exploitation, this chapter shows specific instances when women were able to draw joy and identity from this work and contribute to the welfare of their coreligionists. Lella Umedaly and Noorbanu Nimji were of advanced age when I began this project, so I interviewed their daughters to learn more about what their mothers had hoped to accomplish with their writing. I was able to interview Yasmin and studied her autobiography for further insights.

Food, Race, and the Politics of Emplacement

In her prologue to *The Settler's Cookbook* (2009), Yasmin Alibhai-Brown worries that Asians from East Africa (including Ismailis) "have barely any keepers of our stories."[13] She explains that "[We] had never written our stories, our histories. We are people without a history. And that is kind of a terrible thing."[14] After Asians were expelled from Uganda in 1972, traces of their presence in East Africa were systematically erased: Asian-owned businesses were appropriated, roads renamed, educational curricula rewritten. But that historical record had been limited to begin with. Yasmin, who grew up in Uganda and now lives in London, recalls from her childhood that Indians in Africa knew nothing about their ancestors, many of whom had been brought to the continent as indentured laborers.[15] As she writes in the introduction of her cookbook—a text that is quite literally about satisfying its readers' yearnings, making them feel full—"East African Asians and their children feel the same emptiness [as she herself had felt], historically and geographically disconnected."[16] Yasmin therefore sets out to record this history in her cookbook, gathering personal stories and sharing the memories called to mind by certain foods and recipes.

The Settler's Cookbook is aimed at both diasporic Indian (inclusive of Ismailis) and English audiences. It intersperses recipes with fragments from the history of Asians in Uganda, from the turn of the twentieth century to their expulsion in 1972, and their subsequent efforts to make a new home in Britain. For Yasmin, food has evidentiary value and "bears testimony."[17] In its ingredients, preparation, and modifications, we can recognize changing palates that allude to border crossings and ruptures. The specific food testimonies that we find in *The Settler's Cookbook* thus allow us to glimpse both the intimacies of Indian, Arab, East African, and European interactions and the processes of boundary making, including racism through which boundaries were maintained.

Yasmin treats each recipe in the cookbook as an occasion to divulge the joys and hardships of migration. When she introduces the recipe for *khichiri*, a simple dish of rice and lentils, she tells the story of the Indians who were brought to East Africa in the 1890s as indentured laborers; as these workers built railways and bridges, they ate *khichiri* to keep up their strength.[18] Ismaili Khojas who came to East Africa were not part this indentured labor force, but they did share *khichiri*: they prepared it onboard the dhows that carried them across the Indian Ocean, and it remained a staple food in their households as they tried to scrape together a living in an unfamiliar environment.[19] For a modern Ismaili, *khichiri* thus carries memories of early migrants' efforts to survive and rebuild their lives under conditions of hardship. Other recipes in *The Settler's Cookbook* more directly reveal the scarcity that many migrants endured during the early years of settlement in East Africa. A case in point is Yasmin's recipe for "watery *dhal*," a watered-down lentil dish that signifies both frugality and food paucity.[20] While recipes for *khichiri* and watery *dhal* recount difficulty, others celebrate joyful encounters among Indian settlers, Arab traders, and Africans. These include recipes for steamed *matoke* (plantains) with groundnuts and Indian spices, fried *ngonja* (a variety of Ugandan banana) with cinnamon and coconut cream, and Yasmin's favorite, coconut *dhal*, which combines lentils with the locally plentiful coconut.[21] These foods were prepared when Ismaili women from Gujarat began to shop in the markets of Mombasa or Kampala, creatively mixing Indian spices with locally available produce.

By the mid-twentieth century, the earlier small *dukas* that Indians had set up to sell biscuits, beads, fish, and flour had expanded into larger stores and

factories. When Yasmin was born in 1949, Indian settlers were securely entrenched in Uganda and had come to dominate business enterprise. Racial
difference, as we have seen in chapters 1 and 2, structured the economy and
social life. As tensions intensified among British and Indian settlers and
local populations, the British in particular policed foodways as a means of
delineating boundaries and sustaining hierarchies. Yasmin elaborates how
the British, while enjoying spicy Indian food, utilized it metaphorically to
express contempt toward Indians. In European enclaves, including schools,
administrators posted signs stating "Strong Smells Not Permitted" or
"Malodorous Lunches Not Permitted."[22] British authorities invoked aroma—
or, in stigmatizing language, "smell" or "odor"—to denigrate Indians as filthy
or offensive to the senses.[23] As historian of sensory culture Constance Classen
has argued, "the odour of the other" can be a scapegoat onto which broader
antipathies are displaced.[24] Alex Rhys-Taylor similarly comments that gut
(or visceral) responses to the sensoria of the other are not mere biological
phenomena but are inflected by social histories and cultural experiences.[25]
The British banning of "malodorous lunches" thus both established and
governed racial differences between Indian and white settlers.

In response to British racism, Indians in East Africa coded food with resis-
tive expression. Yasmin tells of dukawallas' wives inventing "Gora chicken"
(literally, white chicken), a form of curry that was "inhumanely hot," which
they would sell only to white bosses to make them weep.[26] We also learn of a
"witchy Indian woman" who concocted a potion for malaria and then added
her own urine to it when white customers sought it. The woman rationalized
her actions as "revenge for their supercilious behavior toward her people."[27]
Indians also invoked smells to express defiance. Once, after encountering a
racist British official at the embassy, Yasmin's mother, speaking in Kuchchhi,
a language that neither the official nor the African security guard posted
nearby could understand, whispered: "They eat pigs, you know, so their
sweat smells bad and they are always heartless. Something in that pig meat
makes you heartless so Allah told us not to eat it."[28] After their expulsion,
as displaced Ugandans tried to settle in England, food and its aroma again
became a node for racist encounters. In 1978, a bus conductor sent Yasmin's
mother off the bus because she "smelled like a curry pot."[29] Yasmin uses her
cookbook and the same language of aroma to fight back: "British ingredients
were cleaner and cooked miraculously fast, but there was something special in Ugandan soil and water. Meat too never smelled as strong as it did in
England, as if it had been wiped with a damp, dirty cloth."[30]

Reflecting on the intersection of racism and food during an interview with me in 2020, Yasmin marvels at how the same "smelly food" that was invoked to insult Indians in the 1970s is now embedded in the English national cuisine: "So chicken tikka is actually, officially, often described as Britain's national food," an obvious contradiction in an era of rising racism and Brexit—"the idea that *we* had smelly food, but *they* could love curry. It is a contradiction. Queen Victoria loved spicy food but when we cooked and ate Indian food, we were smelly. . . . I am sure there are still moments like my mother had, when a Bangladeshi woman from a poor family gets onto the bus."[31]

Yet even as food was deployed as a pretext to deny Ugandan Asians access to basic public services, we see in *The Settler's Cookbook* that through food Asians also cultivated belonging, as they previously had in East Africa. The cookbook is full of examples where Yasmin and her mother "fix" British food, leading it away from its "bland and tepid" origins.[32] Recipes include Jena's shepherd's pie, a version of shepherd's pie that Yasmin's mother repaired "with [a] bit of *garam masala* and magic," and *Jugu* cake, the outcome when Indians in Africa "appropriated recipes from the white memsahib's cookbooks and localized them."[33] Elsewhere in the cookbook, Yasmin lifts Victoria sponges "with lime juice or saffron" and peps up shortbread "with grainy cardamom seeds."[34] She adds grated cheese to kebab mixtures and stuffs roasted chickens with pistachios, figs, almonds, green papayas, spicy effs, or spicy mashed potatoes.[35] By adding spices and playing with the ingredients of British foods, Yasmin and her mother create a distinctive East African British cuisine. From the trauma of displacement and everyday racism, they bring forth a delicious script of belonging.

The Settler's Cookbook neither romanticizes nor disparages the past. The book's narrative entwines displacement and emplacement in productive tension, as ongoing rather than bounded experiences. When I asked Yasmin why she wrote this cookbook-memoir when she had published an autobiography just a few years earlier, she explained that both books emerged out of loss and care. She wrote the autobiography "in a rush, in a panic" after her first marriage to a fellow Asian from Uganda ended and she married an Englishman, with whom she had a daughter. She suddenly worried that her daughter "would grow up, or I could die, and she would never *know*, you know, just what was what. I mean where or who was *I*? So, it [the autobiography] was written in a rush" to impart a "sense of history and memory."[36] The cookbook-memoir emerged from a different loss, when Yasmin's mother passed away in 2006. Yasmin shares, "My mother had been such a force in my life, and when she was no longer there, I felt that the only way I could keep her alive was through my own memories and also through food. Because food has abiding memory . . . all the changes that happen to you are reflected in food. Food tells you a story."[37] Yasmin continues, "[I] wanted the younger generation to know their story. Not just the food but their actual story, the good and the bad. We were deeply racist against Black people, Africans."[38] The cookbook thus fashions intergenerational continuity, not only for Yasmin, her mother, and her daughter, but also for other Asian (including Ismaili) readers who learn about both "the good and the bad." Yasmin offers these food stories also to the British, who often view displaced people as a burden:

> I also wanted the British to know, to read this book and say [to them], "We are here because you were *there*. You [emphasizes and then pauses] brought us from India, my ancestors, to a country, you did *nothing* to help us *feel* African. In fact, you divided us and kept us apart, that resulted in this terrible history . . . and then we come here. Because of your politics we end up here. Because you supported Idi Amin, you brought him into power. He threw us out." So, I wanted that story told.[39]

Through food histories, then, *The Settler's Cookbook* contemplates how colonial and national projects have structured the lives of Asians in East Africa and Britain. It posits belonging as an unfinished project as racism haunts efforts for emplacement, all the while showing that migration can be a pleasurable experience full of experimentation and novel fusions.

Trajectories of Care

When I reached out to interview Noorbanu Nimji, the author of *A Spicy Touch*, I ended up speaking instead with her daughter, Khadija Mangalji. Noorbanu was by that time in her eighties and in poor health. My interview with Khadija was delayed by my own health—I had rescheduled because I was experiencing some back pain at the time—and when we finally connected that was what Khadija wanted to talk about first. She outlined a five-minute stretching routine that had worked for her in the past ("You can do it at the breakfast table").[40] She explained the medicinal qualities of certain spices that reduced inflammation and would thus help my back. I have been following her advice ever since.

I share this episode to illustrate how my connections to the women I interviewed for this book often moved rapidly to the personal, with an intimacy grounded in our shared allegiance to the Ismaili Imam. I did not know Khadija personally; we had communicated only once or twice by email. She knew nothing about me except that I was a fellow Ismaili, writing about her mother's cookbook. That she immediately moved into the role of a caring elder ready to transfer to me her embodied knowledge follows a familiar pattern of women's intergenerational community making: minor gestures of care for (un)known Ismailis facilitate life and living. These are speech acts ("add turmeric to milk") that produce and reiterate a sense of affinity. In fact, Khadija was not the only interlocutor who passed on to me her knowledge of medicinal qualities of food or the Imam's directives about nutrition. I spent numerous days at J.A.'s apartment in Atlanta, and as we prepared meals together she often reminded me that she consumed beef only once a week and avoided drinking tea in the morning in obedience to the *farmans* of Imam Sultan Mahomed Shah.[41] This Ismaili Imam's directives on cooking, hygiene, exercise, and other issues related to women and children's health, circulate in the community both verbally and in written form—one of my interlocutors sent me a twenty-six-page document replete with his *farmans* on these subjects. While not every choice of ingredient or food custom can be traced to the Imam, the corpus of *farmans* unquestionably informs the community's culinary habits. J.A. and Khadija passed on their wisdom to me primarily in the course of conversation, while Khadija's mother, Noorbanu, shared her knowledge of food and its connection to contemporary Ismaili history in both oral and written forms.

Noorbanu Nimji was born in Kenya in 1934, shortly after her parents had migrated there from Gujarat. By 1974, both her father and husband had lost their businesses to nationalization. Fearing that Kenya might follow Idi Amin's example of expelling Asians, Noorbanu's family made its way to Calgary. Then already in her forties, Noorbanu worked hard to support her young family as well as the displaced youth of her community. She went on to write and self-publish four editions of her cookbook between 1986 and 2015. I follow the arc of these cookbooks to trace the intricacies of, and variabilities within, one displaced woman's placemaking activities. Each cookbook illuminates Noorbanu's creative efforts as she strives to regenerate the nascent Ismaili community, experiments with new ingredients, and proposes capacious modes of living in the diaspora. We notice in particular how her activities change over time, from teaching young Ismailis to cook heritage foods in the 1970s to creating food fusions for second-generation Ismailis by the 2010s.

Not long after Noorbanu's family arrived in Calgary, her husband was appointed as *mukhi* of a newly established Ismaili jamatkhana. As explained in a previous chapter, Ismaili Muslims attend jamatkhanas in the early hours of the morning and again in the evening to pray together. Noorbanu became the *mukhiani*—a leadership role typically assigned to the *mukhi*'s wife—and thus assumed responsibility for the needs of female congregants. In everyday Ismaili vernacular, the suffix *maa*, an Urdu term for "mother," is often added to the title of *mukhiani*, marking her as the mother of all congregants. In this capacity, Noorbanu facilitated the settlement of newcomers from East Africa, who continued to move to Calgary throughout the 1970s. She helped them find spices in Canadian grocery stores, guided them to potential jobs, and even hosted some families in her own home until they found permanent housing. Noorbanu's first cookbook emerged from the care work she performed for this nascent community. Among the new arrivals were recently married Ismaili women learning to run their own households and wanting to cook heritage foods for their young families. Since they could no longer turn to their own mothers for help as they had done in the multigenerational homes of East Africa, they reached out to Noorbanu—their "mother" in the context of the Ismaili *jamat*. Khadija recalls that "a lot of them [young Ismaili women] didn't know how to cook. So, they, you know, would ask my mum: 'can you teach us this and can you teach us that?' So my mum said to them, why don't you get a group of people together and then I can show you all at once and then you all will know it." Noorbanu would gather a dozen or so young women for a cooking lesson, and her younger son would type up copies of recipes for the women to take home.

Noorbanu offered cooking classes to successive cohorts of Ismaili women for ten years before she self-published her first cookbook, *A Spicy Touch*, in 1986.[42] Khadija notes that her mother's decision to write the cookbook was deeply influenced by her pastoral care work within the community: "One of the girls told my mom: 'as a *mukhiani maa* you should make a book, you know, you should put all this into a book and it would be so handy for so many people.'" Aimed at "the uninitiated" cook who is nonetheless an insider of sorts and thus not entirely unfamiliar with the ingredients or dishes, this cookbook speaks to someone who has spent her life eating *biryani* and *karela nu saak* but now wants to learn the art of preparing these dishes.[43] Instructions are short and direct and assume some prior knowledge—"Cook until chicken and potatoes are cooked."[44] (By the fourth edition published in 2015, Noorbanu would include detailed instructions—guidance on color, texture, and time—to help the reader discern *when* something is "cooked.") Another clue that the imagined reader of the 1986 *A Spicy Touch* is an insider appears in the glossary, where Noorbanu includes both vernacular Gujarati and English terms to help her readers translate in both directions. The glossary signals the book's status as a bridge between a younger, predominantly English-speaking generation of new cooks and the mothers or grandmothers who know fenugreek seeds as *methi*.[45] Noorbanu explains that she wrote the cookbook to ensure that the foodways of her people are not lost in Canada: "A dish prepared from *A Spicy Touch* is the mirror of the culinary history of a people."[46] She even advertised the cookbook in the community magazine, *Canadian Ismaili* (see the July 1988 issue).[47]

Noorbanu's effort to document the culinary history of Ismailis is analogous to the work of women from other diasporas who wrote cookbooks to ensure the cohesion of their cultural groups. Examining *A Treasure for My Daughter*, a popular Jewish cookbook that similarly presents itself as a guide to inherited foodways, Andrea Eidinger observes that cookbooks of this kind are not "just recipes" but occasions for women to promote certain food customs and shape the ethno-religious identity of their communities.[48] Marlene Epp has analyzed Mennonite cookbooks as texts that codify cultural traditions and reinforce Mennonites' identity as a transnational people.[49] These functions are visible in Noorbanu's first edition as well, as she uses recipes to tell stories about where Ismailis have traveled and describes the specific tastes and textures they have acquired in the course of those journeys. She explains:

> Although the origins of the recipes could still be traced to Northern India, the recipes changed with the immigration of the Ismailis to the shores of Africa in years past, when the Arabic influence was paramount. This added a new dimension to their culinary evolution. More recent travel and immigration to Canada, where plenty of meat and fresh vegetables are available and where emphasis on the nutritional value of food is a watchword, has led to further changes in cooking style.[50]

Noorbanu thus embeds the migration history of her people in dishes like *Kuku Paka*, which combines Indian spices with a coconut and milk sauce to create a Kenyan-Indian curry.

The 1986 edition structures social occasions along with the dishes, revealing the values that Noorbanu hopes her readers will maintain. Noorbanu includes sample menus for a "full meal for invited guests," "a buffet dinner," and a "tea party," expressing an expectation that women would want to—or should want to—uphold traditions of hospitality even in the diaspora. The few photographs that are included in the book depict full meals, prepared for large groups, rather than dishes portrayed in isolation or plated as individual servings, implying that commensality is essential to family and community cohesion. The cover image similarly displays a table laden with food. This emphasis on hospitality becomes all the more significant when viewed against the context of hardship that marked the early days of many displaced Ismailis in Canada, as I heard over and over in my oral history interviews.[51] Often men and women held multiple jobs, and even children had to work after school. Some community members struggled with transportation and lived far from jamatkhanas, and thus had limited contact with fellow Ismailis or family members. The cookbook, then, to some extent, is an aspirational space through which Noorbanu imagines social gatherings that might bring family and community together in abundance, so they can heal together.

Naseem Teja, a young woman who attended Noorbanu's classes in the 1970s, explains her own efforts to replicate Noorbanu's recipes, hinting at its reparative effects:

> I moved to Calgary in my early twenties with a very basic knowledge of East Indian cooking (curry and rice), newly married to someone who loved food but without a parent to teach me dishes I wanted to learn. I realized quickly that she [Noorbanu] was an amazing cook and always willing to share her delicious recipes. She taught us all the tricks to make these dishes turn out the same as hers. I really appreciated her wanting to share all her knowledge with me.[52]

While Noorbanu's "full meal for invited guests" might sound aspirational in a material sense—involving extensive preparation and considerable expense—Naseem's comment reminds us that the aspiration is ultimately not about the number of people around the table but about the bonds that sharing food can create among them. The knowledge being transmitted thus embraces not only the recipe and the technical skills needed to prepare it but also the broader skill of holding family and extended community—the "invited guests"—together. As Theophano observes, "Preparing a dish or a meal is not merely an effort to satisfy physical hunger but often a quest for the good life."[53] By teaching young women how to cook *biryani* and *seero* using the limited and different ingredients available in Calgary, Noorbanu hoped to introduce them to the means through which they could care for their families and *jamats* in unfamiliar settings.

Noorbanu went on to publish three more editions of *A Spicy Touch* in 1992, 2007, and 2015, each consisting of the core recipes from the original cookbook with new material that attended to the evolving tastes and norms around the health of her readers. The successive cookbooks' content—and textual and visual indicators of their intended audiences—reveals how the placemaking activities of women in the migrant generation morphed over time, as Ismaili families gathered around the table increasingly included children and grandchildren who had no direct food memories from India or East Africa. According to Khadija, the second edition (1992) was once again published at the behest of Noorbanu's Ismaili readers—in this case, responding to their desire for additional recipes to those featured in the original text. Khadija explains that her mother "used to make other kinds of food as well," suggesting that the new recipes reflect Noorbanu's actual kitchen practice as opposed to something she created in response to reader demand. To this edition Noorbanu adds "contemporary recipes from Africa, the Middle East and the Orient," giving each her own touch.[54] The third edition (2007), also self-published, imagines a Western audience. Khadija explains that her mother "wanted to make a book that was more for the Western people. You know, because they were all wanting butter chicken recipes." Noorbanu curated the text to display the wide range of Ismaili foodways, showcasing "A Fusion of East African and Indian Cuisine," as this edition is subtitled.[55] Indeed, a prominent function of immigrant cookbooks has been to introduce new culinary cultures to host populations.

The fourth edition of *A Spicy Touch* (first edition self-published in 2015, second edition published by Touchwood Editions in 2020 for distribution in the United States and Canada) continues this project of outreach toward a wider audience. This time Noorbanu brings in as coauthor Karen Anderson, a Canadian food tour operator and food columnist who had attended one of her cooking classes. This edition imagines a white, Western audience as well as an audience of North American–born Ismailis. It includes a lengthy introductory chapter written by Karen, describing Noorbanu's Ismaili faith, her migration journey, and the North Indian, British, and East African influences on her food. The chapter also notes that even before this fourth edition was written, Noorbanu was already a success—having sold more than a quarter-million copies of her first three cookbooks. We learn about the tragedy of the 2013 Great Alberta Flood that destroyed Noorbanu's inventory of previous editions of *A Spicy Touch* cookbooks, creating an impetus for the two friends to write a new collection. But this time their cookbook would be aimed at the "future generations," both Ismaili and otherwise.[56] Karen explains to me in an interview:

> She [Noorbanu] wanted to write a fourth book and make it so that anyone could cook the recipes. Because the first three, especially the first one, does require knowledge of what things are supposed to look like, and how it's supposed to turn out. So, kind of, a cultural phenomenon, because she was really the first person to capture those recipes. And people liked them but, those were women [who] were her peers or maybe daughters of her peers. And by now, we're getting into grandchildren who had never cooked, a lot of them, they don't really know. They're on their own now and they don't really know how things are supposed to turn out. She wanted to write a book that would be for her grandchildren and their children.[57]

This edition therefore includes images of not only prepared dishes (like previous editions) but also spices and lentils, paired with detailed explanatory captions. As its subtitle—"Family Favorites from Noorbanu Nimji's Kitchen"—makes clear, the 2015 iteration of the cookbook nevertheless remains firmly rooted in traditional cuisine. Some older, heritage recipes, such as *Kerala nu Saak*, appear with minimal changes from the version Noorbanu first published in 1986. At the same time we see revisions that recognize a new audience: marking certain dishes as gluten-free, adding visual guides to spices and ingredients, introducing more detailed directions around the textures of ingredients as they are cooked, and tips on how to speed up the cooking process.[58] Khadija notes that while Noorbanu was keen to reproduce the original flavors that would connect her to meals prepared by her own mother and grandmother, she also offered recipe modifications, anticipating readers with varying palates. The fourth edition thus introduces Ismailis—now born in Canada—to the history and tastes of their ancestors while also encouraging the fusions, substitutions, and tactical replacements that are part of Ismaili diasporic experience. Noorbanu explains, "There is not a singular Ismaili cuisine. The food of the Ismaili people is as diverse as the countries and cultures where they live and practice their faith."[59] In theorizing "Ismaili cuisine" as always in-the-making, Noorbanu invites her readers to experiment with the recipes she offers them, blending the foodways they encounter in Canada with the tastes enjoyed by their ancestors (Figure 5.2).

Food studies scholar Kyla Tompkins observes that "[a] recipe, unlike a poem or a novel, will never be taken as complete unto itself: we assume that other, often entirely orally passed-down, iterations preceded it . . . and we assume many other recipes will follow. Recipes are never finished: they morph across time as foodways are handed down and changed, as migration, ecology, technology impact and are impacted by human hunting, farming, cooking and eating cultures."[60] The several iterations of A Spicy Touch epitomize the transformation that Tompkins speaks of. The first version, for

Figure 5.2 Noorbanu and daughter Khadija getting ready for a cooking class.
Courtesy of Khadija Mangalji.

instance, does not contain Noorbanu's favorite *fried mhogo* (cassava), likely because it was inaccessible in Calgary in the 1970s, but by 2015 Noorbanu not only includes it but also presents a "healthier baked version."[61] We can also see her bring various cooking equipment into the mix in the 2015 edition to enable her readers to speed up cooking to match their evolving lifestyles. Noorbanu thus confidently models how an Ismaili diasporic subject may remain rooted in her heritage while also creatively interacting with her environment, performing placemaking through culinary experimentation and modifications to Ismaili foodways.

Noorbanu's culinary influence on the second generation was apparent to me during my fieldwork as many young women and men mentioned cooking with her book by their side. Fareen Jadavji Jessa, who grew up in a household where Noorbanu's cookbooks were always around, considers her an inspiration for her own work as a food blogger: "This is the food that I grew up with—Indian food with East African influences. Noorbanu Nimji's books have been a staple in my house and of most people that I know."[62] A Canadian Ismaili mother and a passionate cook, Fareen blogs at Foodmama.com, where she features recipes from her childhood, new creative fusions that her toddlers like, and dishes influenced by her travels across North America. We see *mogo*, an East African dish of creamy coconut cassava with chicken, alongside salmon burgers and "instant pot *khichri*" that reduces the hour-long cooking process to three minutes.[63] We learn that "saffron almond milk" transports Fareen back to her childhood and that she, like Noorbanu, tries to pass on these scents and tastes of her childhood to her sons: "We inhaled the wonderful aroma [of saffron] and I was taken back to my childhood. Isn't it amazing the power of scent? I was reminded about the saffron milk with almonds that my parents made for me. Many times it was for when we were sick but also some times when just comfort was needed. It was something that I needed to make so my kids could enjoy the fragrant milk, like I did."[64] While Noorbanu's cooking classes and cookbooks emerged from her pastoral care work as *mukhiani*, this vivid childhood memory of saffron and almonds shows us in practice how the work of recreating heritage foods is also part of connecting children to a shared sensorium. Fareen's blogs evidence Noorbanu's crucial role in preserving Ismaili foodways as a link in an ongoing chain of cultural transmission: from oral interactions, to the books that would have been laid out on the counter while Fareen's mother cooked, to now the blogosphere.

Sensory Inheritances

Muneera proudly shows me her mother Lella Umedaly's cookbook, which the family published as *Mamajee's Kitchen* in 2005: "We made this really professional book."[65] In addition to recipes, this self-published cookbook includes dozens of uncaptioned images: of foods, of course, but also of women, men, and children going about their lives, at a playground, on a beach, in a garden. In some of the photographs, hands engage in the task of preparing food. As Muneera looks at one of these—a pair of hands folding flour for a samosa—she names under her breath the relative those hands belong to. She revels in this secret knowledge that only she and other insiders can bring to their experience of the cookbook: "I didn't put any [captions]. You can't tell who those people are, but you can *feel the history*. We did capture a lot of my mother's family history, so our family history."

This sense of felt history is perhaps just what Muneera hoped to capture for her children and grandchildren when she convinced her mother to write the cookbook: "I was thinking about my kids and their kids, and how would they *know* [pauses] my mother." The multisensory experience of preparing and eating food emerged as the best means to achieve this, and the cookbook as an ideal medium for its communication: "How would they know what our food is like? How would they get that 'right taste,' you know?" Muneera implies that the sense of taste—particularly a flavor correctly reproduced—can operate as a connection between generations. "Right taste" enables a form of knowing: as her children savor this recaptured flavor, they would come to *know* their mother and grandmother. Muneera points to food's capacity to introduce us to sensory encounters that are directly ours but also belong, or have belonged, to others.

Scholars of sensory history argue against the common assumption that senses and sensations of the past are beyond recovery, emphasizing instead the replicable quality of sensory experiences. We can explore what sound, smell, touch, taste, and sight meant to particular groups at particular moments.[66] The sense of smell and taste are especially central to intergenerational transmission of culture. Nadia Seremetakis calls food a "passageway," awakening the senses so that one may remember, so that one may know.[67] Rosalyn Eves observes that "every subsequent act of cooking is . . . a reenactment of someone else's movements and a subtle invocation of her memory."[68] *Mamajee's Kitchen* conveys Lella's personal felt history to readers by providing a template they can follow to reenact the movements of her hands kneading flour or grinding masala and through that experience recover sensations of the past. Like Noorbanu, Lella uses a bridge metaphor to explain the past-present-future connections that the cookbook might facilitate: "[the] dishes form a bridge from my past to my grandchildren."[69] Her descendants—biological and communal—can utilize the recipes to evoke the "right taste" and *know* past female kin through a shared sensorium.

Lella Umedaly was born in South Africa in 1930 and moved to Uganda after getting married. Like many Ismailis, she fled to Canada with her young family in 1972. She eventually settled in North Vancouver and opened a daycare in her house, later expanding her business into an early childhood center. Over the years until she retired in 1997, Lella taught at least a thousand children. By then her own children and grandchildren had grown up, and, as she explains in the introduction to her cookbook, they would often call home to ask for "fast, tasty recipes."[70] Since she had learned to cook "by feel, smell, color, texture and the look of the dish," Lella found it difficult at first to pass on her knowledge to them. She and her daughter Muneera therefore decided to codify her cooking experience, a project that took five years.

Each (re)encounter with these recipes takes Lella on a journey: she is transported to her birthplace in South Africa, where she cooked for her siblings; to Uganda, where she became adept at creating new dishes to please a rather stern mother-in-law; and to Canada, where she had to regenerate the taste of home with new ingredients. Lella comments, "With each recipe I remember a person, a story and a feeling. In this book I see so many colors, smell the spices, hear the laughter, and I feel the tears and the challenges that have made me who I am today."[71] The recipe, as an opportunity for sense experience, is thus inseparable from the time and place of earlier interactions.[72] The cookbook transfers culinary instruction but also the sensory details that communicate geographically specific microhistories of Lella's family. Lella includes the recipe for *moong bhajia* specifically to share the tastes of Uganda with her readers: "*Bhajias* were popular in Uganda for many, many years. The best in Kampala, came from Jaffery's opposite the municipal market. We used to go there for this tasty treat often and we missed it when we came to the West, so I have adapted a recipe for these fritters so that we could share that tasty memory with you."[73] She likewise introduces *bharazi* as "coastal Arab cuisine": "Many years ago our family of 7 went to Mombasa, Kenya, and stayed at Whispering Palms cottages where we employed an Arabic woman to cook for us for a few days."[74] Lella connects her Rasso tamarind lentil soup, "a South Indian Tamil recipe," to memories of caring for sick family members: "We make this dish for people who need an immunity boost to fight a fever or cold."[75] From the Portuguese-style fried prawns, which Lella learned to cook from her Portuguese relatives, to the salmon fritters and tilapia masala, which incorporate the abundantly available fish in British Columbia into Indian cuisine, readers are able to follow Lella's recipes and her personal migration journey along with it. The cookbook aptly includes numerous personal photos and thus also operates as a family album, its caption-less nature stirring a desire to turn the pages with an elder who can identify the figures and recall the time and place when a particular photo was taken.

Yet despite the "insider" images and personal reminiscences, the recipes in *Mamajee's Kitchen* also carry with them the memories and experiences of the broader Ismaili community. Lella's recipes for *biryani* and mutton curry, for instance, were developed during the celebrations of the sixty years of Imamat of Sultan Mahomed Shah in Dar es Salaam.[76] Decades later, these recipes offer her readers the opportunity to become a part of this historic experience.[77] Lella also passed on these recipes through cooking classes (Figure 5.3 is a screenshot of one such cooking class). Like Noorbanu's multi-decade effort, Lella leaves behind for coming generations an encounter with the "right

Figure 5.3 Lella and daughter Umeeda cooking together from *Mamajee's Kitchen*.
Courtesy of Umeeda Switlo and Muneera Spence.

taste" of heritage foods and the histories of community ancestors: a sensory inheritance.

Cookbooks as Bridges

Each cookbook considered in this chapter highlights distinct points on the itinerary of emplacement. Yasmin uses *The Settler's Cookbook* to underline how colonial policies have shaped the movement and experiences of Ismailis over the past hundred years. Noorbanu's four iterations of *A Spicy Touch* reveal one displaced woman's contribution to strengthening her community and how it evolved through the decades, as she first helped young Ismaili refugees recreate the taste of home in a new environment and then eventually worked toward *re*-placing Canadian-born Ismailis in East Africa. Lella's cookbook in turn highlights the salience of sensory connections for intergenerational continuity. The culinary nostalgia that we detect in the cookbooks mobilizes personal memory in the service of constructing new communal futures. In other words, the cookbooks—not least in their framing of social occasions, their menus for meals to be consumed in community—furnish readers with what David Sutton describes as "prospective memories," orienting them "toward *future* memories that will be created in the consumption of food."[78] Lella evinces a desire for such prospective memories when she describes her cookbook as forming a bridge from the past to the future. She hopes that her children and other readers will remember her and Ismaili social formations gone by and will carry aspects of that Ismaili culture into their future lives. At the same time, the culinary transfers that I have traced in this chapter retain both the authors' and their young readers' creative agency. Instead of fossilizing cooking into a static "authentic" tradition to be transmitted unmodified from mothers to daughters, the women authors encourage fusions, substitutions, and tactical replacements that keep the process of community formation open and versatile.[79] We can therefore view the authors' act of writing the cookbooks as an ethical practice of taking care of fellow and future Ismailis.

Yasmin, Noorbanu, and Lella's efforts to ensure that younger Ismailis, particularly women, could cook heritage foods might be seen as reproducing or naturalizing women's gendered roles in the domestic sphere.[80] But kitchen work does not always equate to exploitation; it can be empowering, self-affirming, and a unifying force in certain situations. In Noorbanu's case, for instance, we might do well to see her efforts as reflecting the care ethic implicit in her role as faith minister, as *mukhiani maa*, and her desire to ensure the spiritual health of her community. Newcomers would be better able to settle in unfamiliar environments if equipped with the skills to reproduce a taste of home and to confidently experiment with new ingredients. Teaching Naseem the "tricks" of cooking—facilitating a direct replication of a remembered dish—therefore serves a restorative purpose. Nita Kumar and Usha Sanyal, consequently, call on scholars to examine domesticity, and cooking in partic-ular, against larger social and discursive structures to consider how it may con-tribute to women's power or victimhood, their happiness or suffering.[81] Food served to others under conditions of enforcement, for example, is experienced differently than teaching younger women how to make *dhal* quickly so they can balance their responsibilities at both home and work or cooking *biryani* for a religious festival as a practice of *seva* (as we saw in chapter 3). Consuming and sharing heritage foods in a context of displacement where an individual's sense of belonging is fractured may serve a reparative function, psychically and even physiologically, in the gut.[82] These are the mind-body connections that Yasmin alludes to when she says, "Here are the dishes that carry our collective memories."[83] By examining the relationships around cooking, we can intro-duce nuance and reframe how and when it is valued or devalued.

There is yet another lesson to be derived from the cookbooks. Each of the three authors underwent a personal transformation from being anon-ymous home cooks to published experts and teachers. These reinventions model a refusal by the women to be defined by their experience of disloca-tion. The cookbooks became, as coauthor Karen Anderson observes, a legacy for Noorbanu, who ultimately enjoyed minor celebrity status. Karen recalls readers who "would come up to Noorbanu and talk to her and then when they'd leave, she'd sort of wiggle her head and go, 'Oh, I'm a little bit famous' [laughter]." Muneera too spoke of *Mamajee's Kitchen* as giving her mother a legacy and a *place* in history: "I feel like it [the cookbook] gave my mum this kind of authority, a presence, a sort of understanding of her worth, even of history. This cookbook did a good thing. I'm so pleased that it left a legacy for my mother." Lella had a particularly difficult marriage; the cookbook helped her fashion a new self, a writer-self that was entirely her own. And Yasmin, who has now written twelve books on various topics, still identifies the cook-book as her favorite. The three Ismaili authors thus not only restor(y)ed their community but also performed subjectivities not usually associated with refugees.

At the same time, all three enjoyed the opportunity to reinvent themselves due to their social class, education, and location in North America / Britain; for many other Ismaili women, like nani, who remained working class throughout their lives, the opportunity for independent enterprise continued to be limited. For them, transmission of culinary knowledge remains an oral tradition.

6

Placemaking in the Second Generation

As the COVID-19 pandemic intensified in 2020, Ismaili jamatkhanas, like other places of worship in North America, suspended in-person congregational prayers. At the time, Furhana Husani (b. 1978) was serving as a member of the Ismaili Tariqa and Religious Education Board for the United States. In the several months that jamatkhanas remained inaccessible, Furhana and other volunteers launched a virtual program called *Critical Conversations*, allowing Ismailis to come together in cyberspace and remain connected. Furhana could not include the usual topics of Ismaili doctrines that were a mainstay of adult religious education programming: those topics assumed an audience of insiders and hence a public discussion was discouraged. Instead, she focused solely on "social" themes that had an ecumenical, ethical quality. But in the process, the *Critical Conversations* platform broached topics that were considered off-limits until then. It featured Ismaili scholars and activists who reflected on the community's past and present, discussing themes such as gender discrimination within the *jamat*, anti-Blackness in South Asian communities, pursuit of a "model minority" ideal, the previous Imam's positioning in relation to colonial governments, and Ismaili participation in settler colonialism.

Furhana received pushback from some community members who argued that these topics were divisive and disrupted communal harmony. While not averse to debating such issues behind closed doors, a public discussion, it was suggested, had the potential to negatively impact the community's reputation—one that it had crafted so carefully since its arrival in the 1960s. Furhana contended in response that reflecting critically on the Ismaili community's history and present practices was crucial for the community's endurance in the diaspora. In an interview with me, she explains the importance of such critical self-reflection: "Community practice, I think, should always be critiqued because through community practice marginalization happens, and if we're not ensuring that we are an inclusive community—what inclusive communities look like, and what pluralism looks like and the hard work that pluralism requires—then it's just a constant status quo and then people

Rebuilding Community. Shenila Khoja-Moolji, Oxford University Press. © Oxford University Press 2023.
DOI: 10.1093/oso/9780197642023.003.0007

are sent to the margins."[1] For her, conversations about gender, race, and class differences within the *jamat*, or Ismaili participation in settler colonialism and anti-Blackness, can repair rifts within and beyond the community and facilitate its longevity—or emplacement—in North America. Furhana views such discussions as being crucial for the regeneration of both the moral community and the individual: "That struggle is necessary for the community. . . . It's also necessary for individuals' *iman* (faith) because that's how we begin to understand our faith significantly more." Furhana's approach, which emphasizes a reciprocity between the individual and the *jamat*, aligns with that of Islamic studies scholar Maria Dakake. Dakake notes that in Islam, the community is viewed as an environment within which individuals practice, refine, and nurture their virtues, and community in turn is supported by the virtuous acts of its individual members.[2] When Furhana asks Ismailis to engage in "critical conversations," it is a call to practice ethical subjectivities that in turn enhance the robustness of the community.

Furhana speaks from experience. Growing up in Toronto during the 1980s, hers was one of few families of Pakistani origin in a sea of East African Ismailis: "Even though I was the same ethnicity as everybody else, I was very much marginalized in jamatkhana." The notion of being an insider yet outsider remained with her as part of a visceral understanding of center-periphery dynamics *within* the Ismaili community. Her experience was compounded by rampant anti-Brown racism in a Toronto where racial demographics were changing—not least due to immigration—but a multicultural discourse had not yet emerged. South Asians were newly visible and therefore vulnerable. Furhana remembers being pejoratively called "Paki" and seeing her brother get beaten up at school almost daily: "It was an incredibly intolerant society, you know, like I wouldn't get the physical abuse, but I would get a lot of verbal abuse." These early encounters both within and outside the *jamat* have influenced Furhana's understanding of what it takes to fashion an Ismaili sociality across national, ethnic, and linguistic differences, and how to forge emplacement for a racialized and religious minority group in a mostly white, nominally secular (but predominantly Christian) context.

Furhana is one of a dozen second-generation Ismaili women I interviewed for this project. Ranging in age from twenty-five to forty-five, these women's parents fled either East Pakistan or East Africa in the 1970s (or in Furhana's case had ties to both).[3] As second generation, they were born in North America or arrived here at a very young age. While their efforts to sustain the Ismaili sociality share some similarities with the placemaking work of their mothers, both the composition of Ismaili community and the work these women do to sustain it, differ significantly as well. I consider these dynamics in this chapter. Drawing on interviews with second-generation Ismaili women and their cultural and knowledge productions (such as literature, visual arts, scholarly writing, and curricular materials), I ask: What kind of *jamat* do women in the second generation encounter in the American diaspora? How do they make sense of the ethical imperative to care for and support coreligionists? What forms does their care take? How are women's practices shaped by the memory of their parents' displacement and their own experience of growing up as racialized and religious minorities?

Fifty Years Later

Rozina Jivraj (b. 1976)—whose mother, Roshan Pirani, we met in chapter 3—has no direct memories of the makeshift jamatkhana in her family's house in Fort Wayne, although she has heard stories of community members coming together at her home to pray, of her mother making elaborate food spreads (*sufra*), and of her parents taking religious dues all the way to New York City. Her recollection of the next iteration of jamatkhana, in a rented space, is sharper: "It used to be in a building, and I remember the downstairs was for REC (religious education classes). We had a few tables and chairs, and it was only like five or seven kids, I could probably even tell you their names [laughs]. But I remember saying my *dua* for the first time in this jamatkhana when I was four."[4]

The Ismaili community of the 1980s and 1990s, when Rozina was growing up, was very different from the 1970s world of makeshift jamatkhanas that we saw in chapter 3. Gone were the cut-down center tables and *chaddars* of the improvised living room prayer halls, replaced instead by rented offices or even purpose-built structures (Figure 6.1), some of which could accommodate thousands of people. The Imam established social governance institutions, appointed Council leaders as well as *mukhis* and *kamadias*, and regularly visited North America. In the jamatkhanas, religious education classes were offered, and the Ismaili Councils not only provided extensive material support to community members but also became key avenues through which Ismailis could offer their *seva*. It is in this changing milieu that the second generation grew up. By the 2010s when Rozina and I first met in the jamatkhana in Manhattan, there were approximately seventy-five

Figure 6.1 Members of the Ismaili community participating in the construction of the first purpose-built jamatkhana in the United States in Atlanta, Georgia.
Source: *American Ismaili*, March 21, 1989.

jamatkhanas of various sizes in the United States and eighty in Canada, both purpose-built and rented spaces.[5]

I did not know that Rozina's mother, like mine, had been displaced from Dhaka. It was only during my interview with Roshan that I discovered her connection to Rozina. I then approached Rozina for an interview. This is how I recruited several of my twelve interlocutors: they are the daughters of the women I interviewed. Others are acquaintances whom I had met through my institutional volunteer work and discovered that their mothers had fled these two regions when our conversations veered toward my research project. This interview cohort therefore is not representative of second-generation Ismailis. All twelve of my interlocutors have been active in Ismaili institutional volunteer service, as members of either local councils or boards for education, youth development, religious education, or conciliation and arbitration. They are also highly educated—all twelve have earned master's degrees, and three hold doctorates. They are upwardly mobile, and none have experienced the kind of poverty that the women in earlier generations did in India or East Africa (as we saw in chapter 2). Their experience of marginalization, as seen in Furhana's case, emerges from race and religion, not from economic status. Many of the women in this cohort were in college when the attacks of 9/11 took place and remember being called "terrorist." Today their children are growing up in a political environment similarly characterized by anti-Brown racism and Islamophobia. At the same time, they are learning about structural racism and ongoing settler colonialism from North American movements for racial and gender justice, gay rights, and indigenous peoples' struggles.

In contrast to their parents, who might have first found a jamatkhana and then decided on a neighborhood to live, my second-generation interlocutors choose housing, as do other North Americans of their generation, based on distance to work or the quality of local schools. Although a few of them reside within a thirty-minute drive of a jamatkhana, the majority are based much farther away: the nearest jamatkhana might be an hour or even a six-hour commute. Most—even those who live near a jamatkhana—have occupations and lifestyles that prevent them from attending jamatkhana daily. As opposed to their parents' generation, which often established Ismaili housing societies in East Africa or Pakistan, the second generation lives in American neighborhoods where other Ismailis may or may not be present. Whereas ethnonationalist wars and poverty precluded many of the women we encountered in the previous chapters from making permanent homes, the women in the second generation are experiencing a different kind of deterritorialization. They report moving frequently for jobs, which disrupts their relation to a fixed place. Recurring relocations also lead to estrangement from local communities. Thus, the second generation's experiences reflect at once the "success" of situating younger Ismailis in a broader society (where the effects of such dislocations are shared by a high percentage of highly educated individuals) and the feeling of being displaced from Ismaili communities.

But members of this younger cohort are not disengaged: many pray frequently and their volunteer work keeps them connected with the community and its ethical values. Easy travel and ready access to communication technologies also enable them to maintain relationships across continents in ways their mothers could never have imagined. Within the diasporic consciousness of this generation there exists both a sense of belonging to North America and a longing for connection to the ancestral lands of East Africa/India/Pakistan. Some of them have even traveled to these regions for extended visits or to pursue professional or volunteer work.

The *jamat* that the second generation encounters is unmistakably transethnic, transnational, and translingual in character, different from the comparatively homogeneous Khoja *jamat* of earlier generations, most of whom traced their roots to the Sindh-Gujarat corridor and spoke Kuchchhi or Gujarati languages (though they may have also spoken Sindhi, Urdu, and Hindi). Over the last fifty years, Nizari Ismaili demography in North America has shifted: once almost largely Indic, composed of Khojas of the *satpanth* tradition, the community now includes Ismailis from Central Asia and the Middle East who have different intellectual traditions. Since the collapse of the Soviet Union in the 1990s, Ismailis from Central Asia, including Afghanistan, who had been cut off from other Ismailis when living under the Soviet regime, have slowly but steadily been incorporated into the Ismaili transnational community through the Imam's now-regular visits to the region and the establishment of jamatkhanas and Ismaili Councils there.[6] They have more recently made their way to North America to escape political instability in their home regions. War has also pushed Ismailis out of Syria and toward North America and Europe. Moreover, the Ismaili community in America today is composed of not only immigrants and refugees but also Ismailis now born in North America, and there is a significant presence of non-Ismaili spouses and children as well, as rates of exogamy have increased. Members of the second generation thus meet coreligionists from Kabul in prayer halls and Arabic-speaking Ismailis from Salamiyah on volunteer committees; they meet the non-Ismaili spouses of Ismailis in the foyers of jamatkhanas as they all wait to pick up their children after religious education classes.

In the past few decades, the development network established by the Imam has expanded opportunities for diasporic Ismailis to volunteer internationally—to help set up schools and healthcare systems or teach English-language classes. These global service opportunities further extend connections between Indic-origin Ismailis and their non-Indic coreligionists. Today, the community's official communications emphasize that Ismailis live all over the world, belong to many different ethnicities, and speak many different languages. Ismaili institutions work hard to instill this awareness in younger members through religious education curricula, websites, television, and global platforms such as international summer camps, sports tournaments, and artistic alliances.

Second-generation women's participation in, and reproduction of, an Ismaili sociality thus unfolds not only in a diasporic context where Ismailis are a racial and religious minority but also in relation to a *jamat* that is more attuned to its diversity, more globally connected, and much better established within the economies of host countries than the *jamat* of fifty years ago, when their parents first arrived in Atlanta or Toronto.

Entangled Histories

Sadly, when Philando Castile was killed by the police [in 2016], I lived in ____ and wanted to do a session about it in jamatkhana but was not given permission. They [representatives of the Ismaili institutions] said, "We are an apolitical community. This is a political issue." I guess they did not want to take a stance against the police. But I couldn't help feeling that it was my ethical responsibility to speak up. (Sana)[7]

I met forty-year-old Sana in her quiet home in a midwestern city in the United States. Her parents fled Uganda in 1972 and made their way to Toronto. She went on to attend elite universities in Canada and the United States and is a successful professional in the nonprofit sector today. Growing up, in religious education classes, Sana had learned about the Shia tradition of social justice and about Ismaili teachings prohibiting discrimination. Yet when she wanted to discuss the Black Lives Matter movement with other Ismailis in a jamatkhana, she encountered an apparent contradiction between tradition and the expression of those ideals in the actions of the community. She had to forge a new place, outside formal religious sites, to practice what she understood as Ismaili ethics: "I booked a conference room and along with a few other Ismailis held a teach-in where we discussed police brutality and the prison industrial complex as a form of contemporary slavery." Sana emphasizes to me that her actions were an expression of her Shia ethics: "I am doing this work as an Ismaili, as a faithful Ismaili, I might add [laughs]. I am not one of those who has left the community. No. I am very much in it. This is how I live my Ismaili ethics, my Alid (referring to Imam Ali) ethics of social justice, nondiscrimination, equality, you know." Engaging with the ongoing racial politics in the United States compelled Sana to also revisit the history of her ancestors. She explains:

What is interesting is that this path led me to later discover the violence due to which my parents fled Uganda. I knew about how horrible Idi Amin was, but I also learned about how racist Asians were to Africans. Ismailis in East

Africa often did not integrate with locals. Africans were servants or drivers or babysitters or cooks, you know. So Ismailis benefited from their work. That is a defining characteristic of settler colonialism. Indians settled in East Africa and benefited. So now I am on this personal journey, a discovery, about my settlement in Canada or the U.S. I am trying to make sure that my activism against anti-Black racism is not blind to the anti-Black racism practiced by my ancestors in East Africa. You see? Like, they benefited from it, so I have benefited from it too. I am not seeking some kind of redemption or something. I am just making sure that my activism is not blind.

Sana's comments are steeped in the social theory she learned studying sociology and international development at universities in the United States and Canada. But as she applies that knowledge in her effort to understand her ancestors' practices in East Africa, she also repeatedly references the Quran, signaling the influence of religious precepts on her thinking as well: "For me improving race relations is directly about 'enjoining the good' that is mentioned in the Quran." Sana was at first "very uncomfortable" with confronting the colonial policies that had benefited her parents but ultimately concluded that it was her "religious duty to recognize this past" and to "become an ally of Black people in the U.S. today."

Sana's remarks represent the tangled temporalities and ethical sensibilities that I wish to highlight in this section: women of the second generation engage in care and support for coreligionists through not only preservation and transmission of inherited traditions (as we have seen in the previous chapters) but also a critical assessment of the community's internal and external politics. Their placemaking in the here and now (as religious and racialized minorities) and their relationship to the long history of Ismailis depend on reckoning with the community's past(s). Below, I analyze cultural and knowledge productions of some second-generation Ismaili women to illustrate these entangled practices of recovery, memorialization, and self-critique.

Speculating on the Past

"I have been reading this novel for five days, and I still have a third of it to go." I chastise myself that I should be able to get through it faster, thinking of all the journal articles I could have read by now. Only later do I realize why I had to fight my way through Tasneem Jamal's *Where the Air Is Sweet*: every few pages Tasneem's words elicited a visceral, guttural reaction from me. I had to put down the book and rush to another room so my family would not see the tears rolling down my cheeks as I read about Rehmat's death or the moment when Rehmat's daughter-in-law Mumtaz gives her favorite *pacheri* (long scarf) to their African maid, Esteri, with whom Rehmat had grown close over the decades. Mumtaz tells Esteri, "We *mhindi* (a term used for Asians in East Africa) mothers, we are quiet. . . . We have learned to be quiet. We obey our men, even our sons when they become men. But we give our daughters gifts. Things we cherish. . . . Things of value to us, things that have nothing to do with men, or their world. Things men cannot touch, even in their dreams."[8] I recognized this practice. Along with all those memories of making *bhel puri*, my nani had left me her *pacheri*. A few years ago, on a visit to my mother, I had asked for her *pacheri*. I read the novel slowly because the intimate world of Ismaili women that it portrayed was at once familiar and strange to me; it was the first time I was reading about it in print. By tracing hitherto unarchived matrilineal storylines, Tasneem's novel offered a genealogy to readers like me. Reading a text that began as a space for Tasneem to remember her ancestors—their lives in East Africa and their displacement during the 1970s—prompted me in turn to remember the lives of my foremothers in East Pakistan and their own eventual displacement.

Tasneem and I both carry what Marianne Hirsch calls "postmemories" of the traumatic events of 1971–1972.[9] Our connection to the violence of the 1970s is mediated not by personal experience or recall but by the stories we hear, the photographs our older relatives share with us, and the objects from East Africa and East Pakistan that are tucked into suitcases and shoved under beds. We are suspended in a state Nina Fischer describes as one "of knowing but not knowing, of proximity without personal knowledge."[10] We thus remember the past through imagination, creation, and projection. In postmemory work that takes multiple forms, from literature and painting to storytelling. In this section I examine the postmemory work of two Ismaili women—Tasneem Jamal and Sikeena Karmali—who left Uganda and Tanzania, respectively, at a young age.

Tasneem and Sikeena recover the lives of their foremothers not through recall but through imagination and speculation, in a pivot toward creative writing that makes it possible to write about women whose lives are not preserved in the official archives. Saidiya Hartman calls this method "critical fabulation" and explains that it "troubles the line between history and imagination."[11] In Hartman's own work on the lives of Black women at the beginning of the twentieth century, she uses scraps of archival material—a turn-of-the-century photograph of a young girl, for example—to re-create Black women's experiences in Philadelphia and New York, showing how they practiced forms of intimacy and kinship that defied normative understandings of respectability and law. In their novels, Tasneem and Sikeena take us on similar speculative journeys, encouraging readers to think anew about how Ismaili women experienced and remade their lives as settlers in East Africa. The novels envisage Ismaili women of earlier generations not as passive, submissive bodies moving about in men's worlds but as women who refused, resisted, offered aid, and found moments of joy. These novels not only offer a modern reconstruction of Ismaili women but also furnish contemporary Ismailis with new collective memories. At the same time, the authors do not romanticize women; women's lives appear to be constrained by local and colonial patriarchies and its violence. Like Yasmin Alibhai's cookbook (chapter 5), these novels give us a glimpse into the anti-Black racism of Asians while also situating Asians as victims of British racism. Fiction thus becomes a space where second-generation writers and readers work through their trauma—about the violence of displacement, but also about their ancestors' participation in settler colonialism.

Where the Air Is Sweet follows the broad strokes of Tasneem's family's experiences during and after their years in East Africa, in a story arc that shadows them across three continents over a span of fifty years.[12] Tasneem's paternal grandfather moved from Gujarat to Uganda in the 1920s and later brought his wife and child to join him. It took him some time, but he eventually established himself in Uganda, building a business as a petty trader, and the family prospered there until Idi Amin expelled Asians. Tasneem was six years old when her family left for Canada. She says that while the novel's protagonist, Raju, is based on her grandfather, she had no direct memories of him—nor of her grandmother or other extended family she knew in Kampala. She chose fiction as a way to "find them" and tell their stories: "Unlike my parents, I didn't have memories. I felt very robbed. I would hear somebody talk about Kenya or mention Uganda—it was a part of me, but I did not know how to articulate it. I didn't know how to feel entitled to it. Fiction was a way of approaching it."[13] Moreover, fiction allowed Tasneem to convey the deep connection that Asian families like hers felt to Africa, a connection that outsiders rarely understood:

Growing up, when I would tell people I am Indian but from Africa, and when I would tell people that Indians were expelled from Uganda, there would be "Oh, whatever . . . "—there was not a lot of sympathy, the sense was—people were kind of briefly there and then they left. I realized that I needed to explain the emotional connection, and the fact that Indians were tied to the land in some ways. There are also a lot of nuances in the relationship with indigenous populations.[14]

The novel imagines the lives of early Ismaili women settlers in East Africa as we have seen them in chapter 2, their hardships and losses, their ongoing interactions with indigenous Africans, and the sense of loss they experienced after expulsion, both exemplified and amplified by their struggle in Canada. Tasneem found it particularly difficult to craft the character of Raju's wife, Rehmat, whom she based on a grandmother she knew little about. Family stories circulated aplenty about her grandfather (known lovingly as *bapa*), but not so of her grandmother:

> For me it was difficult to write about Rehmat because even my grandmother died when I was still in Uganda, very small. The family lore about her was that she was a saint, she was so lovely, and she was so kind, but then people didn't talk about her. It was all about *bapa bapa*, all the stories of *bapa*. She was just kind of there, she was sort of a presence in the background. And my mother would tell me some stories and that was the launching point for this character [Rehmat]. I was shocked when my mother told me that when my grandparents were young, she [her grandmother] walked out, that she took the kids and left. I was just blown because I had imagined this incredibly passive, almost nonperson, you know, and she was not. There was something there. That took some guts. And also the other launching point was her putting her foot down that she was not going to India [when the expulsion decree was announced]. . . . [F]or me it was trying to see her, find her myself.[15]

We clearly see Tasneem's surprise at discovering her grandmother's assertive stances and her courage; those stories disrupt a community narrative in which past Ismaili women are known largely through the frames of submission and dependence on men. In highlighting Rehmat's quiet modes of resistance—in the novel Rehmat, like the author's grandmother, temporarily separates from her husband and refuses to return to India—Tasneem also endows herself with a history in which women embody admirable qualities including self-respect, autonomy, and courage. She explains that she created Rehmat as "a whole person."

In addition to reimagining Ismaili women of the past, Tasneem turns the novel into a site where she can have tough conversations about racial hierarchy in colonial East Africa and how her ancestors fit into it—conversations that are often evaded in the community. In an exchange between Raju's daughter-in-law, Mumtaz, and a former African employee, Eliab, we hear Eliab spell out the favorable impact of British policies toward Asians: "Would your great Alidina Visram [a prominent Ismaili trader during the British colonial rule] have been so great if he wasn't given advantages by the British? Asian workers are more efficient, the British said. That is why Africans were kept out of cotton ginning and coffee plantation."[16] Eliab also observes that Asians often kept to themselves and spoke in their own languages so Africans would not learn their trade secrets.[17] While Asian men engaged in sexual liaisons with African women, they shuddered at the thought of marrying them. When Raju's friend Hussein brings a local woman to him for "companionship" and Raju hesitates, Hussein degrades her: "You do not need to feel ashamed. These women, they are not the level of our women. They are solely for our needs. Nothing more."[18] Even the friendships between Asian settlers and Africans that exist in Tasneem's novel are contingent. When Mumtaz's husband, Jafaar, speaks of his friendship with an African man named George, he exposes the power imbalance that shaped the friendship's origin: Jafaar was a child trying to learn how to ride a bike and he called out to George to help him because "he was a *kario*. It was his job to serve me."[19] Mumtaz herself confesses that she only encountered Africans as "servants"; she never saw African children otherwise and had no idea about where or how they lived.[20] These scenes enable Tasneem to archive and name the anti-Black racism of her ancestors and acknowledge the favorable treatment they received from the colonizers. But then we also glimpse close friendships such as that between Rehmat and Esteri, which point to those moments when both Asians and Africans tried to forge intimacies somewhere beyond the oppressive structure of colonial racial hierarchies.

When I ask Tasneem what she hoped to convey through such vignettes, she explains that she wanted to show the messiness of settler-indigenous relations, that there were no easy narratives here:

> My sense was that when people would talk of the expulsion, it would be one of two things. It would be "Asians were terrible, they treated Africans

like slaves," or it would be "Asians were complete victims." And of course, none of these things are true, it was a complex dynamic for everyone. So I knew that I wanted to convey the role that Asians played in colonizing and looking down on Africans. But it was not simple, my father very much felt African, but my mother did not have that luxury, they really kept girls away. . . . Asians weren't victims, and they weren't evil perpetrators.

Tasneem here points to broader Asian norms around seclusion that prevented women from meeting members of non-Indian groups. *Where the Air Is Sweet* challenges readers to suspend any expectation of an uncomplicated or reassuring portrait of Ismailis in Africa. It highlights the tension that second-generation Ismailis experience when they remember their ancestors: the effort to hold ancestors accountable for the privilege they gained from their position in the racial hierarchy while also recognizing the violence that was meted out to them by British colonizers and later by Idi Amin. By displaying these intimacies of colonial and racial violence, the novel restores Ismaili ancestors as complex people who lived lives laced with contradictions. Over the years since its first publication in 2014, Tasneem has heard many young Ismailis share that they read the novel to learn about the lives of their parents and grandparents. It has also helped some to better understand the dissonance that they experience. She views the work of the novel as "bearing witness"—"witnessing" here denotes both an effort to preserve lives glimpsed only in fragments and an attempt to assess past generations' actions by locating them in their specific sociopolitical context. This witnessing is a practice of care.

Sikeena Karmali similarly wrote *A House by the Sea* to animate the lives of her ancestors in a fictional reconstruction of their intercontinental migration over the course of the twentieth century. The novel's protagonist, Zahra, like Sikeena herself, is born in Dar es Salaam but flees as a young girl in the 1970s when life in Tanzania becomes difficult for her family. Soldiers rampage through their home, killing the African *ayah* who works for them; their businesses and farms are confiscated by the government. Zahra now lives in London but pines for an "anchor," an "attachment," a place where she can "become whole."[21] Specifically, she wants "a home to call her own."[22] She learns of a house by the sea in Zanzibar that was once bequeathed to her Egyptian grandmother and tries to buy it from its current owners so her parents can live there. The novel follows Zahra's attempts to procure the house and reveals what she learns in the process about her grandmothers—Noor, a young

Ismaili bride who arrived in Zanzibar from Gujarat in the 1930s, and Zahra (the protagonist's namesake), an Arab woman who eloped with a Gujarati Ismaili laborer and converted to the Ismaili faith.

In Sikeena's novel, as Noor boards the cargo ship from India in 1932, she is joined by thirty other Ismaili women who, like her, are headed to the Swahili coast to unite with their Ismaili husbands—"ghosts" to them, as they have never met.[23] Noor does not want to get married. She does not want to go to Africa. But her family is poor and cannot afford the customary dowry: it is not unusual for families in poverty to marry daughters, however reluctantly, to men they have never met. The other Ismaili women also come from impoverished backgrounds—and, like Noor, will never see their families again.[24] On the cargo ship, one young woman is raped by a crew member, her experience concretizing the threat of sexual violence the young women faced during a long journey without the protection of their kinfolk.[25] The other grandmother in Sikeena's novel, the elder Zahra, also experiences violence, though of a different kind. Zahra's husband, Vilayat Khan, fears that her wealthy Arab family will punish him for seducing their daughter, so he tries to hide her from the world.[26] He compels her to remove all aspects of her Arab identity: he does not allow her to speak Arabic and expects her to dress and cook like Gujarati women. When she is caught conversing in Arabic with a vendor, he forbids her from going to the market. Vilayat Khan often slaps and kicks Zahra into compliance. Through the characters of Noor and the elder Zahra, the author imagines both the physical and psychic violence that Ismaili women suffered.

The experience of Ismaili women portrayed in the novel reflects the experience of Asian women more broadly at the time in East Africa. While the details may vary, we find similar evidence of domestic violence in the oral histories collected by Nazira Mawji.[27] Mawji's interlocutors indicate that physical violence was not an exceptional occurrence for this cohort of women settlers. Their husbands beat them, and some prevented them from maintaining contact with their natal families. When I interviewed Sikeena, she explained that she wrote about domestic violence not only because it was rampant then but also because it continues today. Stories like these are passed down from mothers to daughters, in hushed tones. Sikeena explains:

> It's something that is a little bit taboo. We don't talk about it, but it was rampant. It was very, very common. It's something that accompanies warfare and migration and change, and it has historically. My grandmother was

really candid, she told me that these things happened, you know. I know that my paternal grandmother, she was you know, physically abused, she was beaten up by her husband. Everyone knew it and it was sort of, it was a—it was just tolerated. And to be honest, I think it's still tolerated. It's just kind of pushed under the carpet, and it may not be as extreme as it was eighty years ago but it's still there, so I didn't want to leave that out. Because even though it's unpleasant and we would prefer not to deal with it, it is a part of the reality of these women's lives.[28]

The elder Zahra, however, is not defined by her victimhood. She emerges as a healer and as a woman who learns to survive in her surroundings. She befriends Indian and African women and invites them into her home to listen to their stories. They show each other their wounds and apply turmeric paste to their gashes. The women realize that their fates are not so different, that their scars match.[29] Through Zahra, then, the novelist projects agentival capacity onto her foremothers; she speculates deep networks of interpersonal care among women as a way to recover in the face of violence.

This effort to re-story Ismaili women is also visible in the author's portrayal of Noor and her journey from Gujarat to East Africa and later displacement to England and Canada. In Noor we find a "giant of human will" who "crossed four continents and six seas"; her tongue "learned to twist three ways" and she "outwitted tragedy by entering new lands."[30] Noor's character is closely mapped onto the author's own grandmother, who began learning English only after her exile to Canada in the 1970s, striving to become independent even in her sixties, a fact not lost on Sikeena: "It's hard to begin again in your 30s and 40s or whatever it might be. Imagine having to begin again in your 60s and 70s."[31] A character like Noor allows Sikeena to display the strength of Ismaili women to her readers: "I want them [Ismaili readers] to recognize what the women, the matriarchs of their families, how incredible and resilient they were and how much strength it must take. I mean these are women, who some of them have crossed three continents in a lifetime, and they may not have been literate and educated but they were amazing women, because they survived, they were resilient, they learned new languages like my grandmother."[32] Importantly, these women reproduced Ismaili cultures by passing on faith traditions and sustaining them through multiple displacements. Sikeena explains, "You know they were really really *imani* (having faith) in a way that I don't even know if we understand. Because it's faith that got them through. And they're also the ones who kept our faith alive you know. All these little *tasbihs* and things, and habits, they've passed them on through the generations."[33] Sikeena's use of "*imani*" as a trait, points to a key argument of this book: that it is through women's everyday actions, gestures, and habits— their habituated spirituality—that the religious community recreates itself after displacement. By writing about the work of transmitting faith during periods of chaos, Sikeena not only emphasizes how women regenerated the *jamat* but also presents faith as a form of inheritance.

While displaced people carry trauma and loss, Hirsch argues that the next generation does not necessarily experience their postmemorial acts of transfer as a burden.[34] Those acts can also furnish possibilities and fan creativity that can at once be self-making and community making. We see these dynamics in Tasneem and Sikeena's novels. The authors improvise with surviving fragments and flashes of memory to reconstruct Ismaili pasts and create new aesthetic encounters for younger generations through their novels.[35] These projects rewrite Ismaili history in two ways: first, by centering women as protagonists (instead of the male pioneers Ismaili readers more often encounter), and second, by recognizing the violence—both experienced and perpetrated—of settler colonialism, a political experience that is often sidestepped in official community history. The authors transform Ismaili women from the invisible "nonpersons" (as Tasneem notes above) they sometimes seem to be in family memories dominated by stories of fathers and grandfathers, into preservers of tradition whose faith (*iman*) and labor has sustained the Ismaili collective. But Ismaili women are also caught in the colonial-racial matrix of power: experiencing violence and engaging in violence in relation to other groups. This revised story of Ismaili pasts evades the seduction of linear progression from unbelonging to belonging and the simplified portrayals of Ismailis as victims or oppressors. Instead, it shows how colonialism and racism, past and present, have shaped the lives of community members, situating them at the nexus of privilege and subordination.

Engaging a More Recent Past

Whereas Tasneem and Sikeena focus on Ismaili life in East Africa during the early twentieth century, other creative artists and thinkers tackle the community's more recent past, since their arrival in North America in the 1970s. They scrutinize the community's practices for signs of its members' ongoing trauma as racialized and religious minorities and suggest new ways to pursue the elusive goal of emplacement. In the process, they must confront dominant narratives and identities—the image of the grateful refugee, the social expectations of the "model minority," and more. This work of critical reflection emerges in dissertations, in the visual arts, and in new religious education curricula aimed at younger Ismailis.

During the 1970s, the Ismaili Imam issued a *farman* urging his followers who had relocated to Canada to make the new country their homeland.[36] Almas Lalji, who fled Kampala, explains her loyalty to Canada as directly shaped by this *farman*: "Hazar Imam has told us make Canada your home . . . [so we] made it home."[37] Others express how "deeply grateful" they were for Canadian aid and vowed "not to be a burden" and "to give back."[38] The community magazines often reiterated these messages; the editorial of the March 1978 *Canadian Ismaili* notes: "It is . . . most imperative that while we make attempts to uplift our economic well-being we also remember that we are Canadians and that we should not only become Canadians in name but in spirit too."[39] However, not all Ismailis experienced Canada as a land of opportunity. Older women and men often struggled due to limited education and lack of facility in the English language. Several Ismaili men I spoke with described long job searches and extended periods of underemployment. Even so, displaced women—and some of the displaced men I interviewed—said Canada had rescued them. Almas's husband opines that Canada had earned the loyalty of Ismailis by providing them a "good life" and "all the necessities" and by allowing them to build a foundation for themselves and their children.[40] Interlocutors who had settled in the United States voiced similar sentiments. They too were grateful for the opportunity to rebuild their lives.

The second-generation Ismaili women I interviewed have a different relationship to North America. Instead of viewing Canada or the United States as havens—contrasting comparative safety and prosperity in North America against violent dispossession in East Pakistan or East Africa—women in the second generation are more likely to cite their personal experiences of racism and Islamophobia in Toronto or New York and, as a result, see their lives, and the lives of their coreligionists, as shaped by such forms of discrimination. Growing up in Calgary during the 1980s, Shemine Gulamhusein (b. 1987) often overheard comments about her Brown family members at ringette practices—immigrants weren't supposed to do ice sports.[41] She was left out of some team celebrations and was once even asked to put on makeup two shades lighter than her skin tone before joining the rest of her teammates for a group picture.[42] Shemine hid these incidents from her family: she wanted to spare them discomfort, and she wanted to keep skating. She coped by making herself small and invisible, limiting the time she spent in the dressing room to keep herself safe from abuse. Nafisa Dhanani (b. 1980), whose parents fled East Pakistan and made their way to a small rural town in Illinois in the 1980s, remembers similar efforts to try to "fly under the radar" so that "no one [w]ould really see us."[43]

Romana Kassam (b. 1984), who grew up in Toronto, captures analogous sentiments in visual form in a piece called *Salt. Wounds.* In 2018, Romana was invited to participate in an exhibition at Toronto's Metro Convention Centre on the theme of "holidays." She decided to depict how she experienced the season growing up, when "literally the whole world shut down for Christmas," but *khushali*, the birthday celebrations for the Imam, always felt rushed.[44] Romana remembers speeding home from school, eating *biryani* hurriedly, dressing up, and heading to jamatkhana: "It was not a peaceful experience like Christmas." Her painting (Figure 6.2) features an Ismaili woman standing against an Ismaili flag, carrying a *tasbih*. The colorful *shalwar kameez* stands in contrast to the black snow boots that she wears to prevent frostbite. Salt from two shakers trickles onto her. Romana explains what the salt represents:

> When I think of our parents, they fled their countries for survival, they were vulnerable, they were open. So, I looked at that as an open wound. And I looked at colonization as the salt that is pouring over them and eventually stinging the wounds that already exist. Because it was so important for them to fit in, I don't think they have had the opportunity to process what that experience was like. People let go of their cultures to fit in. They compromised. Eventually you put enough salt in the wound and it will never heal.

Romana articulates the vulnerability of migrants: to survive, Ismaili migrants had to fit their lives into the time-space of the dominant settler-colonial society, or perhaps, in different terms, had to stuff their feet into the metaphorical snow boots of Canadian life.

As Shemine, Nafisa, and Romana grew up, they became more vocal about their experience of everyday racial discrimination. Today, they speak against it and resist the pressure to assimilate in the hope that their children, as Nafisa puts it, "will not grow up feeling the same fear and shame."[45] Assimilation, in

Figure 6.2 *Salt. Wounds.* (2018) by Romana Kassam.
Reproduced with permission from the artist.

Romana's diagnosis, had prevented the earlier generation's healing. Reflecting on why this cohort of Ismaili women is less likely to pursue assimilation than their parents, Shemine brings up economic security: "We are able to actually challenge without having the same repercussions of not having food on our tables." We can see in Shemine's reflection a recognition that the earlier generation's assimilative impulses (and the pursuit of a model minority ideal) cannot be disentangled from their experience of financial insecurity, dispossession, and xenophobia.

My second-generation interlocutors are also keenly aware of the state's constitutive role in cultural assimilation that ultimately safeguards white supremacy—through both policymaking and inclusionary messaging that labels some groups as model minorities while excluding and stigmatizing others. They critique community practices and narratives in which Ismailis cast themselves as a "model minority" on the grounds that such self-representations strengthen rather than dismantle racial and class hierarchies. This concern is evident in Salima Bhimani's (b. 1975) reflections on the community's public narratives and its leadership's alliance with the Canadian government. Salima grew up in Canada after her parents fled Uganda, and she would eventually earn a doctorate focusing on diversity, equity, and inclusion. Her doctoral dissertation considers how Ismailis in Canada perform their Muslimness in relation to the state. She finds that to position themselves as "Muslims who are wanted by Canada," Ismailis articulate themselves as "exceptional Muslims."[46] This performance entails depoliticizing Islam and distancing themselves from other Muslims by adopting labels like "modern" and "liberal." The "exceptional Muslim" role is claimed via a metanarrative, or in Salima's phrasing, "sanitized stor[ies]," of Ismaili arrival and successful integration into Canadian life. Those stories, however, omit the routine struggles of Ismailis as members of a racialized minority who also experience Islamophobic discrimination.[47] They also elide the real hardships faced by past and present refugees. Salima recalls, for example, the point system the Canadian state used in the 1970s to determine which Ugandans would be admitted to Canada. Refugees who did not fit the state's image of productive immigrants—the elderly, nonprofessionals, and women whose work was considered extraneous to the labor market—found themselves excluded. Salima's insights are further informed by her research with more recent Ismaili arrivals from Afghanistan, who have limited education and speak little English and are thus often unable to follow the script of rapid employment and assimilation valorized by their East African predecessors. She suggests that the sanitized success stories remain in circulation because they are mutually beneficial for the Canadian state and the Ismaili institutions— Canadian leaders can point to this religious group as one that has successfully integrated, and Ismailis can benefit from the privileges that accrue from being a group with whom the state can partner.

While Salima is sympathetic as to why Ismailis tell these stories, noting that such stories are a necessary component of surviving racialization,[48] she believes that it is only by naming the ongoing hardships experienced by some Ismailis and by speaking openly about the state's constitutive role in creating/ maintaining racial and gendered differences in the service of capital that the community can advance its collective well-being. For Salima this includes recognizing that Ismailis, although they arrived in North America as refugees, are also settlers in a settler-colonial nation and hence participate in the ongoing dispossession of indigenous people. When I interviewed Salima, she explained that by examining the recent history of Ismailis in Canada in her writing and teaching, she hopes to complicate the story that the community tells itself about itself. She elucidates her motivations: "Moving towards justice, for me, begins with looking at yourself. Looking elsewhere is fine, but if you don't look at yourself then that's a problem. Critical social analysis is very important so we can continue to grow."[49]

I view Salima's critical stance in relation to the recent Ismaili past, as she has made that position public in her dissertation, as simultaneously a reflection on and a manifesto for ethical community making. It is a call to the community to assess and reshape its ethics on an ongoing basis, to consider whether, when they have made a place for themselves by conforming their stories to the "model minority" narrative, they have at the same time inadvertently practiced aspirational whiteness. Religious ethics scholars William Schweiker and David Clairmont identify self-criticism as a mode of reflection that tests religious moralities and reveals any distortions of religious teachings that may have crept into individual or community practice; dynamic religious communities undertake such criticism to better orient individual and community conduct.[50] What we see in Salima's scholarship, then, is an effort to analyze and reorient Ismaili community conduct. For this endeavor she draws on the resources (concepts, ideas, orientations) of the tradition itself.

Zahra Somani (b. 1984) brings a similarly self-critical perspective to her ongoing endeavor of creating a new religious studies curriculum for the next generation of Ismailis in America. Zahra is the daughter of Nargis

Somani, whom we met in the second chapter. After fleeing Dhaka, Nargis made a home in Chicago and Zahra was born there.[51] Growing up, Zahra was asked repeatedly to prove her Americanness: "Americans see your skin color and your ethnicity, and they determine whether you are American or not. They would constantly ask [me]: 'Where are you from? Where are you *really* from?'" Her local religious education center did not help much, since its curriculum stressed the community's immigrant rather than its American identity. As Zahra grew older, she found confidence in her sense of belonging in America. Her effort to create a new curriculum for Ismaili religious education centers—one that posits Ismailis as Americans—has emerged from that confidence. Instead of opening the Ismaili North American narrative with the 1970s migration, the American Lived Ismaili Faith (ALIF) curriculum situates the community within a broader history of Muslims on the continent, beginning with the transatlantic slave trade that first brought Muslims from Africa to the shores of the United States. While being careful not to cast an equivalence between the experience of chattel slavery with that of the 1970s migration of Indic Muslims, the curriculum strives to establish affinities between present-day Black and Brown Muslims through this pedagogical move. This story helps younger Ismailis see themselves as part of a longer history of Muslims in North America. Zahra explains:

> It's so important [for us] as a community to re-think, to re-state, or to take a look again at our story. How are we identifying ourselves? So, this new curriculum [ALIF] that Furhana and I are working on is saying we are not actually immigrants. We [Muslims] have been here all along. If I can accept that actually Muslims have been here since [the] 1500s and that my Black brothers and sisters are also Muslims, then how does that change the way in which I enter a protest or the way in which I volunteer? I think all these things are impacted when we're critically thinking about our identity as a community.

Through ALIF, Zahra, along with other second-generation Ismailis, is rewriting the community's recent history so that younger generations of Ismailis can feel emplaced in ways she never did. This emplacement practically means nurturing solidarity with those among whom they live, particularly Black Muslims. This does not mean an erasure of immigrant identity or a minimization of the lineage that Ismailis trace to Arabia as Muslims or that Khojas trace to their ancestral lands in western India. It means seeking additional, multiple, genealogies from which springs a renewed commitment to the Muslim tradition.

The practices of community making documented thus far in this chapter—fiction and curriculum writing, teaching, digital programming, and painting—are different than those described in earlier chapters. Especially noticeable is the absence of reproductive activities like cooking on religious festivals or cleaning the jamatkhanas. This does not mean that such work is no longer being done. As we saw in chapter 3, other community members, especially women, continue to perform the care work that maintains the jamatkhanas and makes possible the celebration of *khushali* or *chandraat*. What we see here are additional activities that are also now required to reproduce the Ismaili sociality in the diaspora. Through their novels (Tasneem and Sikeena), research (Salima and Shemine), curriculum (Zahra), digital programming (Furhana), and artwork (Romana), second-generation Ismaili women practice an ethic of care for the *jamat* that is not a departure from but in *continuity* with the practices of their foremothers. Their products strengthen relatedness and connection by filling gaps in collective knowledge, by opening new avenues for expression within community, and by inviting critical reflection so the community may endure in the diaspora. The work of repair and renewal of religious community is expansive, and involves a wide range of tasks—biological, cultural, and social. These expressions of care spring from women's active engagement with Shia Ismaili moral codes—recall Sana's mobilization of the Alid tradition—as we will see further in the next section.

The Multiple Meanings of *Seva*

Although Furhana, whom we met at the beginning of this chapter, spent considerable time and effort launching digital programming during the 2020 COVID-19 shutdown, she never underestimated the importance of face-to-face, intimate, and local interactions for the reproduction of Ismaili sociality. When we spoke in August 2021, she explained: "In diaspora, so in the North American context, where there are so many other forms of community that can be held, if there isn't a faith community—one that Imam can reach out, touch and guide, help you directly—if that isn't easily accessible for the Imam, it becomes difficult for the community itself to be supported." Using tactile words—a *jamat* that can be "touched" and "held"—Furhana stresses the tangible dimensions of community. Although few of my second-generation interlocutors accessed the jamatkhana daily, they continued to assume the presence of the *jamat* as a tangible entity they could turn to when in need. Anishah Cumber-Taj, a lawyer based in New York, views the Ismaili *jamat* as a "safe haven," though she admits that she currently is more invested in her Brooklyn neighborhood community and works to support local housing projects and reduce food insecurity in New York more generally.[52] Yet she reflects that whenever she moved to a new city—when she first arrived in New York and, before that, in Washington, DC—she immediately looked for the Ismaili *jamat*. She feels deep comfort in knowing that "Ismailis will always be there for me." *Jamat* is thus conceived as a permanent physical entity that she can turn to whenever she decides. Salima Bhimani similarly shared that she chooses when to "dip in and dip out."[53] The comments of both women assume the *jamat*'s permanent presence, even as they elect when and for how long to engage with it.

And yet the *jamat*'s permanence cannot be taken for granted. As this book has shown, the *jamat* is generated and regenerated—both materially and symbolically—through the efforts of its members. For Anishah to find a *jamat* when she first moves to DC or New York, it must exist materially and be produced relationally. This collective fellowship must also withstand the passage of time and be more enduring than other forms of consociation that emerge simply when people find themselves in circumstances where they share their lives with each other, such as work, neighborhood, or school.[54] These latter forms, as anthropologists Amit and Rapport argue, are often ephemeral, partial, and context dependent; they may not transform into ongoing collective identities.[55] That ephemerality and contingency contrast with how Salima and Anishah conceptualize the *jamat*: as a tangible place and a sociality of closeness that subsists through time and space. In Shia Ismaili Islam, the Imam provides that continuity, which is supplemented by the efforts of ordinary Ismailis. Furhana and Shemine name these efforts, *seva*: it is *seva* that sustains the *jamat* in these ways.

Furhana describes *seva* as volunteer activities undertaken by Ismailis to create intimate encounters between coreligionists, similar to the women we met in the previous chapters. For decades she has helped organize summer and winter camps, discussion sessions, service days, and retreats for Ismaili youth: "[I create] opportunities for our young people to come in and serve. [I hope] to build places where people can serve so they can actually begin to care about the community. It's the idea that if we start serving one another, to provide opportunities for the *jamat* to serve one another, then we're able to build this sense of empathy for one another. We're able to get a sense of, why we should care for each other." Shemine, who has also worked actively within Ismaili institutions, likewise sees service or *seva* as a means of communal continuity: "We keep community together by finding people's passions and offering spaces for them to serve or labor in the ways they can be passionate." What Furhana and Shemine are emphasizing is the material, affective, and symbolic production of community through consistent interpersonal encounters. *Seva* appears here as that mode of intimate social and spiritual action through which individual Ismailis serve not only the Imam but also each other—and in doing so, they establish everyday interactions that sustain mutuality. The community produced by *seva*—as Shemine and Furhana describe it—is one where direct physical interaction is a necessary precursor to the sharing of symbols, imaginations, and feelings.

Furhana believes that constructing such a community through *seva* is spiritual work: "For me it's a very spiritual concept. It's the idea of 'oneness.'" Here she mobilizes a key concept in Islam, *tawhid* (oneness), which not only affirms the unicity of God but also points to the oft-repeated notion in the Quran that humans are created from one soul. To sustain the kind of close-knit community that might aspire toward *tawhid*, a core group of individuals must undertake this essential spiritual work. Amit and Rapport explain that the persistence of a social group organized along community lines relies on a group of individuals willing to perform the roles that establish interconnectivity among its members.[56] The social organization can survive shifts in personnel as long as a core group persists. *Seva* by women like Shemine and Furhana (as well as the women we encountered in previous chapters) serves this key purpose of establishing affinity among non-kin so that it survives intercontinental and generational shifts.

At the same time, Furhana and Shemine (along with other second-generation women) imbue additional meanings to *seva* to correspond to their specific and changing circumstances. Without denying the salience of the jamatkhana as what anthropologist Zahra Jamal has called "[a] microcosm of volunteering," some of my interlocutors have tried to craft additional sites of *seva* and avenues for transmitting Ismaili moral codes.[57] Sana's experience is a case in point. When she was denied the opportunity to practice her ethics of racial allyship within the jamatkhana, she created a new site for *seva* and Ismaili sociality. This is not entirely novel; Ismailis have long practiced their ethics outside formal religious institutions. Readers will recall that Farida also invoked *seva* in relation to offering rides to coreligionists (chapter 1) or helping the non-Ismaili neighbor of a friend (chapter 3), practices she performs outside formal Ismaili institutions. In recent decades, as Ismaili institutions have expanded and strengthened, they have become key sites for *seva*. But not everyone is able to render service within these institutions. As we have seen above, many of my second-generation interlocutors live far from jamatkhana and coreligionists, and have limited surplus capital and time (which are often required) to serve voluntarily in senior Ismaili Council positions. They therefore have to figure out new ways to participate in the praxis of *seva*. Shemine, who is an assistant professor of child and youth care at MacEwan University in Alberta, views her scholarly and professional counseling activities for Somali Muslim youth as *seva*. She explains, "I struggle with the institutional definition of what *seva* is. For me, my *seva*, my research, my service is all connected. While it looks like I am being paid for it [research or counseling] a lot of it is entangled. For me it's all kinda just one." Salima expresses similar sentiments: "My entire life is a dedication to the Divine, in service to the Imam. I don't make distinctions on any level. Even the professional work I do is, I feel, in service to the Divine, to humanity, and therefore to the Imam." Furhana further perceives her reproductive activities of cleaning and cooking for her children as also belonging to the domain of *seva*: "Taking care of my children is *seva* because they are Imam's children." Viewing her children as spiritual children of the Imam allows Furhana to consecrate her domestic labor.

Shemine further observes that we often think of *seva* "for the next person, to fulfill *their* needs," and "not for the self." But she articulates care for self as a form of service too: if she is burned out, she cannot provide counseling to the teenage Somali Muslims who show up in her office. Taking a weekend off for rejuvenation is thus spiritual work, *seva*, even though most immediately undertaken for her own self: "It is a spiritual act. If I am not giving to the self in a way that is meaningful, purposeful, exciting, loving, then how do I offer it out?" While the vocabulary of self-care seems at odds with religious traditions' frequent deprioritization of self for the service of others, Shemine's formulation resists the binary of self and other. She privileges self-care not to enhance personal productivity for capitalist accumulation (which is how self-care is often articulated in neoliberal frameworks) but to have more capacity to give, to serve others. Self-care here enhances spirituality and community as opposed to fraying connections to community.

Second-generation women thus claim participation in the devotional praxis of *seva* by extending its definition to include a wider range of activities and new sites of action. They attach religio-moral meanings to routine functions that are usually considered beyond the scope of religion. In the process, they intentionally blur the boundaries between religious and secular, paid and unpaid work, productive and reproductive activities, public and private, self and other. As Salima explains, "You actually have agency and autonomy to decide it [what *seva* means]. Even though we belong to this community that might have had historical definitions around this, we also have agency." In interpreting *seva* expansively, second-generation Ismaili women are not only proposing plural ways of being Ismaili but also illustrating the contingency of religious ethics: ethics are place and time based. Women's definitions of *seva* are informed by their life experiences and shaped by late-stage capitalism and diasporic scattering. By bringing the otherwise undervalued care activities into the realm of religion (as Furhana does) or extending the scope of *seva* to include their daily professional tasks (as Shemine and Salima do), women widen the remit of *seva*. This is one example of how new meanings are ascribed to shared ideologies and symbols. And while second-generation efforts to incorporate a more diverse set of activities under the rubric of *seva* may seem to be a modern innovation, historian Taushif Kara has observed that the spectrum of tasks defined as *seva* in *ginanic* texts is in fact more expansive than its late twentieth-century iteration: *seva* was previously recognized in an array of activities, ranging from "prolonged devotion to the preparation of food, from domestic servility to absolute sacrifice."[58] In that sense, the second generation's reappraisal could be read as a recuperation of an early modern ethic of *seva*.

These changing ascriptions do not necessarily pose a threat to sustaining community. As Anthony Cohen has argued, a community is characterized by common ownership of symbols, but that does not necessarily equate to—or require—sharing meanings or interpretations.[59] What is crucial for the longevity of community, Cohen suggests, is that members preserve a commitment to shared practices of mutuality even as they attach different meanings to them.[60] Second-generation Ismaili women assign a *range of meanings* to the shared symbol of *seva*, meanings that are informed by their specific place, orientation, and circumstance. As meanings are mutable, this project has uncovered different ways of being-in-community across multiple generations. The succession of meaning will continue as each generation remakes *jamat*.

I argued in the first chapter that in examining displaced women's practices of remaking an Ismaili sociality, we learn that Ismaili ethics is not a pregiven or fixed set of codes. It is instead animated through the interpretative efforts of individual Ismailis and shaped by their changing context. This chapter has illustrated these dynamics by focusing on the specific case of second-generation Ismaili women in North America. Second-generation women's practice of an ethical subjectivity is shaped by their parents' experience and by their own experience as highly educated, upwardly mobile Ismailis in a Western, capitalist context. Like earlier generations, they contribute to Ismaili sociality by building/sustaining infrastructure (jamatkhanas and councils), but they are also fashioning additional sites of spiritual kinship, including online platforms and social movements. They create aesthetic and narrative encounters by extending their reach to novels, scholarly books/dissertations, podcasts, and the visual arts, using these modes of expression to both discover their history and document their ongoing experiences as diasporic subjects. As they contend with rampant anti-Brown racism and Islamophobia, they also critically reflect on anti-Blackness among South Asians. They contemplate the ways that their ancestors and Ismaili institutions benefited from racial hierarchies and alliances with colonial authorities and use this analysis to posit new ways of practicing Ismaili ethics in the present. In the process, they personalize religious vocabularies and invest old terms with new meanings. In considering this younger cohort's activities, we observe both continuities and innovations; care and support for coreligionists appear in both familiar and new forms. Ismaili ethics hence emerges as plural and always in-the-making.

7

Conclusion

Spiritual Intimacies

Among contemporary Ismailis, the slogan "One *Jamat*" (One Community) is ubiquitous. It first circulated between 2017 and 2018 when Ismailis across the world celebrated the sixtieth anniversary of the Imamat (spiritual leadership) of Aga Khan IV. The year was marked by celebratory events and the slogan was everywhere: printed on t-shirts, attached to the name of events ("the One *Jamat* dance"), featured in songs streaming on the.ismaili, the official website of Nizari Ismailis ("Journey of One *Jamat*"[1]). Children painted "One *Jamat*" into pictures and adults invited each other to "One *Jamat*" dinners. Ismailis in the United States heard "One *Jamat*"; so did those living in Tajikistan, India, and Germany. In 2018, when I was volunteering at an Ismaili summer camp in Karachi, I saw youth participants from more than fifteen countries spontaneously break into the "One *Jamat*" song. Despite their varying levels of proficiency in English and differences in certain religious rituals, teens from all over the world recognized each other as Ismailis, sharing a common orientation to the Sacred as members of one *jamat*.

In these various utterances, "One *Jamat*" was often used as a descriptor—to name a religious sociality. Yet as we have seen throughout this book, *jamat* is not an a priori construct. It is a material, social, and symbolic formation that requires effort by individuals who both articulate it and exist as its subjective realizations at any particular time and place. "One *Jamat*" is simultaneously a rhetorical appeal (when it appears in songs), an aspiration (the object of many service tasks), and a physical entity (one that my interlocutors often accessed via the jamatkhanas). The slogan invites individuals to identify themselves as members of one *jamat* and to act in ways that produce that sociality. Said differently, it is a call to practice the care and mutuality that I have described throughout this book, where moral guidance (as found in the Quran, *farmans*, or *ginans*) inspires everyday actions (a prepared meal, a ride to the clinic, a kind word) that iterate community. It echoes appeals for intersubjectivity made in the past too through phrases such as "*panje bhai*"

Rebuilding Community. Shenila Khoja-Moolji, Oxford University Press. © Oxford University Press 2023.
DOI: 10.1093/oso/9780197642023.003.0008

and *"panje behno,"* which called on individuals to act in unison like fingers of a hand (*panj*),[2] or a similar call for "patience, understanding and above all unity among the community members" made by the editorial board of the *American Ismaili* in 1979.[3] This book has considered how women, in particular, have understood this call across generations and how they have sustained the *jamat* against, and in the aftermath of, the dislocating effects of wars, forced migration, poverty, and racism. I have focused on a specific cohort of Ismaili women: those who were displaced in the early 1970s from East Pakistan and East Africa and had to remake their lives in the diaspora, primarily in North America, but also in (West) Pakistan and the United Kingdom.

The book expands the definition of migrant placemaking—which is often about subjective attachment to a physical site—to include a consideration of attachment to people and symbols as well. This move enables us to understand women's care activities as sustaining the Ismaili sociality in the here and now as well as symbolically. In Ismaili women's activities—cooking for a lost traveler, establishing a makeshift jamatkhana, reciting *ginans* on a steamer out of Chittagong, telling a miracle story, or writing a cookbook—we glimpse not only the material dimension of placemaking through supporting built infrastructure but also its sensory, aesthetic, somatic, and gustatory dimensions. While in the specific conditions of diaspora each instance of support may, in its own time, advance placemaking, we should view these activities not only in their specificity but also as a constellation of performances undertaken over decades, by countless women. Driving a sick woman to a clinic, helping a widow set up a *duka*, or telling a *moujza* story—done on a daily basis, these small acts reinforce common bonds. We are thus able to grasp how spiritual intimacies are maintained from one generation to the next. Intimacy here, following Lauren Berlant, denotes the closeness that emerges in relationships and sites outside the conventional institutions of intimacy, namely the nuclear family and heterosexual relations.[4] Such additional forms of intimacy are engendered not only through encounters between people but also with memories, stories, spirits/angels, food, buildings, songs, paintings, and photographs.

We have thus learned that religious community is not a given; it is produced during and through a wide range of activities—activities through which women both express and discover Shia Ismaili ethics. This book has accordingly been concerned with showing what ethics *do*. The *jamat* emerges in a new location—and is subsequently sustained—as a result of these ordinary ethical practices that maintain relatedness. This exploration, then, takes ordinary practices as both *expressing* a group's ethos and *creating* that very ethos through shared attachments, dispositions, and orientations. My emphasis on the constitutive nature of ethical action is all the more important because, since my interlocutors share ethnicity, it is easy to default to it as the primary lens through which to understand community actions. But limiting the study of migrant life to ethnicity obscures other motivations and conditions (such as shared congregational life) that also produce relationality. The Ismaili habitus that I have described has been cultivated over decades. Such a habitus, as Saba Mahmood explains, is formed through diligent practice and discipline, such that specific habits (vices and virtues) become rooted in one's character.[5] Thus, while ethnicity cannot be omitted from our understanding of Khoja Ismaili sociality, the sociality also cannot be viewed solely through this lens or we risk overlooking the numerous ways in which Ismailis try to *transcend* ethnicity through ethical conduct. The *jamat* that emerges consequently can be most properly understood as an ethical relation.

Since it is ethical norms (of care, kindness, generosity, sacrifice, and others delineated in this book) that both create and express *jamat*, this arrangement is subject to disruption as well. Such disruption happens when wars, famines, or other conflicts introduce precarity, but it also occurs in the face of abuse. Recall Sumera (chapter 3), who at age seventeen saw an offer of support from a fellow Ismaili turn into sexual harassment. The work of generating mutuality, trust, and friendship must be undertaken repeatedly, across generations, in the face of and against everyday acts of corrosion. By documenting women's practices, I have highlighted how they have marshalled ethical norms for this endeavor. And in considering women from the second generation, I have shown how the practice of critical self-reflection becomes a part of this assemblage. In the process, we have also learned something about how the Shia faith is lived and about nonproductivist approaches to care work. I close with reflections on these additional themes.

Lived Shia Islam

We have seen throughout this book that the Ismaili Imams (Aga Khan III and Aga Khan IV) have emphasized the ethical impulse of Islam and have guided their followers to be united and generous, and to help and support each other, in everyday life. The strong collectivist impetus of Ismaili religious life exists in part due to the central authority of the Imams and as a response to their ongoing moral guidance on interpersonal conduct. Many of my interlocutors spoke of the present Imam's frequent encouragement that each Ismaili be responsible for the welfare of others, mentioning an oft-cited *farman*: "No matter where you are, your responsibilities to your faith, to your *jamat*, to your traditions, remain identical; there is no difference, none whatsoever, in practicing your faith in London, or in Vancouver or in Montreal or in New York rather than in Karachi, Nairobi, Bombay or other parts of the world."[6] Ismailis are thus summoned to recognize themselves as Muslims not only by practicing virtue in relation to the self but also in relation to coreligionists. Community making becomes another kind of virtue or a moral code of the Ismaili tradition that individuals try to practice. Of course, the Imam also directs his followers to enact similar ethics in relation to those who are beyond the community, but each embodiment of obedience to a moral code has its specificity, as Mahmood reminds us, and deserves its own close analysis.[7] My concern in this book has been with community interiority, and I hope others will take up this analysis in relation to Ismaili ethics as practiced in relation to those outside the community.

Women's everyday acts of support for coreligionists not only advance emplacement in the diaspora but also harness belief (*iman*). As David Morgan observes: "Belief, it is important to point out, is not simply assent to dogmatic principles or creedal propositions, but also the embodied or material practices that enact belonging to the group. The feeling that one belongs takes the shape of many experiences, unfolds over time, and is mediated in many forms. Moreover, belonging is nurtured by the aesthetic practices that are designed to generate and refine feeling on the crossed axes of human relationships and human–divine interaction."[8] Morgan's point that "enacting belonging" through material practices is fundamental to belief is supported by this book's observations of Ismaili women. When Merchant tells miracle stories, she conveys Shia Ismaili beliefs related to the Imam's Divine appointment and his *ilm*; when Farida practices patience after a coreligionist fails to show up for an appointment, she undertakes emotional labor that guards against acrimony;[9] when Zahra writes a new curriculum for Ismaili youth, she hopes that they can practice their faith confidently in the American context; when Noorbanu writes a cookbook, she ensures that newly married Ismaili women are able to cook heritage foods at home and for religious festivals; and when Roshan converts her dining room into a makeshift jamatkhana, she facilitates the prayers that draw a congregation together. We are thus reminded that religious communities are formed not only through shared ideologies but also by their members' participation in, and creation of, material culture and affective ties. Women's everyday acts of care are as salient for cultivating belief (*iman*) as dogma or creedal propositions.

And from these practices of Ismaili women, we can also learn something about the ethos of the group. As Francis Clooney has observed, practices are windows into the habits and interpretations of a group; they carry "explanatory and supportive meaning through continuity of tradition."[10] That group ethos becomes rooted in individual character became most apparent to me during my numerous encounters with Laila Datoo (whom we met in chapter 3). When I asked Laila about emptying bedpans for an elderly Ismaili woman at the refugee camp in Italy, she insisted that "it was the right thing to do at the time" and "we were Ismaili." Over the course of our numerous engagements, Laila neither rationalized her care through recourse to *farmans* nor described them using the emic term *seva*. When Ismaili women died onboard dhows heading from India to Zanzibar, other women washed their bodies to prepare them for a funeral. When women in Mombasa showed their wounds to Zahra, she put turmeric paste on them. In these instances, care does not await the invocation of an Ismaili moral code but proceeds as a practice of daily living, as something that one "just does." There is an ongoingness, an ordinariness, and even a pre-personal intensity to these care practices. Such modes of living a faithful life can perhaps be better described in M. Jacqui Alexander's phrasing of lives that have become "habituated to the spiritual."[11] Or, in the words of my interlocutor Dilshad Sadruddin, as she invokes a *farman* she has heard in the jamatkhana: "As *Mawla* says, 'you are in your faith every second that you live on this earth.'"[12] Religion here is not limited to the sites of the jamatkhana or mosque but pervades every moment of living. Such modes of living trouble the assumed separation of faith (*din*) and world (*dunya*). We are instead directed to consider how religious ethics get lodged in individual subjectivity.

My interlocutors' ethical practice springs from but is not reducible to the Shia Ismaili tradition. It is also inflected by other moral codes that they have encountered in their diasporic journeys and by their life circumstances. The concentrated interactions between Ismailis that we observed in East Africa (chapter 2), for instance, were not solely driven by their Imam's *farmans* on unity; these emerged also as the result of colonial policies that separated Asians, Africans, and white settlers. Sana's efforts to create a venue for Ismailis to discuss the Black Lives Matter movement was influenced in part by the Alid tradition of social justice but also by the changing racial politics of the United States (chapter 6). We saw in chapter 2 how women like Hirbai and Tajbibi engaged with philosophical messages that circulated in their milieu—the images of female modesty depicted in the tales of Mahabharata and Ramayana—and incorporated these into their ethical practice. The personalization of *seva* to include reproductive labor and professional work that we have seen Furhana, Salima, and Shemine advance (chapter 6) expresses women's need to give meaning to their daily labor in a context that is different from their ancestors. Women's performance of an Ismaili subjectivity, then, is shaped by multiple intersecting moral codes as well as generational shifts and exigencies of living as gendered, racialized, and classed subjects.

This recognition does not preclude us from observing the discursive dominance of Shia Ismaili teachings in the lives of many of my interlocutors. Women repeatedly cited *farmans* of their Imam on brotherhood, unity, and nutrition; quoted *ginans* on *sreeva*, *seva*, and *iman*; alluded to the Quranic concept of *tawhid* and exhortation to enjoin the good; and explained their actions by reference to the Alid tradition of justice and personal intellectual search. This book thus reveals Ismaili ethical practice as fluid, and Ismaili moral codes as organizing frames furnished by the Imam of the time that are (re)interpreted as practitioners see them intersect with other codes.[13] These organizing frames are shared and transmitted but not reified.

In considering women from the second generation in North America, I have illuminated some of these transmutations, especially as this second generation moves away from the migrant cohort's specific focus on emplacing the community in a new cultural and geographic context. These changes are not ruptures but in continuity with ongoing community life that reshapes individual ethical capacities. As Mahmood reminds us, "Bodily behavior does not simply stand in a relationship of meaning to self and society, but it also endows the self with certain kinds of capacities that provide the substance from which the world is acted upon."[14] The recoding of *seva* that we observed in chapter 6 illustrates how each generation's ethical capacities manifest as different meanings in relation to an ideology broadly shared among Ismaili women of Indic origin. The jamatkhana has remained a salient site of religious practice in North America, though Ismailis are now finding or fashioning additional spaces where they seek to practice their beliefs: among them are digital worlds, rented boardrooms, and streets where they may walk in solidarity with fellow Black Lives Matter movement activists.[15] Likewise, the second generation engages with *moujza* stories in innovative ways, sharing them through digital media (podcasts) and texts (novels, academic books), continuing in the essential faith-sustaining practice of narrating Divine interventions, while transforming a traditional "one-on-one transmission" into a more expansive offering to a wider audience. Sometimes second-generation women will follow familiar patterns of community making and at other times they will craft new ones. This flexibility allows members of a group to identify themselves as Ismaili across generations, adhering to shared religious notions and orientations, even as they practice their Ismaili subjectivities in different ways.

Even when much is culturally shared, forging community takes work. But what happens to spiritual kinship when the axes of difference are multiplied? How do Ismailis from Central Asia or the Middle East participate in community making in their own regions but also in relation to a wider *jamat* in which Indic-origin Ismailis dominate? How are conflicts and clashes overcome? While chapter 6 has begun to offer some ideas, as my interlocutors emphasize the salience of interpersonal connection through service activities, there is room for much more research into this aspect of Ismaili sociality.

Reclaiming Care Work

Certain forms of care—particularly those linked to biological reproduction—are often hidden and stigmatized. Discussing the jamatkhana *safai* (cleaning) committees, anthropologist Zahra Jamal observes that while *safai* is not necessarily a gendered activity—men can and do share in this work—some of her interlocutors considered such feminized tasks as "less worthy" than other volunteer responsibilities like serving on the Ismaili Councils.[16] Jamal thus finds what she calls an "emic hierarchization of volunteers."[17] While such a hierarchy indexes class, immigration status, age, and education levels—not least because certain volunteer roles require significant commitment of time and money—it is also centrally about gender. When an Ismaili congregant dismisses the *safai* committee as a lesser form of spiritual service, that reflects in part a failure to value women's labor. Dorothy Roberts has argued in a different context that dichotomies within women's work depress the value of *all* women's work.[18] Africana studies scholar Judith Casselberry, among others, concurs. Casselberry insists that women's labor is often not even considered labor because gender influences *which* labor becomes legible *as* labor.[19] In her study of African American women members of a Pentecostal church

in New York, she observes that despite the fact that women expended significant effort caring for congregants, and even though the combination of
churchwork and housework generated a heavier burden for them than male
church leaders, they were excluded from church decision-making bodies.
What is needed, then, is a different matrix of valuation. This book is a step in
that direction.

Much of the work described in this book takes the form of routine, often
unglamorous tasks necessary for life-making—peeling the skin from a
chicken before it can be cooked into *biryani*, preparing chai for a traveler,
cleaning an elderly coreligionist's bedpan, mopping the floor of a jamatkhana
kitchen, scrubbing jamatkhana toilets, or changing the diapers of a baby
whose mother has died at a refugee camp. Such acts of care, mostly done
by women, take place largely away from public view. This work happens
in kitchens or bathrooms, often in private homes, and when performed in
the jamatkhana, during times when the rest of the congregants are away
at homes and jobs. Members of the *safai* committees, for example, clean
jamatkhanas during the day or immediately after services, when the building
has emptied out. The ritual blessing we saw delivered by a *mukhi* departing
the jamatkhana in Atlanta (chapter 3) is a further reminder that the *safai*
committee's service continues even after the congregation's leaders go home.
Given this broader invisibility of care activities, it is not surprising that both
the work itself and those who perform it remain undervalued. In fact, in his
intellectual history of *seva*, Kara has observed how notions of servility and
sacrifice embedded in the idea of *seva* (found in the *ginans* but also in Bhakti
literature generally) have sometimes justified "forced labour and monetary
sacrifice of various kinds," especially gendered labor, which elides *seva*'s metaphysical meanings.[20]

But care work (and care in general) has a reparative dimension, as this
book has shown. In the aftermath of wars and forced migration, care begins
the process of renewal. Saidiya Hartman therefore calls care an "antidote
to violence."[21] When, as we have seen, Ismaili women's activities produce
relationality and sociability, they heal past traumas and create connections
between generations. By cooking and packing *biryani* for young, single
Ismaili men (chapter 3), women like Gulzar and Roshan helped them settle
in unfamiliar environments. By washing the *pyalis* from which congregants
would later drink the *abe-shafa*, my interlocutors ensured that a longstanding
ritual practice would continue. By making *seero* and then preserving its
recipe in a cookbook, they nurtured their children's sensory connection to

din (faith). By singing *ginans*, they transmitted Ismaili ideologies housed in hymns. By putting reproductive activities front and center in this book, we have recognized previously hidden subjects (Ismaili women); we have also discovered the centrality of care in creating and sustaining religious communities.

And, as we have seen, for many women, care work has a deeply spiritual dimension. Through these activities women endeavor to realize religious values such as *tawhid*, strengthen their *iman*, and follow the *farmans* of their Imam. When I praise Farida for the hours upon hours she spends cooking and delivering meals, offering rides, visiting the sick, and taking her turn on the *ghusal* committee (whose members perform the ritual cleansing of the body when an Ismaili woman passes on), she inevitably dismisses the praise, as she is "only an instrument." It is not she who helps other Ismailis get to the clinic, track down a discount, or find a job. She instead assigns agency to the Imam: "Imam acts through me. Really, I am just a vessel." In chapter 3, we met Khurshid Bhimani, who similarly insisted that the Imam gives *seva* and so she receives that opportunity as a blessing (*barakah*). These sentiments posit the Imam as an active spiritual force in the world, who facilitates his followers' religious life by giving them opportunities to practice Islamic virtues of generosity, kindness, patience, and goodwill, among others. When we consider such viewpoints, we gain a rather different understanding of care work. We also learn something about what it looks like to live one's life being attentive to *Mawla*. It is a style of religiosity that, as we have seen above, is different from the paradigm of self-cultivation. In this worldview, the Imam is an actant, and the believer's religiosity (which may take the form of care work) is an effect of both her own exertions and the direction afforded to her by the Imam. The individual is not a solitary self, but intimately linked to the Divine, in an experience of Godly presence that Alexander has described as "Sacred accompaniment."[22] Leading life on these terms means orienting to a worldview where human intention and Divine intervention are deeply entangled. In such a life, care work may be received as an opportunity to contribute to a Divine plan. In recognizing the spiritual and reparative dimensions of women's care work—rather than valuing it in relation to creating economic value (as commodity or property)—I have joined scholars like Alexander in refusing to reduce women's work to productivist logics.

Care is not inevitable. The women in my study engaged in care in contexts marked by male domination. They described episodes of domestic violence, lamented the decline of women's-only prayer spaces (*behno majlis* and *sat-sang*), and bemoaned masculine communal norms (such as when Roshan observed that as a divorcee she would not be able to serve as a *mukhiani*). Women have given care even when their own needs have been denied, when their communities have failed—or refused—to protect them. In recognizing the value of women's care work, we need not ignore the ways in which power (patriarchy, for instance) is exercised through its allocation and distribution, as Sandy Grande has observed.[23] Grande reminds us that care work remains imbricated in systems of power including race, heteronormativity, and masculinism.[24] Our task is to highlight the multiple social lives of care and the messy effects that its varying legibility produces. This book has tried to illustrate the value that care work can deliver in forming and sustaining a sociality even when that value goes unrecognized.

An Artifact of Care

I grew up in Pakistan and attended Ismaili religious school in the evenings, five times a week, until I moved to North America at the age of seventeen. That early religious education never touched on the experiences of displaced Ismailis—not those who, like my mother, had fled East Pakistan during the 1971 war, nor the newly arrived Afghan refugees who were living in our midst in Karachi by the 1990s. Displacement and its attendant trauma were mostly absent from the community's public conversations, treated as private matters affecting individuals rather than the Ismaili community as a whole. And aside from a few exceptional women—the wives, daughters, or granddaughters of Prophet Muhammad, or the current Imam's female relatives—I learned little of Shia or Ismaili women. Only when I began to research and write about my mother and grandmother's history of successive displacements did I discover other, similar stories. It is not that these women are forgotten—they are indeed remembered and celebrated by family members. But they have not yet entered the official historical record of Ismailis. It was this potential loss of women's history—recognizing that these women's lives would disappear unrecorded and unarchived—that motivated me to undertake the present study.

At stake here is the cultural memory of the Nizari Ismaili people. If we think of cultural memory as Jan Assman and John Czaplicka define it, "the store of knowledge from which a group derives an awareness of its unity and peculiarity,"[25] then losing or preserving the history of women matters for both present and future. Cultural memory is the reservoir individuals draw upon to view themselves as belonging—and having belonged, over multiple generations—to a coherent and definable group. Through canonical texts, rituals, paintings, monuments, and institutional communications, certain events and episodes are transformed into durable memories, the creation and rehearsal of which is fundamental to consolidating long-term group identity.[26] And what a group chooses to remember or forget is intimately tied to questions of power and gender.[27] As observed in chapter 1, Ismaili cultural memory has centered on Imams and elite men, the rise and fall of Ismaili empires, and doctrinal texts. This book—centering Khoja Ismaili women, everyday life, oral histories, and family texts—accounts for the role that women have played in fashioning the ethical infrastructure of the Ismaili community through the transmission and interpretation of religio-moral codes. Studying older Jewish women in California, anthropologist Barbara Myerhoff similarly describes women's work of this kind as a form of "underground culture" through which values are quietly transmitted in everyday situations.[28] My telling gives modern Ismaili history a palimpsestic quality: this complementary contribution does not ignore the continuous sweep of forty-nine generations of Imams that has reproduced the Ismaili sociality, but recognizes the gendered work ordinary Ismailis contribute to help sustain it. In doing so, it follows Angela Davis, who calls for resisting the "depiction of history as the work of heroic individuals" so that ordinary people may "recognize their potential agency as a part of an ever-expanding community of struggle."[29] I hope not only to have marked the presence of Ismaili women in this recuperative project but also to have illustrated what an Ismaili history from below might look like.

This attention to women's lived ethics moves aside the normative male subject who has often been a stand-in for all human subjects—and, as Zahra Ayubi points out, the focus of works on Islamic ethics, which have tended to treat women as merely instrumental to elite men's ethical endeavors.[30] In Western scholarship on ethics, an overemphasis on rationality has likewise created the conditions for ignoring emotion and care, domains of activity frequently associated with women.[31] This study transforms women's often nonspectacular modes of action and everyday stories into opportunities for moral instruction and reflection. My focus on individual women actors is not intended to downplay the importance of the Ismaili institutional infrastructure. The Ismaili institutions that developed over the course of the twentieth century, including Councils, volunteer committees, and jamatkhanas, have contributed significantly to sustaining the community. But institutions are organizing structures; we still need to know more about the concrete efforts undertaken by the individuals within them. And even with greater knowledge of the work that women do, we still recognize that women's (and men's) efforts and communal institutions can only go so far in creating durable caring societies. Additional supports, from strengthening the welfare state to developing alternatives to capitalist markets, are also required.

By tracing Ismaili women's ethical practices *in* and *for* community, *Rebuilding Community* speaks to broader concerns about how we value (or fail to value) care work, about community as a sociality of concrete practices, about religious life along migratory routes, and about the efforts of refugees to emplace themselves in new locations. Yet in the end, this book's work has been highly specific: witnessing the lives of the women who welcomed me into their homes; shared food with me; sent me photographs, WhatsApp messages, and stories—too many to capture in these pages. This book exists because of their generosity, their memory work, and their desire to leave a record of themselves and their foremothers. And it emerges from my own pursuit of care for them, ensuring that their enormous contribution to Ismaili religious life will not be forgotten. I leave this book in your hands as an artifact of that care.

Notes

Chapter 1

1. This interview was conducted in Urdu in January 2020. Shakar passed away in March 2021.
2. Multiple Indic religious traditions mobilize the concept of *seva* to frame social action in relation to the guidance of *gurus* (teachers). On Sikh approach to *seva*, see Murphy, "Mobilizing Seva," and R. Srivastsan, "Concept of 'Seva' and the 'Sevak' in the Freedom Movement." For an intellectual history of *seva* see Kara, "Abode of Peace: Islam, Empire, and the Khoja Diaspora (1866–1972)."
3. While "East Africa" encompasses a dozen countries in the eastern sub-Saharan region, in this book, it is applied more narrowly to Uganda, Tanzania, and Kenya. According to historian Gijsbert Oonk, the official count for the Indian population of Uganda in 1969 was 74,308. Of this number, 35,000 were British passport holders (mostly protected persons, not British subjects), 8,890 were citizens of India, 253 were citizens of Pakistan, 1,768 were Kenyan citizens, and 26,657 were Ugandan citizens (Oonk, "Gujarati Asians in East Africa, 1800–2000").
4. I follow my interlocutors' gender self-identification. All of them identified as either women or men.
5. Alleyne, "An Idea of Community and Its Discontents: Towards a More Reflexive Sense of Belonging in Multicultural Britain"; Amit, *Realizing Community: Concepts, Social Relationships and Sentiments*.
6. Thomas, "Rebuking the Ethnic Frame: Afro Caribbean and African American Evangelicals and Spiritual Kinship," 226.
7. Gray, "Community as Placemaking: Ram Auctions in the Scottish Borderland," 40.
8. Claudia Moser and Cecelia Feldman write about the effect of a constellation of practices over time in *Locating the Sacred*, 6.
9. See Casselberry, *The Labor of Faith: Gender and Power in Black Apostolic Pentecostalism*.
10. See, for example, Kuepper, Lackey, and Swinerton, "Ugandan Asian Refugees: Resettlement Centre to Community"; Muhammadi, "Gifts from Amin: The Resettlement, Integration, and Identities of Ugandan Asian Refugees in Canada."
11. Schiller and Caglar, "Displacement, Emplacement and Migrant Newcomers: Rethinking Urban Sociabilities within Multiscalar Power," 21. Notable exceptions are the recent collection, Meyer and Van der Veer, *Refugees and Religion: Ethnographic Studies of Global Trajectories*, and Babou, *The Muridiyya on the Move*.

12. On spiritual kinship, see Thomas, *Kincraft: The Making of Black Evangelical Sociality*, and Thomas, Malik, and Wellman, *New Directions in Spiritual Kinship*.

13. Aga Khan, *farman* made in Mumbai, India, March 1, 2018; video clip available at https://ismaililiterature.com/interviews-and-speeches-of-mawlana-hazir-imam/, accessed February 4, 2022.

14. Mittermaier, "Dreams from Elsewhere: Muslim Subjectivities beyond the Trope of Self-Cultivation," 249.

15. See Federici, *Wages against Housework*; Bhattacharya, *Social Reproduction Theory*; Duffy, "Doing the Dirty Work: Gender, Race, and Reproductive Labor in Historical Perspective"; Padios, "Labor." On how unpaid work within the home is further divided into "spiritual and menial" and mapped onto racial lines, see Roberts, "Spiritual and Menial Housework."

16. I am influenced in particular by M. Jacqui Alexander and Sandy Grande's work. Alexander, *Pedagogies of Crossing: Meditations on Feminism, Sexual Politics, Memory, and the Sacred*, and Grande, "Care," in *Keywords for Gender and Sexuality Studies*. See also Raghuram, "Locating Care Ethics beyond the Global North"; Ritchey, *Acts of Care: Recovering Women in Late Medieval Health*.

17. hooks, "Choosing the Margin as a Space of Radical Openness."

18. While the official Ismaili community website claims twelve to fifteen million Ismailis (https://the.ismaili/global/about-us/the-ismaili-community), other estimates are much lower, only a few million (see Devji, "Preface," in *The Ismailis in the Colonial Era*, ix–xvi).

19. Gulam Ali Allana notes that some Ismaili *dais* visited Sindh and Multan as early as the mid-eighth century (Allana, *Ismaili Movement in Sindh, Multan and Gujrat*, 31).

20. Kassam, *Songs of Wisdom and Circles of Dance*, 20; Asani, "From Satpanthi to Ismaili Muslim"; Asani, "The Khojahs of South Asia"; Asani, "The *Ginans*: Betwixt *Satpanthi* Scripture and 'Ismaili' Devotional Literature." According to Allana, the first *pir* to visit the Sindh, Gujarat, Kuchchh, and Kathiawar region was Sayed Nur al-Din (also known as *pir* Satgur Nur) (Allana, *Ismaili Movement in Sindh, Multan and Gujrat*, 42–43).

21. Nanji, "Khojas," 393. Iqbal Akhtar traces the origins of the term *Khwajah* to Sindhi *Khojanu* (to search for), suggesting that it points to the community's perpetual search for economic security and spiritual well-being (Akhtar, *The Khoja of Tanzania*, 34). According to some reports *pir* Sadr al-Din died in the late fourteenth century. Other *satpanthi* groups include *Momnas, Piranapanthis, Shamsis, Guptis, Maulais*, and *Jasnathis* (as noted in Asani, "The *Ginans*," 174).

22. Akhtar, *The Khoja of Tanzania*, 35. While some scholars believe that the majority of Khojas belonged to the Lohana and Bhatia trading castes, others note that they were predominantly low caste (for more see Amiji, "Some Notes on Religious Dissent in Nineteenth-Century East Africa," 603–616).

23. Allana, *Ismaili Movement in Sindh, Multan and Gujrat*, 53; Virani, "Khwajah Sindhi (Khojki): Its Name, Manuscripts and Origin."

24. Allana, *Ismaili Movement in Sindh, Multan and Gujrat*, 60.

25. Asani, "The *Ginans*."

26. Devji cited in Asani, "From Satpanthi to Ismaili Muslim"; see also Masselos, "The Khojas of Bombay"; Hirji, "The Socio-Legal Formation of the Nizari Ismailis of East Africa, 1800–1950."

27. These 1860s estimates are based on transcripts from an 1866 legal challenge to the Imam's authority. By 1876 there were more than seven hundred Ismaili families in Zanzibar (Nanji, "Modernization and Change in the Nizari Ismaili Community in East Africa: A Perspective"). According to Hussain Jasani, Khojas could be found in Mumbai in the 1790s; a later major influx followed the completion of railroad lines in the 1850s (Jasani, "Khojas in Mumbai," lecture at Khaki Lab, November 20, 2021).

28. Walji, "A History of the Ismaili Community in Tanzania," 21; Farida Hussain Noorani, personal interview in Urdu and Gujarati, November 27, 2020; Rashida Moolji, personal interview in Urdu, November 1, 2020. On life on the Gujarat coast see Alpers and Goswami, *Transregional Trade and Traders*; Pradhan, "A Brief History of the Khoja Ismaili Community in Daman, India, from the Portuguese Period to the Present." While the modern Indian state of Gujarat includes the entire peninsula of Kathiawar, the Kuchchh region, and inland territory, nineteenth-century Gujarat referred to only the northeastern part of the peninsula.

29. According to the *Indian Meteorological Memoir* published by the Government of India in 1905, areas affected by famine in 1900 included South Punjab, East Sind, Rajputana, Central India, Berar, Central Provinces, Deccan, Cutch, Kathiawar, and Gujarat (Government of India, *Indian Meteorological Memoir*, 185–186).

30. Akhtar, *The Khoja of Tanzania*, 48.

31. See, for example, Mamdani, *The Voyage of Destiny: From Jamnagar to New York*; Beben and Poor, *The First Aga Khan: Memoirs of the 46th Ismaili Imam*; Tejpar, "The Migration of Indians to Eastern Africa."

32. Numerous oral history accounts and personal interviews, including with Rashida Moolji, November 1, 2020, and Daulat Delawala, November 2, 2020; Shariffa Keshavjee in Salvadori, *We Came in Dhows*, vol. 3, 173. See also Walji, *A History of the Ismaili Community*, 30.

33. Akhtar, "Religious Citizenship: The Case of the Globalised Khoja."

34. For more on the journeys that Ismailis undertook see Mawani, "The Coming of Ismailis to East Africa," 3.

35. Rashida Moolji, personal interview in Urdu, November 1, 2020.

36. Lalani and Dhalla, *A Journal of Life in Kathiawad, Gujarat & Buganda, Uganda: Habib Rahemtulla Lalani—1910–1997*, part 3.

37. Rehmat, personal interview in Urdu, July 5, 2019.

38. S.A., personal interview in English, December 17, 2019.

39. Laila Bandali, personal interview in English, November 18, 2020.

40. Zakaria, *1971: A People's History from Bangladesh, Pakistan and India*, 80. Estimates of deaths from the 1970 cyclone range as high as three hundred thousand to five hundred thousand.

41. Cutts, *The State of World Refugees 2000*; one *New York Times* journalist reported some six thousand displaced people at one camp in Karachi (Sterba, "For Hungry Bihari Refugees in Karachi, Future Is Bleak").

42. Saikia, *Women and the Making of Bangladesh*. See also Cutts, *The State of World Refugees 2000*, 67.

43. Noordin Alibhai and Mumtaz Alibhai, personal interview in Urdu, December 22, 2019.

44. On forced migrants in camps near the Bangladesh-India border, see Zakaria, *1971*, and Goethe Institute's Oral History Project, http://www.goethe.de/ins/in/lp/prj/inm/mvi/enindex.htm, accessed December 17, 2020.

45. Amirali Moolji, personal interview in Urdu, April 10, 2020; Noordin Alibhai and Mumtaz Alibhai, personal interview in Urdu, December 22, 2019; Kamaluddin Ali Muhammad, personal interview in English, January 4, 2020.

46. Noordin Alibhai served as chairman of the Rehabilitation Committee for Ismailis from Uganda, Burma, and East Pakistan; Hameed Husain also recalls Ismaili volunteers in Karachi who arranged transportation, temporary homes, furniture, and school admission for Ismailis from East Pakistan (Husain, *Journey with the Gods*, 141–142).

47. Gregory, *South Asians in East Africa*, 34; Asians in East Africa were a heterogeneous group, belonging to different religious and ethnic traditions. For more on their histories and differences see Morris, *The Indians in Uganda*; Mamdani, *Imperialism and Fascism in Uganda*; Mangat, *A History of the Asians in East Africa*; Bertz, *Diaspora and Nation*; and Aiyar, *Indians in Kenya: The Politics of Diaspora*.

48. Mamdani, "Class Struggles in Uganda," 31. See also Brennan, *Taifa: Making Nation and Race in Urban Tanzania*.

49. For more see Kelley, "What Did Cedric Robinson Mean by Racial Capitalism?"

50. Mawji, "Raced and Gendered Subjectivities in the Diasporas: Exploring the Role of Generationally Transferred Local 'Subjugated' Knowledges in the Education of Canadian Ismaili Women of Indian East African Heritage," 170–171.

51. Mamdani, *Imperialism and Fascism*, 31–32.

52. Winders, "Molloy: Reflecting on the Ugandan Refugee Movement."

53. British subjects also found it difficult to re-enter the United Kingdom. The Commonwealth Immigrants Act of 1968 required a demonstration of "close connection," which in practice meant that only those with at least one parent or grandparent born in Britain would be allowed entry. On these restrictions, see Brah, *Cartographies of Diaspora: Contesting Identities*.

54. In public remarks delivered in both Kenya and Tanzania, Aga Khan IV repeatedly urged his followers to show loyalty to their adopted countries. During a 1966 visit to Tanzania he said, "Some spiritual children have been worried about their future. Some have been thinking of moving out of Tanzania, but I do not recommend this.... But what I am sure about is that each and everyone of you, everyday whenever possible, should in your daily habits and in your daily way of living show to the people of Tanzania that you are loyal citizens of this country.... [Y]ou must continue to work in Tanzania sincerely and loyally." Elsewhere he said, "Concerning the future of my Jamats also in Kenya and in Uganda . . . [i]t is more important than ever before that you should try, each one of you, to make it quite clear, in your everyday contacts, that you are citizens, loyal citizens of Tanzania and that you intend to help citizens of

Tanzania as you have done in the past. I say each one of you should make this effort" (as cited in Mukadam and Mawani, "Diaspora Revisited: Second-Generation Nizari Ismaili Muslims of Gujarati Ancestry," 159).

55. Iqbal Paroo, for instance, repeated "I am African" multiple times during our interview (Iqbal Paroo, personal interview in English, December 14, 2020).

56. Decker, *In Idi Amin's Shadow: Women, Gender and Militarism in Uganda*; Hundle, "Exceptions to the Expulsion: Violence, Security, and Community among Ugandan Asians, 1971–1979."

57. Cutts, *The State of World Refugees 2000*, 69. See also Molloy, "40th Anniversary Lecture: Uganda Asian Refugee Movement 1972." According to Karim Karim, the first Ismaili in Canada was a Pakistani student who arrived in 1952 (Karim, "At the Interstices of Tradition, Modernity and Postmodernity"). See also Meghji, "Rediscovering a Lost Piece of History—First Steps in the Migration of Tanzanian Ismailis to Canada."

58. See, for instance, Bhushan, "NRIs Remember Dark Days of Idi Amin"; Dowden, "Short-Sighted Demagogue Who Played the Race Card"; Premji, "From Refugee to Canadian Citizen: A Ugandan Tells the Story of His 1972 Journey to Winnipeg."

59. Coulson, *Tanzania: A Political Economy*.

60. For an account of nationalization and its impact on young Asians' educational and professional progress see Ladha, *Memoirs of a Muhindi*.

61. See Kassamali's account in Mukadam and Mawani, "Living in a Material World: Religious Commodification and Resistance," 58.

62. Bertz, *Diaspora and Nation*.

63. Manby, *Struggles for Citizenship in Africa*.

64. BBC, "More Kenyan Asians Flee to Britain," February 4, 1968. See Bahadurali Sumar's story in Premji, "From Refugee to Canadian Citizen." Despite the general environment of fear, some Ismailis remained in East Africa and continued to express strong commitments to their African identity. During a 1986 interview Salim Manji, an Ismaili from Kenya, dismissed the popular accusation that Asians have always had "one leg out of the country." He exclaimed: "There is no fallback position and none is sought. Ours is a long-term commitment in terms of generations" (as cited in Fitzgerald, "Kenya's Asians: Needed but Not Wanted. They're Victims of Their Own Success").

65. According to one estimate, in 1979 there were seven thousand Ismailis in the United Kingdom. See "Editorial" *Ismaili Forum 4*, no. 1 (1979): 2.

66. The nonprofit Project for Public Spaces defines placemaking as "the process of creating quality places that people want to live, work, play and learn in." See also Whyte, *The Social Life of Small Urban Spaces*; Nejad, Walker, and Newhouse, "Indigenous Placemaking and the Built Environment: Toward Transformative Urban Design"; McGaw, Pieris, and Potter, "Indigenous Place-Making in the City."

67. See advertisement by Ismaili Hotel in *Africa Ismaili 1*, no. 3 (1969): 3.

68. G.V., personal interview in Gujarati and English, June 9, 2021.

69. Horst, *Transnational Nomads: How Somalis Cope with Refugee Life in the Dadaab Camps of Kenya*.

70. Ibid., 204.
71. Ma Vang, "Rechronicling History."
72. Greg Noble as cited in Vasquez and Knott, "Three Dimensions of Religious Place Making in Diaspora," 338; Tweed, *Our Lady of the Exile: Diasporic Religion at a Cuban Catholic Shrine in Miami*; see also Peña, *Performing Piety: Making Space with the Virgin of Guadalupe*.
73. Tobin, "Self-Making in Exile"; Perkins, *Muslim American City: Gender and Religion in Metro Detroit*.
74. Alibhai-Brown, *The Settler's Cookbook*, 1, 16, 41, and 67.
75. Daftary, *The Isma'ilis: Their History and Doctrines*, 2–3. For more on this episode, see Virani, "The Eagle Returns: Evidence of Continued Ismai'li Activity at Alamut and in the South Caspian Region Following the Mongol Conquests"; and Jamal, *Surviving the Mongols: The Continuity of Ismaili Tradition in Persia*.
76. Daftary, *The Isma'ilis*, 2–3.
77. See more at iis.ac.uk. For a survey see Andani, "A Survey of Ismaili Studies Part 1" and Andani, "A Survey of Ismaili Studies Part 2."
78. Some ethnographic studies include Steinberg,. *Isma'ili Modern: Globalization and Identity in a Muslim Community*; Remtilla, "Re-producing Social Relations: Political and Economic Change and Islam in Post-Soviet Tajik Ishkashim"; Jamal, "Work No Words: Voluntarism, Subjectivity, and Moral Economies of Exchange among Khoja Ismaili Muslims"; Dossa, "(Re)imagining Aging Lives: Ethnographic Narratives of Muslim Women in diaspora"; Mastibekov, *Leadership and Authority in Central Asia: The Ismaili Community in Tajikistan*; Iloliev, *The Ismaili-Sufi Sage of Pamir*. Recent books published by the Institute of Ismaili Studies include Vellani, *People of Faith*, and Kabani, *Ismaili Festivals*.
79. Work on Ismaili communities includes Virani, "Taqiyya and Identity in a South Asian Community"; Asani, "From Satpanthi to Ismaili Muslim"; Hirji, "The Socio-Legal Formation of the Ismailis"; Kassam, "The Gender Policies of Aga Khan III and Aga Khan IV"; Karim, "Ismaili Engagements with Contemporary Canadian Society"; Tejpar, "The Migration of Indians to Eastern Africa"; Poor, *Authority without Territory: The Aga Khan Development Network and the Ismaili Imamate*; Nanji, "Modernization and Change"; Mamodaly and Fakirani, "Voices from Shia Imami Ismaili Nizari Muslim Women"; Grondelle, *The Ismailis in the Colonial Era: Modernity, Empire and Islam*; Bhimani, "Mapping the Assembly of Muslim Exceptionality and Exceptional Muslims in Colonial Modernity"; Merchant, "Between a Rock and a Hard Place: Shia Ismaili Muslim Girls Negotiate Islam in the Classroom"; Trovão, "Doing Family, Gender, Religion and Raced Identities across Generations."
80. Community efforts include those of Zahir Dhalla, Malik Merchant, Nimira Dewji, Mumtaz Ali Tajddin, and Iqbal Dewji, among others. Memoirs include those by Mahmood Mamdani, Mohamed Keshavjee, Mansoor Ladha, Shelina Zia-Shariff, Nazlin Rahemtulla, Tasneem Jamal, and Nazlin Rahemtulla, among others.
81. A key community-sponsored text—Daftary and Hirji, *The Ismailis: An Illustrated History*—begins with a chapter on "The Advent of Islam and the Early Shi'a." The chapter surveys the life of the Prophet, his migration from Mecca to Medina, Muslim

conquests and wars, succession after the Prophet's death (including Shi'a claims to leadership), and doctrinal development, then discusses early Ismailis and the Fatimid State. In addition to information on the Imams, this introduction to Ismaili history discusses *dais* (mostly male) such as Nasir Khursrow, Qadi Numan, Rashid al-din Sinan, and Nasir al-din al-Tusi. Parin Dossa observes that women are largely absent from both canonical Ismaili texts (like the one considered above) and vernacular versions of Ismaili history. For instance, Mumtaz Tajddin's project curating "101 Ismaili Heroes" (2003) includes not a single female hero, although the cover image features eight women (For more see Dossa, "(Re)imagining Aging Lives"; Tajddin, *101 Ismaili Heroes*, vol. 1, *Late 19th Century to Present Age*, available http:// heritage.ismaili.net/node/20663, accessed August 1, 2022). For an account of the community's didactic practices see Mukherjee, *Ismailism and Islam in Modern South Asia: Community and Identity in the Age of Religious Internationals*.

82. For more see Ebrahim, "The Three Kings without Crowns"; Paroo, "Pioneering Ismaili Settlement in East Africa" (Private papers, January 1970); Tejpar, "The Migration of Indians to Eastern Africa." The pioneer terminology is also used for refugees who arrived in Canada: as an example, see Meghji, "Rediscovering a Lost Piece of Ismaili History."

83. See *Ismaili Forum 4*, no. 1 (1979): cover image; *Ismaili Forum 4*, no. 2 (1979): "The 20th Century East African Ismaili Emigres," 3–5.

84. Feminist scholars have long called for a gendering of history that accounts for women's ways of knowing and being. See Bornat and Diamond, "Women's History and Oral History: Developments and Debates"; Abu-Lughod, *Writing Women's Worlds: Bedouin Stories*, 14–15.

85. Mawji, "Raced and Gendered Subjectivities in the Diasporas"; Dossa, *Afghanistan Remembers: Gendered Narrations of Violence and Culinary Practices*; Dossa, "(Re)imagining Aging Lives"; Jiwa, "Voices from the diaspora: Identity Formation of Ismaili Girls and Women in Canada"; Mukadam and Mawani, "Excess Baggage or Precious Gems?" For a general introduction to the early settlement of Ismailis in the United States, see Ross-Shariff and Nanji, "Islamic Identity, Family, and Community," and Nanji, "The Nizari Ismaili Muslim Community in North America."

86. Paroo, "Aga Khan III and the British Empire"; Kassam, "The Gender Policies"; Keshavjee, "The Redefined Role of the Ismaili Muslim Woman *through Higher Education and the Professions*"; Khoja-Moolji, "Redefining Muslim Women: Aga Khan III's Reforms for Women's Education."

87. Henig, *Remaking Muslim Lives: Everyday Islam in Postwar Bosnia and Herzegovina*, 29.

88. Berlant, "Intimacy," 282.

89. See, for example, Paroo, "Aga Khan III and the British Empire"; Bhimani, "Mapping the Assembly of Muslim Exceptionality and Exceptional Muslims in Colonial Modernity"; Kara, "Abode of Peace"; Grondelle, *The Ismailis in the Colonial Era*.

90. See, for example, Cohen, *Belonging: Identity and Social Organisation in British Rural Cultures*, 12; Gupta and Ferguson, *Culture, Power, Place: Explorations in Critical Anthropology*, 13.

91. Thomas, Malik, and Wellman, *New Directions in Spiritual Kinship*.

92. Seeman, "Kinship as Ethical Relation: A Critique of the Spiritual Kinship Paradigm."

93. Wellman, "Substance, Spirit, and Sociality."

94. Aga Khan, interview, *Politique Internationale*, 2011–2012. In the Islamic worldview, as Ismaili studies scholar Azim Nanji explains, the covenantal relationship with God is sustained through both ritualistic prayers and everyday conduct (Nanji, "Islamic Ethics," 107).

95. Particularly, Virginia Held's *The Ethics of Care*.

96. For more see Amir-Moezzi, *The Spirituality of Shi'i Islam*.

97. Dilshad Sadruddin, personal interview in Urdu, January 9, 2019.

98. Ismaili Constitution, author's collection.

99. On everyday circumstances and ethics see Schielke and Orient, "Second Thoughts about the Anthropology of Islam, or How to Make Sense of Grand Schemes in Everyday Life."

100. See, for example, Prasad, *Poetics of Conduct: Oral Narratives and Moral Being in a South Indian Town*; Sajoo, *Muslim Ethics: Emerging Vistas*; Reinhart, *Lived Islam: Colloquial Religion in a Cosmopolitan Tradition*; McGuire, *Lived Religion: Faith and Practice in Everyday Life*. On religious ethics see Bucar and Stalnaker, *Religious Ethics in a Time of Globalism*; Schweiker and Clairmont, *Religious Ethics: Meaning and Method*.

101. Keane, "Ethics as Piety."

102. Prasad, *Poetics of Conduct*, 226.

103. Ibid. See also Das, "Ordinary Ethics."

104. On this idea see also Mittermaier, *Giving to God: Islamic Charity in Revolutionary Times*.

105. J.A., personal interview in Urdu, December 23, 2019, and subsequent conversations and homestays in December 2020, December 2021, March 2022.

106. On how personal agency meets Divinely preordained futures and material contingencies, see Menin, "The Impasse of Modernity: Personal Agency, Divine Destiny, and the Unpredictability of Intimate Relationships in Morocco."

107. Mittermaier, *Giving to God*, 7.

108. Lambek, "Toward an Ethics of the Act," 63.

109. Moran-Thomas, *Traveling with Sugar: Chronicles of a Global Epidemic*, 20.

110. Thomas, "Strangers, Friends, and Kin," 75.

111. Ibid.

112. Alexander, *Pedagogies of Crossing*; Hammer, *Peaceful Families: American Muslim Efforts against Domestic Violence*; Narayan, *Storytellers, Saints, and Scoundrels*; Moran-Thomas, *Traveling with Sugar*, 23; Eichler-Levine, *Painted Pomegranates and Needlepoint Rabbis: How Jews Craft Resilience and Create Community*, 16.

113. Lugones, *Peregrinajes/Pilgrimages: Theorizing Coalitions against Multiple Oppressions*.

114. Halbwachs, *The Collective Memory*, 68.

115. On individual stories forming collective history see Pandurang, "Scrutinising the Past: A Review of Socio-Literary Narratives of the East African Asian Diasporic Experience," 48.

116. Hirsch and Smith, "Feminism and Cultural Memory."

117. See, for example, Rupani, "Immigration and Citizenship in Canada," in issue 4 of *Ismaili Forum* published in 1979; Esmail, "Learning under the Fatimids" in the first issue of *The American Ismaili* published in 1979; Nanji, "Some Lesser Known Daiʾs and Their Tombs in the Indian Subcontinent," in the third issue of *The American Ismaili* published in 1979. Furthermore, *The American Ismaili 1*, no. 3 (1979) includes articles on "Employment with the Federal Government" (p. 28) and "Sources of Financial Aid for Ismaili Students" (p. 69); we also learn about a *mukhi kamadia* conference held in New York in June 1979 (p. 34) and another one held in California in October of the same year (p. 37). The July 11, 1976, issue of *Canadian Ismaili* includes an article entitled "To Succeed in Business Focus on Marketing" (p. 15), a children's story (p. 13–14), and information about heart disease and education loan schemes. The March 1978 issue of *Canadian Ismaili* (vol. 1, no. 1) provides information about "Jamatkhanas in Western Canada," "Canada's New Immigration Law," and "Hypertension in Perspective in Our Community." In 1976, two educational supplements were published by the Ismailia Education Board for Ontario in February and July that provide information about career planning and financial assistance.
118. Modi and Pandurang, "Women as an Invisible Constituency"; Seidenberg, *Mercantile Adventures: The World of East African Asians 1750–1985*.

Chapter 2

1. Gulzar Kassam (Puribai's granddaughter), personal interview in English, November 3, 2020.
2. Adatia and King, "Some East African Firmans of H. H. Aga Khan III," 184. See also Aziz, *Aga Khan III: Selected Speeches and Writings*.
3. Yasmin Hirji (Nur's daughter), personal interview in English, November 16, 2020.
4. Arab and Indian philanthropists, including Ismailis, established charitable health associations to address the needs of the local population. These facilities often had a loose relationship with the colonial government and operated in parallel with the Colonial Medical Service. For more see Greenwood, *Beyond the State: The Colonial Medical Service in British Africa*.
5. During the same visit, the Imam told Puribai's two sons to head inland as there were better economic prospects there. A year later, when he saw the two men were still in Zanzibar, he reminded the family of his instruction; one of the sons, Badruddin Velji, left for Lindi the next day. Puribai eventually moved to join him there.
6. Asani, "From Satpanthi to Ismaili Muslim"; Hirji, "The Socio-Legal Formation of the Nizari Ismailis of East Africa."
7. Hirji, "The Socio-Legal Formation of the Nizari Ismailis of East Africa."
8. On the schism see Rizvi and King, "Some East African Ithna-Asheri Jamaats (1840–1967)"; Amiji, "Some Notes on Religious Dissent in Nineteenth-Century East Africa."

9. For more see Ruthven, "Aga Khan III and the Ismaili Renaissance"; Paroo, "Aga Khan III and the British Empire."

10. Nanji, "Khojas," 393; Hirji, "The Socio-Legal Formation of the Nizari Ismailis of East Africa"; Hickling, *Disinheriting Daughters, Applying Hindu Laws of Inheritance to the Khoja Muslim Community in Western India, 1847–1937*; Purohit, *The Aga Khan Case*; Shodhan, "Legal Formulation of the Question of Community."

11. Lambek, "Introduction," in *Ordinary Ethics*, 23.

12. On the role of jamatkhanas see community text: Remtilla, *Ismaili Identity and Jamatkhanas in East Africa*.

13. I am grateful to Habib's daughter Shirin Karsan for sharing her father's journals with me. The journals have been translated from Gujarati to English by Zahir Dhalla.

14. Lalani and Dhalla, *A Journal of Life in Kathiawad, Gujarat & Buganda, Uganda*, part 4, 11.

15. On the connection between meals and kinship see Carsten, *After Kinship: New Departures in Anthropology*; Wellman, "Substance, Spirit, and Sociality."

16. Lalani and Dhalla, *A Journal of Life*, part 4, 11.

17. Christie, *Cholera Epidemics in East Africa*.

18. Ibid., 341.

19. Ibid., 342.

20. Iqbal Akhtar dates the establishment of this house for poor Khoja Ismaili women based on a doorway inscription. See Akhtar, *The Khoja of Tanzania*, 111.

21. As noted in Salvadori, *Through Open Doors: A View of Asian Cultures in Kenya*, 225.

22. Akhtar, "The Narrative Prayers (Kahani) of the African Khoja," 221.

23. Amiji, "Some Notes on Religious Dissent in Nineteenth-Century East Africa," 606.

24. Between 1887 and 1921, the total population of Indians in East Africa increased—as a result of both natural reproduction and continued migration—from 6,345 to 54,434. Robert Gregory notes that by 1962, there were 366,013 Asians in East Africa (Gregory, *South Asians in East Africa*, 13; Gregory, *Quest for Equality: Asian Politics in East Africa, 1900–1967*, 4).

25. Christie, *Cholera Epidemics in East Africa*, 337.

26. For more on the lives of Asian settlers, see Seidenberg, *Mercantile Adventurers*; Patel, *Challenge to Colonialism: The Struggle of Alibhai Mulla Jeevanjee for Equal Rights in Kenya*; Oonk, "Gujarati Asians in East Africa"; Markovits, "Indian Merchant Networks outside India in the Nineteenth and Twentieth Centuries."

27. Mumtaz Akberali, "Memories of Zanzibar," http://znzmumtaz.50webs.com/.

28. Shamji as cited in Keshavjee, *Bwana Mzuri: Memories of Hasham Jamal, a Pioneer in Kisumu*, 43. Other examples of Ismaili women in business include Labai Vellani, who came to Zanzibar seeking a divorce from her husband. Hearing that her life would be in danger if she returned to India, she decided to remain in Zanzibar. She became an Ismaili man's second wife and contributed to the family income by helping to run her husband's business. Similarly, when Khatijabai Naran's husband passed away while she was pregnant with their fourth child, she began spending her days rolling cigarettes, which her older son delivered to buyers after school; she later established a *duka*. See details at https://khojawiki.org/Remti_Hassanali_Nasser_Welji. See

also Nusri Hassam, *Sultan Habib Kassam Dewji Family*, December 14, 2011, http://theismailisoftanga50s60s.blogspot.com/p/family-write-ups.html. Evidence of other Ismaili women managing their family's *dukas* in Nairobi, Dar es salaam, and German East Africa can be found in Nair, "At Home, at Work," unpublished paper.

29. Bahadur Kassam, personal interview in English, November 11, 2020.

30. For an account of Alladin and Prembai, who purchased land from German officials, see Patney, *Ties of Bandhana: The Story of Alladin Bapu*, 74–76. See also Mukadam and Mawani, "Excess Baggage," 153; Verjee, "Flag at Half-mast" in Salvadori, *We Came in Dhows*, vol. 2, 34.

31. Adatia and King, "Some East African Firmans," 188.

32. Ebrahim Jamal writes of Kisumu during the 1910s and 1920s in Salvadori, *We Came in Dhows*, vol. 2, 11.

33. Risk of illness sent some settlers back to the larger towns. For more on life in Moshi, see Patney, *Ties of Bandhana*.

34. Many Ismaili women also moved inland with their husbands. After her marriage, Nurbanu Gulamhussein Moledina (b. 1914) moved to the small rural town of Mpigi in Uganda, where husband and wife worked together until they had saved enough to start their own provisions store in Kampala ("Nurbanu Gulamhussein Moledina," http://khojawiki.org/Nurbanu_Gulamhussein_Moledina). When Patlibai (d. 1957) arrived in Mombasa from Gujarat in 1910 with her husband and two children, a relative advised them they would find better trading opportunities in Masaka, so the family undertook the challenging journey by train to Lake Victoria, then by boat to Entebbe and on to Bukakata, and then via palanquin to Masaka. Patlibai was among the first Indian women in Masaka (Dhalla, "Sherbanu Lalani," 14).

35. This account is pieced together from interviews with Maniben's daughter and son-in-law, an unpublished memoir written by her son and daughter-in-law, a family trust document titled "Fulfilling a Dream: Mohammedally and Maniben Rattansi Educational Trust," and oral history accounts gathered in Rattansi Family, "Cultural Confusions," in Salvadori, *We Came in Dhows*, vol. 3, 46.

36. Rattansi Family, "Cultural Confusions," 46.

37. Keshavjee, *Bwana Mzuri*, 15; Shariffa Keshavjee, personal interview in English, March 19, 2021, and July 24, 2021.

38. Hirbai's husbands' names were Dhanjibhai and Ebrahim Samji (last name is spelled as Shamji in some records too). Shariffa Keshavjee, email communication, July 25, 2021.

39. Shamji as cited in Keshavjee, *Bwana Mzuri*, 43.

40. Alibhai, "Tajbibi Abualy Aziz (1926–2019) A Satpanthi Sita." I thank Ali Asani for introducing me to Mohamed Abualy Alibhai.

41. Asani, "From Satpanthi to Ismaili Muslim." For more see Stewart, "In Search of Equivalence: Conceiving Muslim-Hindu Encounter through Translation Theory."

42. Reinhart, *Lived Islam*.

43. Dhalla, "Sherbanu Lalani," 23.

44. Lalani and Dhalla, *A Journal of Life*, part 4, 17–19.

45. Shirinbai's husband, Hasham Jamal, served as president for the years 1905–1914, 1920–1925, and 1931–1946. From 1946 to 1962, he remained "honorary president."

Reported by Shirinbai's granddaughter in Shariffa Keshavjee, *Bwana Mzuri,* 22, with further information via personal communication with Shariffa Keshavjee on March 20, 2021.

46. Mawani, "The Jamat Khana as a Source of Cohesiveness in the Ismaili Community in Kenya," 57.

47. Shirin Karsan, email communication, April 12, 2022.

48. Gulzar Kassam, email communication, November 29, 2020. See also the case of the Verjee cousins in Verjee, "English School Boys," in Salvadori, *We Came in Dhows,* vol. 2, 58–59.

49. Keshavjee, "The Elusive Access to Education for Muslim Women in Kenya from the Late Nineteenth Century to the 'Winds of Change' in Africa (1890s to 1960s)"; Khoja-Moolji, "Redefining Muslim Women: Aga Khan III's Reforms for Women's Education"; Kassam, "The Gender Policies of Aga Khan III and Aga Khan IV."

50. Khoja-Moolji, *Forging the Ideal Educated Girl: The Production of Desirable Subjects in Muslim South Asia.* On concerns about women's education, see oral histories collected by Mawji, "Raced and Gendered Subjectivities *in the Diasporas,*" 43.

51. Cited in Noormohamed-Hunzai, *A Bridge between Two Epochs,* 88.

52. Cited in Malick, *His Royal Highness Prince Aga Khan,* 211.

53. Aga Khan, *India in Transition,* 354 and 258.

54. *Farman* made in 1915, cited in Kassam, "The Gender Policies," 258.

55. *Farman* made in Zanzibar, 1925, cited in Adatia and King, "Some East African Firmans," 187.

56. Kassam, "The Gender Policies," 258.

57. "The Aga Khan Schools in Tanzania," https://www.agakhanschools.org/tanzania.

58. See *farman* made in Rajkot, 1923, cited in Noormohamed-Hunzai, *A Bridge between Two Epochs,* 93. Both Aga Khan III and Aga Khan IV invested extensively in the countries where Ismailis resided, seeking to improve the lives of their followers and of the broader communities within which they lived. Aga Khan III, for instance, established insurance companies, investment trusts, and building societies in East Africa, which provided resources to the less wealthy members of his community to secure loans and housing. Aga Khan IV further established social service institutions such as schools, clinics, and hospitals, which served Ismailis and non-Ismailis alike. He provided aid to governments during disasters—such as in the aftermath of the cyclone in East Pakistan in 1970—and he promoted industrial development. In his *farmans,* he called on Ismailis to build bridges with other communities and to remain loyal citizens of their newly independent nations. Both the Imams have also been active in anticolonial movements and political diplomacy, with Aga Khan III serving as a president of the All India Muslim League and the League of Nations; both have also served as mediators between political entities.

59. Morris, *The Indians in Uganda.*

60. An Aga Khan School for boys was established in Mombasa in 1918, with funds from the Imam and a grant from the British colonial government. The following year, a school for girls was also established. Walji notes that by 1933 government grants covered up to 50 percent of the cost of education in Aga Khan Schools in some districts.

Walji, "A History of the Ismaili Community," 189. See also Keshavjee, "The Redefined Role of the Ismaili Muslim Woman."

61. Keshavjee, *Bwana Mzuri*, 31.

62. Keshavjee, *Bwana Mzuri*, 31. See also Meherwanji, "She Came on Her Own," in Salvadori, *We Came in Dhows*, vol. 2, 164–165; Keshavjee, personal interview in English, March 17, 2021.

63. Jamal, "When Kendu Bay Had a jamatkhana," in Salvadori, *We Came in Dhows*, vol. 2, 178–179.

64. Sakarkhanu Lalji, "A Girl Growing Up in Migori," in Salvadori, *We Came in Dhows*, vol. 2, 181.

65. Gulab Gudka, "A Nice Atmosphere," in Salvadori, *We Came in Dhows*, vol. 2, 172.

66. Keshavjee, *Bwana Mzuri*, 32.

67. *Saak* is curry and *khawo* means eating, but this phrase is also used colloquially to refer to curry and rice.

68. Shariffa Keshavjee, personal interview in English, March 17, 2021.

69. Mawji, "Raced and Gendered Subjectivities," 43; Keshavjee, "The Elusive Access to Education."

70. Trovão, "Doing Family, Gender, Religion and Raced Identities across Generations," 113.

71. Gulzar Kassam, personal interview in English, November 3, 2020.

72. Gulzar Kassam, email communication, November 29, 2020.

73. See *The Official Gazette of the Colony and Protectorate of Kenya*, 1935, 182.

74. Mohamed Abualy Alibhai, email communication, September 19, 2021.

75. Gulbano Jiwan Hirji, a student at the Ismailia Mission Centre, cited in Alibhai, "Tajbibi Abualy Aziz."

76. Yasmin Hirji, personal interview in English, November 16, 2020.

77. Dhalla, *My Tanga Days*, 27.

78. On more about these and other reforms see Asani, "Improving the Status of Women through Reforms in Marriage Contract Law."

79. Nair, "At Home, at Work;" Seidenberg, *Mercantile Adventurers*.

80. Aga Khan III, *Message to the World of Islam*.

81. Noormohamed-Hunzai, *A Bridge between Two Epochs*, 84.

82. Aga Khan III as cited in Calderini, "Female Seclusion and the Veil: Two Issues in Political and Social Discourse," 56.

83. Noormohamed-Hunzai, *A Bridge between Two Epochs*, 96.

84. Dhalla, "Sherbanu Lalani," 18.

85. Noormohamed-Hunzai, *A Bridge between Two Epochs*, 86.

86. *Farman* by Aga Khan III made in Mombasa on June 17, 1945, cited in Noormohamed-Hunzai, *A Bridge between Two Epochs*, 113.

87. Calderini, "Female Seclusion and the Veil," 56.

88. Keshavjee, *Bwana Mzuri*, 33.

89. Kassam-Remtulla, "(Dis)placing Khojahs," 11.

90. Umeeda Switlo, interview February 21, 2014, Oral History Archives, Pier 21.

91. Kara, personal communication, January 2, 2022.

92. Mawji, "Raced and Gendered Subjectivities," 135.

93. Alibhai-Brown, "Racism Is Not Just a White Problem."

94. Paroo, "Playing Politics with the Youth: Aga Khan III's Use of Colonial Education and the Ismaili Girl Guide Movement in British Colonial Tanganyika, 1920–1940."

95. Dhalla, "Sherbanu Lalani," 24.

96. Mawji, "Raced and Gendered Subjectivities," 135–136.

97. Keshavjee, *Into that Heaven of Freedom: The Impact of Apartheid on an Indian Family's Diasporic Journey.*

98. Ismail, "Varas Allidina Visram the Uncrowned King of Uganda," 5.

99. *Farman* made in Nairobi, 1945, as cited in Noormohamed-Hunzai, *A Bridge between Two Epochs*, 107.

100. By 1957 the Aga Khan had personally contributed two hundred thousand pounds to the society, funding the construction of schools, clinics, and mosques throughout East Africa (Aziz, *Aga Khan III*, 1998); Aliaa Paroo points out that Aga Khan Schools began admitting African students by 1953 (Paroo, "Playing Politics with the Youth," 545).

101. Kara, "Abode of Peace," 147.

102. Nanji, "Modernization and Change," 135. On the Aga Khan's advising his community to obtain Ugandan citizenship, see also Grondelle, *The Ismailis in the Colonial Era*; on how other Indians made decisions related to citizenship see Oonk, "Gujarati Asians in East Africa."

103. Somjee, *Bead Bai*; Somjee, *Home between Crossings*. See also Padurang, "Imaginings of Khoja, Maasai and Swahili Aesthetics in Artist Ethnographer Sultan Somjee's Narratives."

104. Delgado and Stefancic, *Critical Race Theory*, 8.

105. Manjapra, *Colonialism in Global Perspective*, 13.

106. G.V., personal interview in English, June 9, 2021; Almas Lalji, personal interview in English, January 20, 2020. Almas found a job in Toronto the first week she was looking. Her husband's educational background was in earth sciences, and he had some trouble finding a job. Thus, for the first five to six months in Canada, Almas was the primary earner for her family.

107. Roshan Kajani, personal interview in Urdu, November 4, 2020.

108. Karima (pseudonym), personal interview in English and Urdu, April 9, 2020.

109. J.A., personal interview in Urdu, December 23, 2019, and subsequent conversations in December 2020, December 2021, March 2022.

110. Merchant, *Mountains before Me.*

111. Kamaluddin Ali Muhammad, email communication, June 6, 2021; Madad Ali estimates there were five hundred Ismailis in Mymensingh in 1970 (personal interview in Urdu, July 2, 2019); Anwar Somani estimates the jamat in Chittagong as including fifteen hundred (personal interview in Urdu, December 19, 2019); Ayeleen Ajanee Saleh estimates about fifteen to twenty thousand Ismailis in East Pakistan by the late 1960s (Saleh, "A Case Study of the Ismaili Jamat in Bangladesh").

112. Mumtaz Noordin, personal interview in Urdu, December 22, 2019.

113. Saleh, "A Case Study of the Ismaili Jamat in Bangladesh," 24.

114. Enayet Jiwani, personal interview in English, May 5, 2020.

115. Husain, *Journey with the Gods*, 22.

116. In 1960, the Imam also visited West Pakistan to attend the opening ceremony for a residential society in Karimabad. That society would later house several displaced families, including my mother's family, who moved there in the early-1970s.

117. Speech by Aga Khan IV in 1970 in Dhaka, first published in *Ismaili Mirror*, 1970, Special Edition, http://ismaili.net/heritage/node/34607, accessed July 13, 2021.

118. Speech by Aga Khan IV during a civic reception arranged by Dacca Municipal Corporation as cited in *Ismaili Forum*, Souvenir issue (1979): 18.

119. Malek Batada, personal interview in Urdu, January 4, 2020.

120. Z.H., personal interview in Urdu, December 23, 2019.

121. Saleh, "A Case Study of the Ismaili Jamat in Bangladesh," 11.

122. Nargis Somani, personal interview in Urdu, February 13, 2021.

123. Dilshad Sadruddin, personal interview in Urdu, January 9, 2019.

124. Interview recording shared by Sherbanu's son, Aziz Ajani, 2019.

125. Noorjehan Hadi (Dolat Valliani's daughter), personal interview in Urdu, July 18, 2021.

126. Farida Khoja and Zarin Taj Huda, personal interview in Urdu, July 18, 2021. A boys academy was managed by the Aga Khan Education Board as well.

127. Zarin Taj Huda, personal interview in Urdu, July 18, 2021.

128. As cited in Saleh, "A Case Study of the Ismaili Jamat in Bangladesh," 18.

129. Ibid.

130. Zarintaj Sultan, personal interview in Urdu and English, December 23, 2021.

131. Farida Merchant, personal interview in English, April 6, 2021.

132. Merchant, *Mountains before Me*, 49.

133. Ibid., 35–36.

134. Saleh, "A Case Study of the Ismaili Jamat in Bangladesh," 37; Mehrunissa and Sultan Ali Rajwany, personal interview in Urdu, December 17, 2019.

135. S.D., personal interview in Urdu, January 8, 2019.

136. *Ginan* text and translation from Zarina Kamaluddin and Kamaluddin Ali Muhammad, *Ginan with English Translation and Glossary*.

137. Munira Dhanani, personal interview in English, January 14, 2020.

138. Mawji, "Raced and Gendered Subjectivities," 30, 223, 229.

139. Ibid., 215.

140. K.F., personal interview in Urdu, July 7, 2020, and March 24, 2021.

Interlude

1. Z.H., personal interview in Urdu, December 23, 2019.

2. Karima (pseudonym to protect anonymity), personal interview in English, April 9, 2020.

3. Munira Dhanani, personal interview in English, January 14, 2020.

4. Umeeda Switlo, personal interview in English, May 26, 2020.

Chapter 3

1. I have constructed this account based on personal interviews and email communications with Sakarkhanu's son-in-law, Dr. Mohammad Manji, November 10–17, 2020; biographical notes written by Sakarkhanu's daughter for Khoja Wiki; and photos and documents her family shared with me.

2. See Dunn, "Islam in Sydney: Contesting the Discourse of Absence"; Krause and Bastida, "Church-Based Social Relationships, Belonging, and Health among Older Mexican Americans"; Wu et al., "Religion and Refugee Well-Being: The Importance of Inclusive Community."

3. Horst and Grabska, "Introduction: Flight and Exile"; Adam and Ward, "Stress, Religious Coping and Wellbeing in Acculturating Muslims."

4. Jacobsen and Kumar, *South Asians in the Diaspora*, xiii.

5. Mawani, "Sanctuary for the Soul: The Centrality of the Jamatkhana in Religious Identity Formation"; Mazumdar and Mazumdar, "Religious Placemaking and Community Building in Diaspora."

6. Moser and Feldman, *Locating the Sacred*, 1.

7. Thrift, "But Malice Aforethought," 136, 146.

8. Tuan, *Topophilia: A Study of Environmental Perceptions, Attitudes, and Values*, 4.

9. Sherbanoo Ajani, audio interview, 2019. Shared with me by her son, Aziz Ajani.

10. J.A., personal conversation in Urdu in Atlanta jamatkhana, March 21, 2022.

11. Shia Ismaili Tariqa Board for Pakistan, *Ginan Sharif with Translation*, part I.

12. Mawani, "The Jamatkhana: Exploring its Prehistories and Hegemony in the Twentieth Century"; See also Mawani, *Beyond the Mosque: Diverse Spaces of Muslim Worship*, 86.

13. In smaller congregations and for certain *majalis* (religious gatherings), women have been appointed as *mukhiani* or *kamadiani* independent of their relationship to men.

14. Hirji, "The Socio-Legal Formation of the Nizari Ismailis," 143. For more about the constitutions that established these Councils see Nanji, "Modernization and Change in the Nizari Ismaili Community in East Africa." Earlier the Imam had appointed *punjebhais* (literally "five brothers") to adjudicate disputes.

15. Hirji, "Socio-Legal Formation of the Nizari Ismailis," 152.

16. For how rituals intersect with women's daily life see Dossa, "Ritual and Daily Life: Transmission and Interpretation of the Ismaili Tradition in Vancouver."

17. The jamatkhana in Zanzibar, for instance, used to have a separate entrance and prayer space for women. For a detailed study of jamatkhanas in Kenya see Mawani, "The Jamat Khana as a Source of Cohesiveness."

18. Wealthy families often donated money to support the construction of jamatkhanas, in addition to grants received from the Imam. While women patrons of jamatkhanas were not numerous, they did exist. In 1937, a Mrs. Virbai donated twenty-five thousand shillings to build a jamatkhana, a school, a library, and a traveler's residence in Jinja ("Pride of Jinja," *Golden Jubilee Africa Number*, 1885–1935, Golden Jubilee edition). Women also participated in other ways, including by supporting husbands who were directly engaged in construction. When a new jamatkhana was constructed in Iringa in the 1930s, a woman named Bachibai "would hold the lantern" while her

husband did the masonry work: "Tak-tak-tak, the children would hear their father hammering on the stones next door" (Mohammad Manji, personal interview in English, November 10, 2020).

19. Keshavjee, *Bwana Mzuri*, 33.

20. Message from Imam dated August 23, 1952, cited in Noormohamed-Hunzai, *A Bridge between Two Epochs*, 118.

21. Mawani and Velji, "Towards a Tradition of Service."

22. The literary section continued to function as the Vidhya Vinod Club and was later renamed as the Recreation Club Institute.

23. Mawani and Velji, "Towards a Tradition of Service."

24. Shirin Sondhi (daughter of Maniben Rattansi), personal interview in English, November 7, 2020, and November 10, 2020.

25. Laila Bandali, personal interview in English, November 18, 2020, followed by email communication, September 28, 2021.

26. Nazira Mawji, personal interview in English, November 25, 2020.

27. Shaida Adatia, personal interview in English, November 17, 2020.

28. Dhalla, *My Tanga Days*, 150.

29. By the late twentieth century greater numbers of women were trained and authorized by the Ismaili institutions as *waezin*.

30. Salma Tejpar, personal interview in English, December 3, 2020, and May 6, 2022, followed by email communication, June 29, 2021, and May 7, 2022.

31. Salma Tejpar, email communication, June 29, 2021.

32. Salma Tejpar, email communication, May 7, 2022.

33. "Religious Discussion Held at Countess Bhachibai Tejpar's Residence on Mar 26/65 at 9 p.m.," private papers.

34. The Sanskrit term "*satsang*" denotes being in the company of good people or in the company of truth.

35. Nazira Mawji, personal interview in English, November 25, 2020.

36. This home for unmarried mothers also appears in Shelina Zia-Shariff's memoir, *Nairobi Days*; the author identifies her grandmother as one of the women who volunteered for the facility.

37. Salma Tejpar, personal interview in English, May 6, 2022, and email communication, May 7, 2022.

38. Nazira Mawji, personal interview in English, November 25, 2020. In contrast to Khoja Ismailis, Khoja Ithnasharis have retained some sacred spaces that are not controlled by their councils. Akhtar writes about *mehphils* (shrines dedicated to Shia saints or a martyr of Karbala) in Dar es Salaam that serve as communal gathering spaces for older women. Such spaces exist alongside the mosque and the *imamvado* (a communal hall for the observance of rites and rituals). See Akhtar, *The Khoja of Tanzania*.

39. On this point also see Alia Paroo, "Knowing One Another: Honoring Our Women and Foremothers," Critical Conversations, Ismaili Tariqa and Religious Education Board for USA, March 7, 2021.

40. Fatima as quoted in Trovão, "Doing Family, Gender, Religion and Raced Identities across Generations," 107.

41. Fariyal Ross-Sheriff, personal interview in English, January 16, 2023.

42. Among the first Ismailis to become residents in the United States were college students and professionals from India, Pakistan, and several African countries, who were allowed entry under the Immigration and Nationality Act of 1965. The act modified the National Origins Formula that had previously restricted immigration to primarily from northern and western Europe. Alyshea Cummins notes that the first Ismaili to arrive in Canada was a Pakistani, Safarali Ismaily, who settled in Ottawa in 1952 (Cummins, "Making space through public engagements Canadian Ismaili Muslims," 296).

43. Shirin Karsan, personal interview in English, December 19, 2019.

44. Sumera (pseudonym), personal interview in Urdu and English, January 13, 2020.

45. Editors, "Editorial," *Canadian Ismaili* (July 1976): 5.

46. According to an institutional update in the *American Ismaili* (December 1979, vol. 1, no. 3), jamats could now be found in Atlanta, Boston, Chicago, Cleveland, Columbia, Des Moines, Connecticut, Edison, East Lansing, Fort Wayne, Fort Lauderdale, Lancaster, Miami, Minneapolis, Milwaukee, New York, Normal, Orlando, Philadelphia, Royersford, Spartanburg, Tampa Bay, Washington, and Poughkeepsie. The article further notes that "religious classes are held in most established jamatkhanas."

47. For another account of a makeshift jamatkhana see Dhalla, *The Willowdale Jamatkhana Story*; Shirin Sadrudin Jaffer established one in Los Angeles as early as April 1967.

48. Gulzar Kassam, personal interview in English, December 15, 2020.

49. Iqbal Paroo, personal interview in English, December 14, 2020.

50. R.K., personal interview in English, January 6, 2020.

51. Naila Jamal, personal interview in English and Urdu, January 6, 2020.

52. Hubbard, "Space/Place," 42.

53. Lefebvre, *The Production of Space*, 105. See also Anttonen, "Space, Body, and the Notion of Boundary."

54. Rehmat Nanji, interviewed by a relative, December 14, 2020, shared with me by Rehmat.

55. This account is based on interviews with Kulsum and Daulat's daughters (Roshan Pirani, personal interview in English and Urdu, July 20, 2021, and Shiroz Virani, personal interview in English, November 20, 2020, and email communication on July 10, 2022).

56. Roshan Pirani, personal interview in English and Urdu, July 20, 2021.

57. In the 1980s, it was organized at a building at the intersection of Wester Masterson Avenue and Calhoun Street, and in the 1990s, at North Coliseum Boulevard.

58. *Anant akhado* is a *ginan* by *pir* Hasan Kabirdin. For more see Kamaluddin and Muhammad Ali, *Anant Akhado and Anant Na Nav Chugga*. See Nelson, "Sensing the Sacred: Anglican Material Religion in Early South Carolina," for more on how objects and rituals mark a change from common to scared time.

59. Jones, "The Makeshift and the Contingent: Lefebvre and the Production of Precarious Sacred Space," 179.

60. Ibid., 190.

61. Rozina Jivraj cited in Shahzia Pirani-Mellstrom, Fort Wayne Ismaili Muslim Jamat 1972–2015, PowerPoint, August 2022.

62. Sumera (pseudonym), personal interview in Urdu and English, January 13, 2021.

63. Mawani, "The Jamat Khana as a Source of Cohesiveness," 7.

64. Berlant, "Intimacy," 284 (emphasis in original).

65. Other ships that Ismailis boarded from Chittagong included the SS *Rustam* and the SS *Ohrmazd*.

66. Interviews with J.A., Enayet Lalani, Farida Merchant, and Roshan Pirani.

67. See Coward and Goa, *Mantra: Hearing the Divine in India and America*; Qureshi, *Sufi Music of India and Pakistan: Sound, Context, and Meaning in Qawwali*.

68. Srinivas, *In the Presence of Sai Baba*, 77–78.

69. Laila Datoo, personal interview in English, November 30, 2020.

70. *Ginan* text and translation from Kamaluddin and Muhammad Ali, *Ginan with English Translation and Glossary*.

71. Khurshid Bhimani, personal interview in English, February 3, 2021.

72. An editorial published in the March 1977 issue of *Canadian Ismaili* reiterates this message: "An extract from Mowlana Sultan Mohamed Shah's firman gives the Ismaili volunteer the supreme driving motive in his service to this community: 'he that serves me most becomes nearer to me'" (3–4).

73. Leila Hirji, personal interview in English, February 20, 2021.

74. See also Kayikci, *Islamic Ethics and Female Volunteering*, 3.

75. Mol, Moser, and Pols describe care as a style and mode of living in *Care in Practice: On Tinkering in Clinics, Homes, and Farms*, 13.

76. Jamal, *Embodying Ethics, Performing Pluralism: Volunteerism among Ismailis in Houston, TX*.

77. K.F., personal conversation in Urdu, July 7, 2020; follow-up on March 24, 2021.

78. Fieldnotes, November 2019, Atlanta jamatkhana *safai*.

79. Ghosh, "A World of Their Very Own: Religion, Pain and Subversion in Bengali Homes in the Nineteenth Century," 214.

80. Ibid., 214–215.

81. Mawji, "Raced and Gendered Subjectivities," 206.

82. Ibid., 247.

83. See the story of Fatima in Trovão, "Doing Family," 106–107.

84. Keshavjee, "The Redefined Role of the Ismaili Muslim Woman," 218–219.

85. Ibid.

86. Fieldnotes, Atlanta jamatkhana, November 2019.

87. *Kumb* is a small bowl and *pyali* is a small cup used for the *ab-e-shifa* ceremony.

88. Congregants continue to address women and men who have served as *Mukhi*, *Mukhiani*, *Kamadia*, and *Kamadiani* with these honorifics long after their official terms have concluded.

Chapter 4

1. Shamsuddin [last name withheld to protect anonymity], personal interview in Urdu, January 8, 2019.
2. Erll, "Locating the Family in Cultural Memory Studies," 307.
3. Mittermaier, "Dreams and the Miraculous," 111.
4. For more see al-Nu'man, *Da'a'im al-Islam* and Amir-Moezzi, *The Spirituality of Shi'i Islam*. Shia Imam Ja'far as-Sadiq said, "It is through us that God is served, through us that He is obeyed, and through us that He is disobeyed. He, therefore who obeys us, has indeed obeyed God, and he who disobeys us has disobeyed God. Obedience to us [the Imams] was determined by God for His creation from before [the time of creation]. Thus no act from any person is acceptable to Him except through our agency, no person is shown mercy except through us, and no man is subjected to punishment except through us, for we are the gateway to God and His proof, His custodians in respect of His creation, the guardians of His secret, and the repository of His knowledge" (cited in Qadi Nu'man, *Da'a'im al-Islam*, 75).
5. Butticci and Mittermaier, "Afterword." See also Kasmani, "On Un/Worlding: Fakirs, Fairies and the Dead in Pakistan"; Kasmani, "Grounds of Becoming: Fakirs among the Dead in Sehwan Sharif, Pakistan"; Selim, "Learning the Elsewhere of 'Inner Space.'"
6. Narayan, *Storytellers, Saints, and Scoundrels*.
7. See Zargar, *The Polished Mirror: Storytelling and the Pursuit of Virtue in Islamic Philosophy and Sufism*; Lawless, *God's Peculiar People*; Star and Finke, *Acts of Faith: Explaining the Human Side of Religion*.
8. Singleton, "'Your Faith Has Made You Well': The Role of Storytelling in the Experience of Miraculous Healing."
9. Dein, "Miracles, Media, Mezuzot: Storytelling among Chabad Hasidim."
10. See Quran, chapter 21, verse 69; chapter 7, verses 104–109.
11. See Quran, chapter 5, verse 27; chapter 7, verse 16.
12. For more on miracles, dreams, and visions in Islam see Thomas, "Miracles in Islam"; Weddle, *Miracles: Wonder and Meaning in World Religions*; Yazicioglu, *Understanding the Qur'anic Miracle Stories in the Modern Age*; Green, "The Religious and Cultural Roles of Dreams and Visions in Islam"; Ewing, "The Dream of Spiritual Initiation and the Organization of Self: Representations among Pakistani Sufis"; Kasmani, "Pilgrimage of the Dream."
13. Renard, *Friends of God: Islamic Images of Piety, Commitment, and Servanthood*, 95.
14. Renard, *Islam and the Heroic Image*, 119. Some Muslim schools of thought are skeptical of saintly marvels and question the existence of otherworldly creatures such as jinns, emphasizing instead rational religious sensibilities. See also Doostdar, *The Iranian Metaphysicals*.
15. Pierce, *Twelve Infallible Men*, 106.
16. Sikander Ali Khoja, personal interview in Sindhi, December 20, 2020.
17. Nünning, "Making Events—Making Stories—Making Worlds," 201.
18. Ibid.

19. In a *ginan pir* Sadr al-din says: *Eji duldul ghode Ali chadshe shaha, chadshe shaha, Chadi chaud bhavan manhe varatiyo* (O brother! Mawla Ali will ride Duldul horse and will spread in the fourteen worlds). Translation from Kamaluddin and Kamaluddin, *50 Ginans with English Translation and Glossary,* vol. 7.

20. Schaefer, *Religious Affects,* 3, 9, 17.

21. Shams, personal interview in Urdu, July 6, 2019.

22. Husain, *Journey with the Gods,* unpublished memoir.

23. Ibid., 151–153.

24. Ibid., 153.

25. Z.H., personal interview in Urdu, December 23, 2019.

26. Chavoshian, "Dream-Realities."

27. Jamal, "Work No Words," 72.

28. Grondelle, *The Ismailis in the Colonial Era,* 96–97.

29. Ibid., 99.

30. For more see Miserez, *Prince Sadruddin Aga Khan.*

31. Laila Datoo, personal interview in English, November 30, 2020.

32. Gilsenan, *Saint and Sufi in Modern Egypt,* 32. For more on sacred narrative genres see Chen, "A Discussion on the Concept of 'Sacred Narrative.'"

33. N.A., personal interview in Urdu, December 22, 2019.

34. A couple of years later, I met Zarintaj Sultan, who shared a verse from a *ginan* to make a similar point about a woman who had helped her get admission to nursing school: "You know how it says, *maannas rupe saaheb* (the Lord will take human form), so it was *Mawla* in her form" (Zarintaj Sultan, personal interview in Urdu and English, December 23, 2021).

35. Merchant, *Mountains before Me,* 58.

36. Ibid., 67.

37. Ibid., 125, 104.

38. Ibid., 144.

39. Ibid., 169.

40. Almas Lalji, personal interview in English, May 2, 2020; see also her interview with Shezan Muhammedi for the Uganda Collection Oral History Project at Carleton University, May 12, 2015.

41. Rossbina Nathoo, personal interview in English, January 14, 2020; see also her interview with Shezan Muhammedi for the Uganda Collection Oral History Project at Carleton University, July 20, 2015.

42. Zarintaj Huda, personal interview in Urdu, December 25, 2019. The belief that the Imam's guidance protects Ismailis was expressed not only by those Ismailis who fled East Pakistan or East Africa in the 1970s but also by those who fled violence related to the partition of India in the 1940s and 1950s. Farida Hussain Noorani (b. 1945) recalls her family's quandary when Imam Sultan Mahomed Shah asked her older brother to move the entire family from Gujarat to Pune. Her family—not unlike the family of Roshan Kajani, whom we met in chapter 2—was quite wealthy, owning seven mills and five shops; their house had ten rooms. Mystified yet dutiful, the family packed up their lives and moved to Pune. There they struggled at first, because they had been

able to bring only limited savings with them. When I asked Farida Noorani why her parents made this move, which seemed at odds with their interests, she immediately answered, "Because the Imam said so. *He knows the future.*" Reflecting further, she explained that it was in Pune that she was able to attend an English-language convent school, an opportunity that would not have been available to her in Gujarat and that has served her well in life. She explains, "The Imam wanted his *jamat* to live in cities where they could get better education." The Imam's knowledge of the future had set her family on a prosperous trajectory, "*Shukar*" (Farida Hussain Noorani, personal interview in Urdu and Gujarati, November 27, 2020. Special thanks to Nuhad Pirani for arranging this interview).

43. Madad Ali, personal interview in Urdu, July 20, 2019.

44. Mittermaier, "Dreams and the Miraculous," 112.

45. Gilsenan, *Recognizing Islam*, 75.

46. Anthony Shenoda cited in Mittermaier, "Dreams and the Miraculous," 114. Emphasis in original.

47. For more about this incidence see Muhammad and Kamaluddin, *Golden Memories: A Short Autobiography*, 43.

48. The Shams steamer was part of the Crescent Shipping Lines Limited, which belonged to Muhammad Amin Muhammad Bashir Limited, owned by a Punjabi family from Lahore (Amirali Moolji, email communication, December 14, 2020). On her last emergency voyage from East Pakistan in 1971—carrying 3,500 passengers and likely no cargo—the Shams steamer was briefly stuck in the port of Chalna but managed to escape. The ship operated until 1994, carrying passengers (often for Hajj) and cargo from Karachi to the Arabian Peninsula. See "Crescent Shipping Lines Ltd," http://pakistan-national-shipping.blogspot.com/2013/05/crescent-shipping-lines-ltd.html.

49. Farhana Esmail, personal interview in English, August 27, 2021.

50. On the transmission of Hindu teachings see Narayan, *Storytellers, Saints, and Scoundrels*.

51. Narayan, "Haunting Stories." See also Narayan, "Placing Lives through Stories: Second Generation South Asian Americans."

52. Nünning, "Making Events—Making Stories—Making Worlds," 192.

Chapter 5

1. *Bhel puri* is a popular street food with origins in Gujarat, formerly home to a large Ismaili Muslim population. It consists of deep-fried puff pastries (*puri*), deep-fried strings of chickpea flour (*sev*), puffed rice, onions, spices mixed with tamarind, and a cilantro-based sauce (chutney).

2. See Dossa, *Afghanistan Remembers: Gendered Narrations of Violence and Culinary Practices*, 32; Ahad, "Post-Blackness and Culinary Nostalgia in Marcus Samuelsson's *Yes, Chef*," 7.

3. Howes, "Introduction," in *Empire of the Sense*, 5. See also Walmsley, "Race, Place and Taste: Making Identities Through Sensory Experience in Ecuador," 56.

4. Tomczak, "On Exile, Memory and Food," 230.

5. On this topic see Tompkins, "Literary Approaches to Food Studies"; Cho, *Eating Chinese: Culture on the Menu in Small Town Canada*.

6. Umedaly and Spence, *Mamajee's Kitchen* (2005); Nimji, *A Spicy Touch*, vol. 1, *Indian Cooking with a Contemporary Approach* (1986); Nimji, *A Spicy Touch*, vol. 2, *Contemporary Indian, African, and Middle Eastern Cuisine* (1992); Nimji, *A Spicy Touch*, vol. 3, *A Fusion of East African and Indian Cuisine* (2007); Nimji and Anderson, *A Spicy Touch*, vol. 4, *Family Favourites from Noorbanu Nimji's Kitchen* (2015/2020); Alibhai-Brown, *The Settler's Cookbook: A Memoir of Love, Migration and Food* (2009).

7. Sack, *Whitebread Protestants: Food and Religion in American Culture*, 62.

8. Alibhai-Brown, *The Settler's Cookbook*, 221; Umedaly, *Mamajee's Kitchen*, 170; Nimji, *A Spicy Touch I*, 74, 99, 100.

9. Black, "Recipes for Cosmopolitanism: Cooking across Borders in the South Asian Diaspora," 3–4. See also Wheaton, "Finding Real Life in Cookbooks: The Adventures of a Culinary Historian"; Tompkins, "Consider the Recipe."

10. Bailey-Dick, "The Kitchenhood of All Believers: A Journey into the Discourse of Mennonite Cookbooks"; Gold, *Danish Cookbooks: Domesticity and National Identity, 1616–1901*; Eves, "A Recipe for Remembrance: Memory and Identity in African-American Women's Cookbooks."

11. Theophano, *Eat My Words: Reading Women's Lives through the Cookbooks They Wrote*, 6.

12. Eves, "A Recipe for Remembrance," 282.

13. Yasmin Alibhai-Brown, personal interview in English, October 8, 2020; Alibhai-Brown, *The Settler's Cookbook*, 14.

14. Alibhai-Brown, *The Settler's Cookbook*, 14.

15. Ibid.

16. Ibid., 13.

17. Ibid., 41, 16. See also Tompkins, "Literary Approaches to Food Studies," 245.

18. Alibhai-Brown, *The Settler's Cookbook*, 59.

19. About traveling by *dhow* in 1901, Nanji Mehta recalls, "When the wind raised heavy waves, we were put to great trouble while cooking. On such days we satisfied ourselves with fried buns, boiled grams [*khichiri*] and other eatables that could be easily prepared" (Nanji Mehta, "My First Dhow Voyage 1901," in Salvadori, *We Came in Dhows*, vol. 1, 13). Karsonbhai Premji Gangji Bhudia recalls how his family lived in their early days in Mombasa in 1937: "Usually about 10-15 men would live together in one 'house', which would consist simply of one large room. Living conditions in our house were typical, except we were a particularly large group, about 30 people, both grown men and some schoolboys like myself. We slept on cotton mattresses, about three inches thick, laid out on the floor. During the day they would be rolled up, out of the way. People had very few possessions, usually two or three sets of shirts and trousers. . . . [T]he kitchen was in one corner of the room; the stove was three stones,

the fuel was firewood. In our household I did the cooking. After school I and the other school boys would prepare the food for everyone in the household. The main meal was in the evening. The food consisted of boiled beans ('kichdi') and chapatis and yoghurt and milk. The was our diet except on every eleventh day (Ekadasi days) when we would eat boiled potatoes and groundnuts and dates. In the morning our breakfast was leftovers and tea" (Karsonbhai Premji Gangji Bhudia cited in "Cramped Quarters," in Salvadori, *We Came in Dhows*, vol. 1, 131). Writing about her own experience of heading back to India in the 1940s, Mankunwarba Jethwa explains, "Kichree was the food most people made since it was so easy to prepare" (Mankunwarba Jethwa, "A Maritime Miracle," in Salvadori, *We Came in Dhows*, vol. 1, 13).

20. Alibhai-Brown, *The Settler's Cookbook*, 72.
21. Ibid., 62, 225.
22. Ibid., 102, 175.
23. Ibid.
24. Classen, "The Odor of the Other: Olfactory Symbolism and Cultural Categories," 134; Rhys-Taylor, "Disgust and Distinction: The Case of the Jellied Eel," 237.
25. Rhys-Taylor, "Disgust and Distinction."
26. Alibhai-Brown, *The Settler's Cookbook*, 78.
27. Ibid., 80.
28. Ibid., 20.
29. Ibid., 10.
30. Ibid., 27., 8,
31. Alibhai-Brown, personal interview in English, October 8, 2020.
32. Alibhai-Brown, *The Settler's Cookbook*, 15, 166.
33. Ibid., 15, 225.
34. Ibid., 166–167.
35. Ibid., 167.
36. Alibhai-Brown, personal interview in English, October 8, 2020.
37. Ibid.
38. Ibid.
39. Ibid.
40. Khadija Mangalji, personal interview in English, April 1, 2020.
41. *Farmans* about consumption of beef made on April 18, 1925, in Nairobi and on July 13 and July 12, 1945, in Dar es Salaam.
42. The printer advanced the cost of the initial print run.
43. Nimji, *A Spicy Touch*, vol. 1, back cover.
44. Ibid., 82.
45. Ibid., 1, 7.
46. Ibid., 1, 3.
47. See advertisement in *Canadian Ismaili*, July 1988, p. 36.
48. Eidinger, "*A Treasure for My Daughter* and the Creation of a Jewish Cultural Orthodoxy in Postwar Montreal."
49. Epp, "Eating across Borders: Reading Immigrant Cookbooks," 64, 56.
50. Nimji, *A Spicy Touch*, vol. 1, 3.

51. Shirin Karsan, personal interview in English, December 9, 2019; Rashida Haji, personal interview in English, November 16, 2020; Munira Dhanani, personal interview in English, January 14, 2020.

52. Naseem Teja, email communication, January 8, 2021. Shared with me by Khadija Mangalji.

53. Theophano, *Eat My Words*, 7.

54. Nimji, *A Spicy Touch*, vol. 2, publisher's jacket copy.

55. This is the subtitle for the third edition of *A Spicy Touch*. See Nimji, *A Spicy Touch*, vol. 3.

56. Nimji and Anderson, *A Spicy Touch*, vol. 4 (2020 edition), 15.

57. Karen Anderson, personal interview in English, April 1, 2020.

58. See for instance Nimji and Anderson, *A Spicy Touch*, vol. 4 (2020 edition), 12, 151. These additions may in part also reflect the publisher (or the food writer coauthor) standardizing Noorbanu's recipes to fit publishers' conventions for cookbooks.

59. Nimji and Anderson, *A Spicy Touch*, vol. 4 (2020 edition), 12.

60. Tompkins, "Consider the Recipe," 440.

61. Nimji and Anderson, *A Spicy Touch*, vol. 4 (2020 edition), 68.

62. Jadavji, "A Spicy Touch and Chana Wagharia," https://foodmamma.com/2016/01/a-spicy-touch-and-chana-wagharia/, accessed July 18, 2022.

63. Jadavji, "Instant Pot Khichri."

64. Jadavji, "Saffron Almond Milk."

65. Muneera Spence, personal interview in English, March 23, 2020.

66. Smith, "Preface: Styling Sensory History," 471.

67. Seremetakis, "The Memory of the Senses," 4.

68. Eves, "A Recipe for Remembrance," 291.

69. Umedaly and Spence, *Mamajee's Kitchen*, 178.

70. Ibid.

71. Ibid.

72. Hurst and Lawrence, "(Re)Placing, Remembering, Revealing," 305.

73. Umedaly and Spence, *Mamajee's Kitchen*, 36.

74. Ibid., 102.

75. Ibid., 116.

76. Ibid., 99.

77. On "connective sensory histories" inscribed in food see Ray, "Migration, Transnational Cuisines, and Invisible Ethnics," 210.

78. Sutton, *Remembrance of Repasts*, 28.

79. On culinary motherlines see Sarkar, "Religious Recipes: Culinary Motherlines of Feasts and Fasts in India," 75.

80. On how women's culinary activities reproduce their subordination within the domestic sphere see Bose, *Women in the Hindu Tradition: Rules, Roles and Exceptions*; Appadurai, "Gastro-Politics in Hindu South Asia."

81. Kumar and Sanyal, "Introduction," in *Food, Faith, and Gender in South*, 3.

82. Locher, Yoels, Maurer, and van Ells, "Comfort Foods: An Exploratory Journey into the Social and Emotional Significance of Food," 280.

83. Alibhai-Brown, *The Settler's Cookbook*, 17.

Chapter 6

1. Furhana Husani, personal interview in English, August 7, 2021.
2. Dakake, "What Do We Owe to Others?"
3. Furhana Husani's maternal grandfather, Isaack Moosa, was born in India but after partition established his business in Dhaka. Her maternal grandmother, Shirin Moosa, was born in Zanzibar but at a young age was sent to Karachi to be raised by her grandfather because her parents could not afford to keep all their children. While Isaack worked in East Pakistan, his wife and children, including Furhana's mother, mostly stayed in West Pakistan. During the 1970s, Isaack's business was nationalized and he eventually had to flee Dhaka. The family stayed on in Karachi for a bit but soon Furhana's mother along with her brother headed to London and then to Toronto in search of economic stability. In Toronto, Furhana's mother married an Ismaili man, and Furhana was born in 1978. Furhana says, "There's so much migration in my family [laughing]. So, we have family that's in East Africa and then a whole family that's in Pakistan as well."
4. Rozina Jivraj, personal interview in English, August 31, 2021.
5. According to Jamal, by 2008 there were seventy-five jamatkhanas in the United States (Jamal, "Work No Words," 226); according to Cummins, by 2012 there were eighty jamatkhanas in Canada (Cummins, "Alleviating the Clash of Ignorance(s): *An Ismaili Muslim Initiative in Canada*," 92).
6. For more see Steinberg, *Ismaili Modern*.
7. I am using a pseudonym and have modified some details as requested by this interlocutor. Personal interview in English, 2020.
8. Jamal, *Where the Air Is Sweet*, 236.
9. Hirsch, *The Generation of Postmemory: Writing and Visual Culture after the Holocaust*. On postmemories of second-generation Sikhs see Devgan, "Re-Presenting Pasts: Sikh Diasporic and Digital Memories of 1984."
10. Fischer, *Memory Work: The Second Generation*, 6.
11. As cited in Okeowo, "How Saidiya Hartman Retells the History of Black Life."
12. Based on personal interview with Tasneem Jamal on August 27, 2021, and her interview with TVO, July 21, 2014.
13. Tasneem Jamal, personal interview in English, August 27, 2021.
14. Ibid.
15. Ibid.
16. Jamal, *Where the Air Is Sweet*, 191.
17. Ibid., 192.
18. Ibid., 27.
19. Ibid., 108.
20. Ibid., 107.
21. Karmali, *A House by the Sea*, 31, 42, 47.
22. Ibid., 203.
23. Ibid., 63.
24. Ibid., 63.

25. Ibid., 64.

26. Ibid., 170.

27. Mawji, "Raced and Gendered Subjectivities."

28. Sikeena Karamali, personal interview in English, August 10, 2021.

29. Karmali, *A House by the Sea*, 172, 196.

30. Ibid., 190.

31. Sikeena Karamali, personal interview in English, August 10, 2021.

32. Ibid.

33. Ibid.

34. Hirsch, "Stateless Memory," 419.

35. On creative work as self-determining see Ohito, "Some of Us Die: A Black Feminist Researcher's Survival Method for Creatively Refusing Death and Decay in the Neoliberal Academy"; Sierschynski, "Improvising Identity, Body, and Race."

36. Archival footage in private collections.

37. Almas Lalji, personal interview in English, January 20, 2020.

38. Rossbina Nathoo, personal interview in English, January 14, 2020; see also interviews with Rossbina Nathoo, and Zul and Yasmin Rupani, in the Ugandan Asian Archive Oral History Project.

39. Editors, "Editorial," *Canadian Ismaili 1*, no. 1 (1978): 3.

40. Mohamed, interviewed by Shezan Muhammadi, May 12, 2015, the Ugandan Asian Archive Oral History Project.

41. Ringette is a noncontact winter team sport played on an ice rink. Gulamhusein, "Living in the In-Between as an Ismaili Muslim Woman," 110. I also draw on my interview with Shemine conducted on August 10, 2021.

42. Gulamhusein, "Living in the In-Between as an Ismaili Muslim Woman," 111.

43. Nafisa Dhanani, personal interview in English, August 16, 2021.

44. Romana Kassam, personal interview in English, September 7, 2021.

45. Nafisa Dhanani, personal interview in English, August 16, 2021.

46. Salima Bhimani, personal interview in English, June 2, 2020.

47. Bhimani, "Mapping the Assembly of Muslim Exceptionality," 284–285.

48. Salima Bhimani, email communication, July 17, 2022.

49. Salima Bhimani, personal interview in English, June 2, 2020.

50. Schweiker and Clairmont, *Religious Ethics*, 239.

51. Zahra Somani, personal interview in English, June 2, 2020.

52. Anishah Cumber-Taj, personal interview in English, August 27, 2021.

53. Salima Bhimani, personal interview in English, June 2, 2020.

54. Amit and Rapport, *The Trouble with Community*.

55. Ibid.

56. Ibid., 23.

57. Jamal, "Work No Words," 225.

58. Kara, "Abode of Peace," 58.

59. Cohen, *The Symbolic Construction of Community*.

60. Ibid., 21.

Chapter 7

1. The Ismaili, "Journey of One Jamat: Expressions from Various Artists," https://the.ismaili/diamond-jubilee/journey-one-jamat-%E2%80%94-volume-1-usa, accessed April 18, 2022.
2. I thank Nargis Virani for help with this translation.
3. Editors, "Editorial," *American Ismaili 1*, no. 3 (1979): 2.
4. Berlant, "Intimacy."
5. Mahmood, "Ethics and Piety."
6. Cited in Mukadam and Mawani, "Excess Baggage or Precious Gems? The Migration of Cultural Commodities," 164.
7. Mahmood, *Politics of Piety*, 29.
8. Morgan, "The Look of Sympathy: Religion, Visual Culture, and the Social Life of Feeling," 141.
9. Sociologist Arlie Hochschild defines emotional labor as the effort undertaken "to induce or suppress feeling in order to sustain the outward countenance that produces the proper state of mind in others" (Hochschild, *The Managed Heart*, 20).
10. Clooney, "Practices," 78–85.
11. Alexander, *Pedagogies of Crossing*, 297 and 325.
12. Dilshad Sadruddin, personal interview in Urdu, January 9, 2019.
13. For more on morals as organizing frames see Crawley, "Review of: The Labor of Faith by Judith Casselberry."
14. Mahmood, *Politics of Piety*, 27.
15. This pattern resonates with what scholars of North American religions call a "post-denominational age," where formal institutions are a small part of religious communities. See Eichler-Levine, *Painted Pomegranates and Needlepoint Rabbis*, 16.
16. Jamal, "Work No Words," 235.
17. Ibid., 246.
18. Roberts, "Spiritual and Menial Housework."
19. Casselberry, *The Labor of Faith*.
20. Kara, "Abode of Peace," 56.
21. Saidiya Hartman cited in Maclear, "Something So Broken: Black Care in the Wake of Beasts of the Southern Wild," 603.
22. Alexander, *Pedagogies of Crossing*, 354.
23. Grande, "Care."
24. Ibid.
25. Assman and Czaplicka, "Collective Memory and Cultural Identity," 130.
26. Thomson, "Memory and Remembering in Oral History," 86.
27. Hirsch and Smith, "Feminism and Cultural Memory," 6.
28. Myerhoff, *Number Our Days: A Triumph of Continuity and Culture among Jewish Old People in an Urban Ghetto*, 268.
29. Davis, "Black Power, Feminism and the Prison-Industrial Complex."
30. Ayubi, *Gendered Morality*, 240
31. Jaggar, "Feminist Ethics: Problems, Projects, Prospects."

Bibliography

Abu-Lughod, Lila. *Writing Women's Worlds: Bedouin Stories*. Oakland: University of California Press, 2008.

Adatia, A. K., and Noel King. "Some East African Firmans of H. H. Aga Khan III." *Journal of Religion in Africa* 2, no. 3 (1969): 179–191.

Aga Khan, His Highness Prince Karim. Farman made in Ahmedabad, India, February 25, 2018. Video clip. https://ismaililiterature.com/interviews-and-speeches-of-mawl ana-hazir-imam/.

Aga Khan, His Highness Prince Karim. Interview. *Politique Internationale*, 2011–2012. https://www.akdn.org/speech/his-highness-aga-khan/his-highness-aga-khan-life-service-development.

Aga Khan, His Highness Prince Karim. Speech in 1970 Dhakka first published in *Ismaili Mirror*, 1970– Special Edition. http://ismaili.net/heritage/node/34607, accessed July 13, 2021.

Aga Khan, Sultan Mahomed Shah. *India in Transition, A Study in Political Evolution*. New York: G. Putnam, 1918.

Aga Khan, Sultan Mahomed Shah. *Message to the World of Islam*. Karachi: Ismailia Association of Pakistan, 1977.

Ahad, Badia. "Post-Blackness and Culinary Nostalgia in Marcus Samuelsson's *Yes, Chef.*" *American Studies* 54, no. 4 (2016): 5–26.

Aiyar, Sana. *Indians in Kenya: The Politics of Diaspora*. Cambridge, MA: Harvard University Press, 2015.

Akberali, Mumtaz. "Memories of Zanzibar." http://znzmumtaz.50webs.com/, accessed July 11, 2022.

Akhtar, Iqbal. *The Khoja of Tanzania*. Leiden: Brill, 2016.

Akhtar, Iqbal. "The Narrative Prayers (*Kahani*) of the African Khoja." *Narrative Culture* 1, no. 2 (2014): 217–238.

Akhtar, Iqbal. "Religious Citizenship: The Case of the Globalised Khoja." *African Sociological Review* 18, no. 1 (2014): 27–48.Al-Nu'man, Abu Hanifah. *The Pillars of Islam: Da'a'im al-Islam of al-Qadi al-Nu'man*. Translated by Asaf Ali Asghar Fyzee and Ismaili Poonawala. New Delhi: Oxford University Press, 2002.

Alexander, M. Jacqui. *Pedagogies of Crossing: Meditations on Feminism, Sexual Politics, Memory, and the Sacred*. Durham, NC: Duke University Press, 2006.

Alibhai-Brown, Yasmin. "Racism Is Not Just a White Problem." *INews*, November 10, 2020. https://inews.co.uk/news/long-reads/racism-south-asian-prejudices-black-lives-matter-753885.

Alibhai-Brown, Yasmin. *The Settler's Cookbook: A Memoir of Love, Migration and Food*. London: Portobello Books, 2009.

Alibhai, Mohamed. "Tajbibi Abualy Aziz (1926–2019) A Satpanthi Sita." *Olduvai Review*, March 2020. https://theolduvaireview.com/tajbibi-abualy-aziz/, accessed July 11, 2022.

Allana, Gulam Ali. *Ismaili Movement in Sindh, Multan and Gujrat*. Karachi: Zaki Son's Printers, 2008.

Alleyne, Brian. "An Idea of Community and Its Discontents: Towards a More Reflexive Sense of Belonging in Multicultural Britain." *Ethnic and Racial Studies* 25, no. 4 (2002): 607–627.

Alpers, Edward, and Chhaya Goswami. *Transregional Trade and Traders. Situating Gujarat in the Indian Ocean from Early Times to 1900*. Oxford: Oxford University Press, 2019.

Amiji, Hatim. "Some Notes on Religious Dissent in Nineteenth-Century East Africa." *African Historical Studies* 4, no. 3 (1971): 603–616.

Amir-Moezzi, Mohammad Ali. *The Spirituality of Shi'i Islam*. London: I. B. Tauris, 2011.

Amit, Vered. *Realizing Community: Concepts, Social Relationships and Sentiments*. New York: Routledge, 2002.

Amit, Vered, and Nigel Rapport. *The Trouble with Community*. London: Pluto Press, 2002.

Andani, Khalil. "A Survey of Ismaili Studies Part 1: Early Ismailism and Fatimid Ismailism." *Religion Compass* 10, no. 8 (2016): 191–206.

Andani, Khalil. "A Survey of Ismaili Studies Part 2: Post-Fatimid and Modern Ismailism." *Religion Compass* 10, no. 11 (2016): 269–282.

Anttonen, Veikko. "Space, Body, and the Notion of Boundary: A Category-Theoretical Approach to Religion." *Temenos* 41, no. 2 (2005): 185–201.

Appadurai, Arjun. "Gastro-Politics in Hindu South Asia." *American Ethnologist* 8, no. 3 (1981): 494–511.

Asani, Ali. "From Satpanthi to Ismaili Muslim." In *A Modern History of the Ismailis: Continuity and Change in a Muslim Community*, edited by Farhad Daftary, 95–128. London: I. B. Tauris, 2011.

Asani, Ali. "The *Ginans*: Betwixt *Satpanthi* Scripture and 'Ismaili' Devotional Literature." In *Non Sola Scriptura*, edited by Bruce Fudge, Kambiz GhaneaBassiri, Christian Lange, and Sarah Savant, 169–193. New York: Routledge, 2022.

Asani, Ali. "Improving the Status of Women through Reforms in Marriage Contract Law: The Experience of the Nizari Ismaili Community." In *The Islamic Marriage Contract*, edited by Asifa Quraishi and Frank Vogel, 285–295. Cambridge, MA: Harvard University Press, 2009.

Asani, Ali. "The Khojahs of South Asia." *Cultural Dynamics* 13, no. 2 (2001): 155–168.

Assman, Jan, and John Czaplicka. "Collective Memory and Cultural Identity." *New German Critique* 65 (Spring-Summer 1995): 125–133.

Ayubi, Zahra. *Gendered Morality*. New York: Columbia University Press, 2019.

Aziz, K. K. *Aga Khan III: Selected Speeches and Writings of Sir Sultan Muhammed Shah*. Vol. 1. London: Routledge, 1998.

Babou, Cheikh. *The Muridiyya on the Move*. Athens: Ohio University Press, 2021.

Bailey-Dick, Matthew. "The Kitchenhood of All Believers: A Journey into the Discourse of Mennonite Cookbooks." *Mennonite Quarterly Review* 79, no. 2 (2005): 531–547.

BBC. "More Kenyan Asians Flee to Britain." *BBC Online*, February 4, 1968. http://news.bbc.co.uk/onthisday/hi/dates/stories/february/4/newsid_2738000/2738629.stm.

Beben, Daniel, and Daryoush Poor. *The First Aga Khan: Memoirs of the 46th Ismaili Imam, a Persian Edition and English Translation of Muhammad Hasan al-Husayni's Ibrat-afza*. London: Bloomsbury, 2018.

Berlant, Lauren. "Intimacy." *Critical Inquiry* 24, no. 2 (1998): 281–288.

Bertz, Ned. *Diaspora and Nation*. Honolulu: University of Hawaii Press, 2015.

Bhattacharya, Tithi. *Social Reproduction Theory: Remapping Class, Recentering Oppression*. London: Pluto, 2017.

Bhimani, Salima. "Mapping the Assembly of Muslim Exceptionality and Exceptional Muslims in Colonial Modernity." PhD diss., University of Toronto, 2013.

Bhushan, Kul. "NRIs Remember Dark Days of Idi Amin." *Hindustan Times*, June 4, 2007. https://www.hindustantimes.com/india/nris-remember-dark-days-of-idi-amin/story-sHMv5nZRthQ9d4ta4HUQdM.html.

Black, Shameem. "Recipes for Cosmopolitanism: Cooking across Borders in the South Asian Diaspora." *Frontiers: A Journal of Women Studies* 31, no. 1 (2010): 1–30.

Bornat, Joanna, and Hanna Diamond. "Women's History and Oral History: Developments and Debates." *Women's History Review* 16, no. 1 (2007): 19–39.

Bose, Mandakranta. *Women in the Hindu Tradition: Rules, Roles and Exceptions*. London: Routledge, 2010.

Brah, Avtar. *Cartographies of Diaspora: Contesting Identities*. London: Routledge, 1996.

Brennan, James. *Taifa: Making Nation and Race in Urban Tanzania*. Athens: Ohio University Press, 2013.

Bucar, Elizabeth, and Aaron Stalnaker. *Religious Ethics in a Time of Globalism*. New York: Springer, 2012.

Butticci, Annalisa, and Amira Mittermaier. "Afterword." *Religion and Society: Advances in Research* 11, no. 1 (2020): 176–185.

Calderini, Simonetta. "Female Seclusion and the Veil: Two Issues in Political and Social Discourse." In *Islam and the Veil: Theoretical and Regional Contexts*, edited by Theodore Gabriel and Rabiha Tannan, 48–62. London: Continuum, 2011.

Carsten, Janet. *After Kinship: New Departures in Anthropology*. Cambridge: Cambridge University Press, 2004.

Casey, Edward. "Body, Self, and Landscape: A Geophilosophical Inquiry into the Place World." In *Textures of Place: Exploring Humanist Geographies*, edited by Paul Adams, Steven Hoelscher, and Karen Till, 403–425. Minneapolis: University of Minnesota Press, 2001.

Casselberry, Judith. *The Labor of Faith: Gender and Power in Black Apostolic Pentecostalism*. Durham, NC: Duke University Press, 2017.

Chavoshian, Sana. "Dream-Realities." *Religion and Society* 11, no. 1 (2020): 148–162.

Chen, Lianshan. "A Discussion on the Concept of 'Sacred Narrative.'" *Journal of Chinese Humanities* 3, no. 1 (2017): 35–47.

Cho, Lily. *Eating Chinese: Culture on the Menu in Small Town Canada*. Toronto: University of Toronto Press, 2010.

Christie, James. *Cholera Epidemics in East Africa*. London: Macmillan and Co., 1876.

Classen, Constance. "The Odor of the Other: Olfactory Symbolism and Cultural Categories." *Ethos* 20, no. 2 (1992): 133–166.

Clooney, Francis. "Practices." In *The Blackwell Companion to Religious Ethics*, edited by William Schweiker, 78–85. Oxford: Blackwell, 2005.

Cohen, Anthony. *Belonging: Identity and Social Organisation in British Rural Cultures*. Manchester: Manchester University Press, 1982.

Cohen, Anthony. *The Symbolic Construction of Community*. New York: Tavistock Publications, 1985.

Coulson, Andrew. *Tanzania: A Political Economy*. Oxford: Oxford University Press, 2013.

Coward, Harold, and David Goa. *Mantra: Hearing the Divine in India and America*. New York: Columbia University Press, 2004.

Crawley, Ashon. "Review of: The Labor of Faith by Judith Casselberry." *Hypatia* 36, no. 3 (2021): 1–4.

Cummins, Alyshea. "Alleviating the Clash of Ignorance(s): An Ismaili Muslim Initiative in Canada." PhD diss., Wilfrid Laurier University, 2012.

Cummins, Alyshea. "Making Space Through Public Engagements: Canadian Ismaili Muslims." In *Bloomsbury Handbook of Religion and Migration*, edited by Rubina Ramji and Alison Marshall, 123–138. United Kingdom: Bloomsbury Press, 2022.

Cutts, Mark. *The State of World Refugees 2000: Fifty Years of Humanitarian Action*. Oxford: Oxford University Press, 2000.

Daftary, Farhad. *The Isma'ilis: Their History and Doctrines*. Cambridge: Cambridge University Press, 1990.

Daftary, Farhad, and Zulfikar Hirji. *The Ismailis: An Illustrated History*. London: Institute of Ismaili Studies, 2008.

Dakake, Maria. "What Do We Owe to Others?" *The Maydan*, November 9, 2021. https://themaydan.com/2021/11/what-do-we-owe-to-others-the-meaning-of-muslim-communal-ethics-in-a-contemporary-context/.

Das, Veena. "Ordinary Ethics." In *A Companion to Moral Anthropology*, edited by Didier Fassin, 133–149. Hoboken, NJ: Wiley, 2015.

Davis, Angela. "Black Power, Feminism and the Prison-Industrial Complex." *The Nation*, August 27, 2014. https://www.thenation.com/article/archive/qa-angela-davis-black-power-feminism-and-prison-industrial-complex/.

Decker, Alicia. *In Idi Amin's Shadow: Women, Gender and Militarism in Uganda*. Athens: Ohio University Press, 2014.

Dein, Simon. "Miracles, Media, Mezuzot: Storytelling among Chabad Hasidim." *Religions* 7, no. 9 (2016): 1–17.

Delgado, Richard, and Jean Stefancic. *Critical Race Theory*. New York: New York University Press, 1995.

Devgan, Shruti. "Re-Presenting Pasts: Sikh Diasporic and Digital Memories of 1984." PhD diss., Rutgers University, 2015.

Devji, Faisal. "Preface." In *The Ismailis in the Colonial Era: Modernity, Empire, and Islam, 1839–1969* edited by Marc Van Grondelle, ix–xvi. New York: Columbia University Press, 2009.

Dewji, Nimira. "Early Ismaili Settlers of East Africa First Established a Foothold in Zanzibar." https://nimirasblog.wordpress.com/2019/08/22/early-ismaili-settlers-of-east-africa-established-a-foothold-in-zanzibar/, August 22, 2019, accessed May 28, 2021.

Dhalla, Zahir. *My Tanga Days*. Scotts Valley, CA: CreateSpace Independent Publishing Platform, 2017.

Dhalla, Zahir. *Sherbanu Lalani*. Unpublished memoir.

Dhalla, Zahir. *The Willowdale Jamatkhana Story*. Toronto: Kitabu Publications, 2014.

Doostdar, Alireza. *The Iranian Metaphysicals*. Princeton, NJ: Princeton University Press, 2018.

Dossa, Parin. *Afghanistan Remembers: Gendered Narrations of Violence and Culinary Practices*. Toronto: University of Toronto Press, 2014.

Dossa, Parin. "(Re)imagining Aging Lives: Ethnographic Narratives of Muslim Women in Diaspora." *Journal of Cross-Cultural Gerontology* 14, no. 3 (1999): 245–272.

Dossa, Parin. "Ritual and Daily Life: Transmission and Interpretation of the Ismaili Tradition in Vancouver." PhD thesis, University of British Columbia, 1985.

Dowden, Richard. "Short-Sighted Demagogue Who Played the Race Card." *The Independent*, August 4, 1992. https://www.independent.co.uk/news/world/shortsigh ted-demagogue-who-played-the-race-card-idi-amin-expelled-the-asians-20-years-ago-richard-dowden-africa-editor-explains-why-the-decision-was-supported-by-ugandans-1538196.html.

Duffy, Mignon. "Doing the Dirty Work: Gender, Race, and Reproductive Labor in Historical Perspective." *Gender & Society* 21, no. 3 (2007): 313–336.

Dunn, Kevin. "Islam in Sydney: Contesting the Discourse of Absence." *Australian Geographer* 35, no. 1 (2004): 333–353.

Ebrahim, Mohib. "The Three Kings Without Crowns." https://simerg.com/special-series-i-wish-id-been-there/the-three-kings-without-crowns/, 2010, accessed July 13, 2021.

Editors. "Editorial." *Canadian Ismaili* (July 1976): 5.

Editors. "Editorial." *Canadian Ismaili* (March 1977): 3–4.

Editors. "Editorial." *Canadian Ismaili* 1, no. 1 (1978): 3.

Editors. "Editorial." *American Ismaili* 1, no. 3 (1979): 2.

Editors. "Editorial." *Ismaili Forum* 4, no. 1 (1979): 2.

Eichler-Levine, Jodi. *Painted Pomegranates and Needlepoint Rabbis: How Jews Craft Resilience and Create Community.* Chapel Hill: University of North Carolina Press, 2020.

Eidinger, Andrea. "Gefilte Fish and Roast Duck with Orange Slices: *A Treasure for My Daughter* and the Creation of a Jewish Cultural Orthodoxy in Postwar Montreal." In *Edible Histories, Cultural Politics: Towards a Canadian Food History*, edited by Franca Iacovetta, Valerie Korinek, and Marlene Epp, 189–208. Toronto: University of Toronto Press, 2012.

Epp, Marlene. "Eating across Borders: Reading Immigrant Cookbooks." *Histoire Sociale/ Social History* 48, no. 96 (2015): 45–65.

Erll, Astrl. "Locating the Family in Cultural Memory Studies." *Journal of Comparative Family Studies* 42, no. 3 (2011): 303–318.

Esmail, Aziz. "Learning under the Fatimids." *American Ismaili* 1, no. 3 (1979): 20.

Eves, Rosalyn. "A Recipe for Remembrance: Memory and Identity in African-American Women's Cookbooks." *Rhetoric Review* 24, no. 3 (2005): 280–297.

Ewing, Katherine. "The Dream of Spiritual Initiation and the Organization of Self: Representations among Pakistani Sufis." *American Ethnologist* 17, no. 1 (1990): 56–74.

Federici, Silvia. *Wages against Housework.* London: Power of Women Collective, 1975.

Fischer, Nina. *Memory Work: The Second Generation.* London: Palgrave Macmillan, 2015.

Fitzgerald, Mary. "Kenya's Asians: Needed but Not Wanted. They're Victims of Their Own Success." *Christian Science Monitor*, August 21, 1986.

Ghosh, Anindita. "A World of Their Very Own: Religion, Pain and Subversion in Bengali Homes in the Nineteenth Century." In *Behind the Veil: Resistance, Women and the Everyday in Colonial South Asia*, edited by Anindita Ghosh, 191–221. Ranikhet: Permanent Black, 2011.

Gilsenan, Michael. *Recognizing Islam: An Anthropologist's Introduction.* London: Routledge, 1982.

Gilsenan, Michael. *Saint and Sufi in Modern Egypt.* Oxford: Oxford University Press, 1973.

Glick-Schiller, Nina, Ayse Caglar, and Thaddeus Gulbrandsen. "Beyond the Ethnic Lens: Locality, Globality, and Born-Again Incorporation." *American Ethnologist* 33, no. 4 (2006): 612–633.

Goethe Institute's Oral History Project. http://www.goethe.de/ins/in/lp/prj/inm/mvi/enindex.htm, accessed December 17, 2020.

Gold, Carol. *Danish Cookbooks: Domesticity and National Identity, 1616–1901.* Seattle: University of Washington Press, 2006.

Government of India. *Indian Meteorological Memoir 16,* no. 2, 185–186. Calcutta: Office of the Superintendent of Government Printing, 1905.

Grande, Sandy. "Care." In *Keywords for Gender and Sexuality Studies,* edited by the Feminist Collective, 43–46. New York: New York University Press, 2021.

Gray, John. "Community as Placemaking: Ram Auctions in the Scottish Borderland." In *Realizing Community,* edited by Vered Amit, 38–59. New York: Routledge, 2002.

Green, Nile. "The Religious and Cultural Roles of Dreams and Visions in Islam." *Journal of the Royal Asiatic Society* 13, no. 3 (2003): 287–313.

Greenwood, Anna. *Beyond the State: The Colonial Medical Service in British Africa.* Manchester: Manchester University Press, 2019.

Gregory, Robert. *South Asians in East Africa: An Economic and Social History, 1890–1980.* Nashville, TN: Westview Press, 1993.

Gregory, Robert. *Quest for Equality: Asian Politics in East Africa, 1900–1967.* New Delhi, India: Orient Longman, 1993.

Grondelle, Van. *The Ismailis in the Colonial Era: Modernity, Empire and Islam.* London: Hurst and Company, 2009.

Gulamhusein, Shemine. "Living in the In-Between as an Ismaili Muslim Woman." PhD diss., University of Victoria, 2018.

Gupta, Akhil, and James Ferguson. *Culture, Power, Place: Explorations in Critical Anthropology.* Durham, NC: Duke University Press, 1997.

Halbwachs, Maurice. *The Collective Memory.* Translated by Francis J. Ditter and Vida Yazdi Ditter. New York: Harper & Row, 1980.

Hammer, Juliane. *Peaceful Families: American Muslim Efforts against Domestic Violence.* Princeton, NJ: Princeton University Press, 2019.

Held, Virginia. *The Ethics of Care.* Oxford: Oxford University Press: 2006.

Henig, David. *Remaking Muslim Lives: Everyday Islam in Postwar Bosnia and Herzegovina.* Chicago: University of Illinois Press, 2020.

Hickling, Carissa. *Disinheriting Daughters: Applying Hindu Laws of Inheritance to the Khoja Muslim Community in Western India, 1847–1937.* Manitoba: University of Manitoba Press, 1998.

Hirji, Zulfiqar. "The Socio-Legal Formation of the Nizari Ismailis of East Africa, 1800–1950." In *A Modern History of the Ismailis: Continuity and Change in a Muslim Community,* edited by Farhad Daftary, 129–160. London: I. B. Tauris, 2011.

Hirsch, Marianne. *The Generation of Postmemory: Writing and Visual Culture after the Holocaust.* New York: Columbia University Press, 2012.

Hirsch, Marianne. "Stateless Memory." *Critical Times* 2, no. 3 (2019): 416–434.

Hirsch, Marianne, and Valerie Smith. "Feminism and Cultural Memory: An Introduction." *Signs* 28, no. 1 (2002): 1–19.

Hochschild, Arlie. *The Managed Heart.* Oakland: University of California Press, 2012.

hooks, bell. "Choosing the Marin as a Space of Radical Openness." *Framework* 36, no. 1 (1989): 15–23.

Horst, Cindy. *Transnational Nomads: How Somalis Cope with Refugee Life in the Dadaab Camps of Kenya.* New York: Berghahn Books, 2008.

Horst, Cindy, and Katarzyna Grabska. "Introduction: Flight and Exile." *Social Analysis* 59, no. 1 (2015): 1–18.

Howes, David. "Introduction." In *Empire of the Sense*, edited by David Howes, 1–20. New York: Berg, 2005.

Hubbard, Phil. "Space/Place." In *Cultural Geography: A Critical Dictionary of Key Concepts*, edited by David Atkinson, 34–40. London: I. B. Tauris, 2005.

Hundle, Anneeth. "Exceptions to the Expulsion: Violence, Security, and Community among Ugandan Asians, 1971–1979." *Journal of Eastern African Studies* 7, no. 1 (2013): 164–182.

Hurst, Rachel, and Jane Lawrence. "(Re)Placing, Remembering, Revealing." In *Memory and Architecture*, edited by Eleni Bastea, 293–316. Albuquerque: University of New Mexico Press, 2004.

Husain, Hameed. *Journey with the Gods*. Unpublished memoir.

Iloliev, Abdulmamad. *The Ismaili-Sufi Sage of Pamir: Mubarak-i Wakhani and the Esoteric Tradition of the Pamiri Muslims*. New York: Cambria Press, 2008.

Ismail, Abbas. "The 20th Century East African Ismaili Emigres." *Ismaili Forum* 4, no. 2 (1979): 4–5.

Ismail, Abbas. "Varas Allidina Visram the Uncrowned King of Uganda." *Ismaili Forum* 4, no. 1 (1979): 3–5.

The Ismaili. "Journey of One *Jamat*: Expressions from Various Artists," November 3, 2017. https://the.ismaili/diamond-jubilee/journey-one-jamat-%E2%80%94-volume-1-usa, accessed April 18, 2022.

Jacobsen, Knut, and Pratap Kumar. "Preliminary Material." In *South Asians in the Diaspora*, edited by Knut Jacobsen and Pratap Kumar, i–xl. Leiden: Brill, 2018.

Jaggar, Alison. "Feminist Ethics: Problems, Projects Prospects." In *Feminist Ethics*, edited by Claudia Card, 78–104. Lawrence: University Press of Kansas, 1991.

Jamal, Nadia. *Surviving the Mongols: The Continuity of Ismaili Tradition in Persia*. New York: I. B. Tauris, 2002.

Jamal, Tasneem. *Where the Air Is Sweet*. Toronto: HarperCollins Publishers, 2014.

Jamal, Zahra. *Embodying Ethics, Performing Pluralism: Volunteerism among Ismailis in Houston, TX*. Cambridge, MA: Pluralism Project, 2003.

Jamal, Zahra. "Work No Words: Voluntarism, Subjectivity, and Moral Economies of Exchange among Khoja Ismaili Muslims." PhD diss., Harvard University, 2008.

Jasani, Hussain. "Khojas in Mumbai." Lecture at Khaki Lab, November 20, 2021.

Jessa, Fareen. "Instant Pot Khichri." *Food Mama blog*, April 25, 2017. https://foodmamma.com/2017/04/instant-pot-khichri/.

Jessa, Fareen. "Saffron Almond Milk." *Food Mama blog*, February 15, 2021. https://foodmamma.com/2021/02/saffron-almond-milk/.

Jessa, Fareen. "A Spicy Touch and Chana Wagharia." *Food Mama blog*, January 29, 2016. https://foodmamma.com/2016/01/a-spicy-touch-and-chana-wagharia/.

Jiwa, Rizwana. "Voices from the Diaspora: Identity Formation of Ismaili Girls and Women in Canada." Master's thesis, Simon Fraser University, 2003.

Jones, Rhys. "The Makeshift and the Contingent: Lefebvre and the Production of Precarious Sacred Space." *Society and Space* 37, no. 1 (2019): 177–194.

Kabani, Shiraz. *Ismaili Festivals*. London: Institute of Ismaili Studies, 2021.

Kamaluddin, Zarina, and Kamaluddin Ali Muhammad. *Anant Akhado and Anant Na Nav Chugga with English Translation and Glossary*. Karachi: K. A. Printers, 2010.

Kamaluddin, Zarina, and Kamaluddin Ali Muhammad. *Ginan with English Translation and Glossary*. Vol. 1. Karachi: Z. A. Printer, 2011.

Kara, Taushif. "Abode of Peace: Islam, Empire, and the Khoja Diaspora (1866–1972)." PhD diss., University of Cambridge, 2021.

Karim, Karim. "At the Interstices of Tradition, Modernity and Postmodernity: Ismaili Engagements with Contemporary Canadian Society." In *A Modern History of the Ismailis: Continuity and Change in a Muslim Community*, edited by Farhad Daftary, 265–294. London: I. B. Tauris, 2011.

Karmali, Sikeena. *A House by the Sea*. Montreal: Vehicule Press, 2003.

Kasmani, Omar. "Grounds of Becoming: Fakirs among the Dead in Sehwan Sharif, Pakistan." *Culture and Religion* 18, no. 2 (2017): 77–89.

Kasmani, Omar. "On Un/Worlding: Fakirs, Fairies and the Dead in Pakistan." *Affect and Colonialism*, August 10, 2021. https://affect-and-colonialism.net/video/on-un-world ing-fakirs-fairies-and-the-dead-in-pakistan/.

Kasmani, Omar. "Pilgrimage of the Dream." In *Muslim Pilgrimage in the Modern World*, edited by Babak Rahimi and Peyman Eshaghi, 133–148. Chapel Hill: University of North Carolina Press, 2019.

Kassam-Remtulla, Aly. "(Dis)placing Khojahs." Master's thesis, Stanford University, 1999.

Kassam, Tazim. *Songs of Wisdom and Circles of Dance: Hymns of the Satpanth Isma'ili Muslim Saint, Pir Shams*. New York: State University of New York Press, 1995.

Kassam, Zayn. "The Gender Policies of Aga Khan III and Aga Khan IV." In *A Modern History of the Ismailis*, edited by Farhad Daftary, 247–264. London: I. B. Tauris, 2011.

Kayikci, Merve. *Islamic Ethics and Female Volunteering*. London: Palgrave, 2020.

Keane, Webb. "Ethics as Piety." *Numen* 61, no. 2–3 (2014): 221–236.

Kelley, D. G. Robin. "What Did Cedric Robinson Mean by Racial Capitalism?" *Boston Review*, January 12, 2017.

Keshavjee, Mohamed. *Into that Heaven of Freedom: The Impact of Apartheid on an Indian Family's Diasporic Journey*. Toronto: University of Toronto Press, 2016.

Keshavjee, Rashida. "The Elusive Access to Education for Muslim Women in Kenya from the Late Nineteenth Century to the 'Winds of Change' in Africa (1890s to 1960s)." *Paedagogica Historica* 46, no. 1–2 (2010): 99–115.

Keshavjee, Rashida. "The Redefined Role of the Ismaili Muslim Woman through Higher Education and the Professions." PhD diss., University of Toronto, 2004.

Keshavjee, Shariffa. *Bwana Mzuri: Memories of Hasham Jamal, a Pioneer in Kisumu*. Privately published, 2005.

Khoja-Moolji, Shenila. *Forging the Ideal Educated Girl: The Production of Desirable Subjects in Muslim South Asia*. Oakland: University of California Press, 2018.

Khoja-Moolji, Shenila. "Redefining Muslim Women: Aga Khan III's Reforms for Women's Education." *South Asia Graduate Research Journal* 20, no. 1 (2011): 69–94.

Krause, Neal, and Elena Bastida. "Church-Based Social Relationships, Belonging, and Health among Older Mexican Americans." *Journal for the Scientific Study of Religion* 50, no. 2 (2011): 397–409.

Kuepper, William, Lynne Lackey, and Nelson Swinerton, "Ugandan Asian Refugees: Resettlement Centre to Community," *Community Development Journal* 11, no. 3 (1976): 199–208.

Kumar, Nita, and Usha Sanyal. "Introduction." In *Food, Faith, and Gender in South*, edited by Usha Sanyal and Nita Kumar, 1–28. New York: Bloomsbury, 2020.

Ladha, Mansoor. *Memoirs of a Muhindi: Fleeing East Africa for the West*. Regina: University of Regina Press, 2017.

Lalani, Habib, and Zahir Dhalla, *A Journal of Life in Kathiawad, Gujarat & Buganda, Uganda: Habib Rahemtulla Lalani—1910–1997*. Parts 1 through 4. February 7, 2017. https://ismailimail.blog/2017/02/07/a-journal-of-life-in-kathiawad-gujarat-buganda-uganda-habib-rahemtulla-lalani-1910-1997/

Lambek, Michael. "Introduction." In *Ordinary Ethics: Anthropology, Language, and Action*, edited by Michael Lambek, 1–36. New York: Fordham University Press, 2010.

Lambek, Michael. "Toward an Ethics of the Act." In *Ordinary Ethics: Anthropology, Language, and Action*, edited by Michael Lambek, 39–63. New York: Fordham University Press, 2010.

Lawless, Elaine. *God's Peculiar People*. Lexington: University of Kentucky Press, 1988.

Lefebvre, Henri. *The Production of Space*. Oxford, England: Blackwell, 1991.

Locher, Julie, William Yoels, Donna Maurer, and Jillian van Ells. "Comfort Foods: An Exploratory Journey into the Social and Emotional Significance of Food." *Food and Foodways* 13, no. 4 (2005): 273–297.

Lugones, Maria. *Peregrinajes/Pilgrimages: Theorizing Coalitions against Multiple Oppressions*. Lanham, MD: Rowman and Littlefield, 2003.

Maclear, Kyo. "Something So Broken: Black Care in the Wake of Beasts of the Southern Wild." *ISLE: Interdisciplinary Studies in Literature and Environment* 25, no. 3 (2018): 603–629.

Mahmood, Saba. "Ethics and Piety." In *A Companion to Moral Anthropology*, edited by Didier Fassin, 221–241. Hoboken, NJ: Wiley, 2012.

Mahmood, Saba. *Politics of Piety*. Princeton, NJ: Princeton University Press, 2004.

Malick, Qayyum. *His Royal Highness Prince Aga Khan: Guide, Philosopher and Friend of the Islamic World*. Karachi: Ismailia Association for Pakistan, 1969.

Mamdani, Amirali. *The Voyage of Destiny: From Jamnagar to New York*. Bloomington, IN: Xlibris Corporation, 2012.

Mamdani, Mahmood. "Class Struggles in Uganda." *Review of African Political Economy* 2, no. 4 (1975): 26–61.

Mamdani, Mahmood. *Imperialism and Fascism in Uganda*. London: Heinemann Educational Books, 1983.

Mamodaly, Adil, and Alim Fakirani. "Voices from Shia Imami Ismaili Nizari Muslim Women: Reflections from Canada on Past and Present Gendered Roles in Islam." In *Women in Islam: Reflections on Historical and Contemporary Research*, edited by Terence Lovet, 213–236. New York: Springer, 2012.

Manby, Bronwen. *Struggles for Citizenship in Africa*. New York: Zed Books, 2009.

Mangat, J. S. *A History of the Asians in East Africa*. Oxford: Clarendon Press, 1969.

Manjapra, Kris. *Colonialism in Global Perspective*. Cambridge: Cambridge University Press, 2020.

Markovits, Claude. "Indian Merchant Networks outside India in the Nineteenth and Twentieth Centuries: A Preliminary Study." *Modern Asian Studies* 33, no. 4 (1999): 883–911.

Masselos, Jim. "The Khojas of Bombay." In *Caste and Social Stratification among Muslims in India*, edited by Imtiaz Ahmad, 97–116. Delhi: Manohar, 1978.

Massey, Doreen. *For Space*. London: Sage, 2005.

Mastibekov, Otambek. *Leadership and Authority in Central Asia: The Ismaili Community in Tajikistan*. Abingdon: Routledge, 2014.

Mawani, Parin. "The Coming of Ismailis to East Africa." *Africa Ismaili* 5, no. 19 (1976): 3.

Mawani, Parin. "The Jamat Khana as a Source of Cohesiveness in the Ismaili Community in Kenya." Master's thesis, University of Nairobi, 1975.

Mawani, Rizwan. *Beyond the Mosque: Diverse Spaces of Muslim Worship*. New York: Bloomsbury, 2019.

Mawani, Rizwan. "The Jamatkhana: Exploring Its Prehistories and Hegemony in the Twentieth Century." Paper presented at the International Ismaili Studies Conference, 2017.

Mawani, Rizwan, and Nashila Velji. "Towards a Tradition of Service." *Ismaili Canada* 2, (2012): 39–43.

Mawani, Sharmina. "Sanctuary for the Soul: The Centrality of the Jamatkhana in Religious Identity Formation." In *Perspectives of Female Researchers*, edited by Sharmina Mawani and Anjoom Mukadam, 75–98. Berlin: Logos Verlag, 2016.

Mawji, Nazira. "Raced and Gendered Subjectivities in the Diasporas: Exploring the Role of Generationally Transferred Local 'Subjugated' Knowledges in the Education of Canadian Ismaili Women of Indian East African Heritage." PhD diss., University of Toronto, 2018.

Mazumdar, Shampa, and Sanjoy Mazumdar. "Religious Placemaking and Community Building in Diaspora." *Environment and Behavior* 41, no. 3 (2009): 307–337.

McGaw, Janet, Anoma Pieris, and Emily Potter. "Indigenous Place-Making in the City." *Architectural Theory Review* 16, no. 3 (2011): 296–311.

McGuire, Meredith. *Lived Religion: Faith and Practice in Everyday Life*. Oxford: Oxford University Press, 2008.

Meghji, Sadru. "Rediscovering a Lost Piece of Ismaili History – First Steps in the Migration of Tanzanian Ismailis to Canada." *Simerg*, February 16, 2014. https://simerg.com/liter ary-readings/rediscovering-a-lost-piece-of-ismaili-history-first-steps-in-the-migrat ion-of-tanzanian-ismailis-to-canada/, accessed July 14, 2021.

Menin, Laura. "The Impasse of Modernity: Personal Agency, Divine Destiny, and the Unpredictability of Intimate Relationships in Morocco." *Journal of the Royal Anthropological Institute* 21, no. 4 (2015): 892–910.

Merchant, Farida. *Mountains before Me*. Unpublished memoir.

Merchant, Natasha. "Between a Rock and a Hard Place: Shia Ismaili Muslim Girls Negotiate Islam in the Classroom." *Diaspora, Indigenous, and Minority Education* 10, no. 2 (2016): 98–111.

Meyer, Birgit, and Peter van der Veer, eds. *Refugees and Religion: Ethnographic Studies of Global Trajectories*. London: Bloomsbury, 2021.

Miserez, Diana. *Prince Sadruddin Aga Khan*. Leicestershire: Book Guild Limited, 2017.

Mittermaier, Amira. "Dreams and the Miraculous." In *A Companion to the Anthropology of the Middle East*, edited by Soraya Altorki, 107–124. Hoboken, NJ: Wiley & Sons, 2015.

Mittermaier, Amira. "Dreams from Elsewhere: Muslim Subjectivities beyond the Trope of Self-Cultivation." *Journal of the Royal Anthropological Institute* 18, no. 2 (2012): 247–265.

Mittermaier, Amira. *Giving to God: Islamic Charity in Revolutionary Times*. Oakland: University of California Press, 2019.

Modi, Renu, and Mala Pandurang. "Women as an Invisible Constituency." *South Asian Diaspora* 9, no. 2 (2017): 179–192.

Mol, Annemarie, Ingunn Moser, and Jeannette Pols. *Care in Practice: On Tinkering in Clinics, Homes, and Farms*. New York: Columbia University Press, 2010.

Molloy, Michael. "40th Anniversary Lecture: Uganda Asian Refugee Movement 1972." University of Western Ontario, 2012. http://www.youtube.com/watch?v=NtPKNxymY.

Moran-Thomas, Amy. *Traveling with Sugar: Chronicles of a Global Epidemic.* Oakland: University of California Press, 2019.

Morgan, David. "The Look of Sympathy: Religion, Visual Culture, and the Social Life of Feeling." *Material Religion* 5, no. 2 (2015): 132–155.

Morris, H. S. *The Indians in Uganda.* London: Weidenfeld and Nicolson, 1968.

Moser, Claudia, and Cecelia Feldman. *Locating the Sacred.* Oxford: Oxbow Books, 2014.

Muhammad, Kamaluddin Ali, and Zarina Kamaluddin. *50 Ginans with English Translation and Glossary.* Karachi: Shia Imami Ismaili Tariqah and Religious Education Board for Pakistan, 1999.

Muhammad, Kamaluddin Ali, and Zarina Kamaluddin, *Golden Memories: A Short Autobiography.* Karachi: A. S. Enterprises, 2016.

Muhammadi, Shezan. "Gifts from Amin: The Resettlement, Integration, and Identities of Ugandan Asian Refugees in Canada." PhD diss., University of Western Ontario, 2017.

Mukadam, Anjoom, and Sharmina Mawani. "Diaspora Revisited: Second-Generation Nizari Ismaili Muslims of Gujarati Ancestry." In *Global Indian Diasporas: Exploring Trajectories of Migration and Theory*, edited by Gijsbert Oonk, 195–210. Amsterdam: Amsterdam University Press, 2007.

Mukadam, Anjoom, and Sharmina Mawani. "Excess Baggage or Precious Gems? The Migration of Cultural Commodities." In *Muslims in Britain: Race, Place and Identities*, edited by Peter Hopkins and Richard Gale, 150–168. Edinburgh: Edinburgh University Press, 2009.

Mukadam, Anjoom, and Sharmina Mawani. "Living in a Material World: Religious Commodification and Resistance." In *Religion, Consumerism and Sustainability*, edited by Lyn Thomas, 55–71. London: Palgrave Macmillan, 2011.

Mukherjee, Soumen. *Ismailism and Islam in Modern South Asia: Community and Identity in the Age of Religious Internationals.* Cambridge: Cambridge University Press, 2017.

Murphy, Anne. "Mobilizing Seva." In *South Asians in the Diaspora*, edited by Knut Jacobsen and Pratap Kumar, 337–372. Leiden: Brill, 2018.

Myerhoff, Barbara. *Number Our Days: A Triumph of Continuity and Culture among Jewish Old People in an Urban Ghetto.* Ann Arbor: University of Michigan Press, 1992.

Nair, Savita. "At Home, at Work: Indian Immigrant Women in Colonial East Africa (c.1920–1940)." Unpublished paper. http://sites.cortland.edu/wagadu/wp-content/uploads/sites/3/2016/11/wagaduvol10SavitaNair.pdf.

Nanji, Azim. "Islamic Ethics." In *A Companion to Ethics*, edited by Peter Singer, 106–118. Oxford: Blackwell, 1991.

Nanji, Azim. "Khojas." In *Encyclopedia of Islam and Muslim World.* Vol. 2, edited by Richard Martin, 393. New York: MacMillan Reference Books, 2016.

Nanji, Azim. "Modernization and Change in the Nizari Ismaili Community in East Africa: A Perspective." *Journal of Religion in Africa* 6, no. 2 (1974): 123–139.

Nanji, Azim. "The Nizari Ismaili Muslim Community in North America: Background and Development." In *The Muslim Community in North America*, edited by Earle Waugh, Sharon Abu-Laban, and Regula Qureshi, 148–164. Edmonton: University of Alberta Press, 1983.

Nanji, Azim. *The Nizari Ismaili Tradition in the Indo-Pakistan Subcontinent.* Delmar: Caravan Books, 1978.

Nanji, Azim. "Some Lesser Known Dai's and Their Tombs in the Indian Subcontinent." *American Ismaili* 1, no. 3 (1979): 17–20.

Narayan, Kirin. "Haunting Stories." In *South Asians in the Diaspora: South Asians in the Diaspora*, edited by Knut Jacobsen and Pratap Kumar, 415–434. Leiden: Brill, 2018.

Narayan, Kirin. "Placing Lives through Stories." In *Everyday Life in South Asia*, edited by Diane Mines and Sarah Lamb, 472–486. Indianapolis: Indiana University Press, 2010.

Narayan, Kirin. *Storytellers, Saints, and Scoundrels: Folk Narrative in Hindu Religious Teaching*. Philadelphia: University of Pennsylvania Press, 1989.

Neal, Sarah, and Sue Walters. "Rural Be/longing and Rural Social Organizations: Conviviality and Community-Making in the English Countryside." *Sociology* 42, no. 2 (2008): 279–297.

Nejad, Sarem, Ryan Walker, and David Newhouse. "Indigenous Placemaking and the Built Environment: Toward Transformative Urban Design." *Journal of Urban Design* 25, no. 4 (2020): 433–442.

Nelson, Louis. "Sensing the Sacred: Anglican Material Religion in Early South Carolina." *Winterthur Portfolio* 41, no. 4 (2007): 203–238.

Nimji, Noorbanu. *A Spicy Touch*. Vol. 1, *Indian Cooking with a Contemporary Approach*. Calgary, Canada: Spicy Touch Publishing, 1986.

Nimji, Noorbanu. *A Spicy Touch*. Vol. 2, *Contemporary Indian, African, & Middle Eastern Cuisine*. Calgary, Canada: Spicy Touch Publishing, 1992.

Nimji, Noorbanu. *A Spicy Touch*. Vol. 3, *A Fusion of East African and Indian Cuisine*. Calgary, Canada: Spicy Touch Publishing, 2007.

Nimji, Noorbanu, and Karen Anderson. *A Spicy Touch*. Vol. 4, *Family Favourites from Noorbanu Nimji's Kitchen*. Victoria: Touchwood Editions, 2020.

Noormohamed-Hunzai, Rashida. *A Bridge between Two Epochs*. Vancouver: Metropolitan Fine Printers, 2018.

Nünning, Ansgar. "Making Events—Making Stories—Making Worlds." In *Cultural Ways of Worldmaking*, edited by Vera Nünning, Ansgar Nünning, Birgit Neumann, and Mirjam Horn, 189–214. Berlin: De Gruyter, 2010.

Ohito, Esther. "Some of Us Die: A Black Feminist Researcher's Survival Method for Creatively Refusing Death and Decay in the Neoliberal Academy." *International Journal of Qualitative Studies in Education* 34, no. 6 (2020): 515–533.

Okeowo, Alexis. "How Saidiya Hartman Retells the History of Black Life." *New Yorker*, October 19, 2020. https://www.newyorker.com/magazine/2020/10/26/how-saidiya-hartman-retells-the-history-of-black-life.

Oonk, Gijsbert. "Gujarati Asians in East Africa, 1800–2000: Colonization, Decolonization and Complex Citizenship Issues." *Diaspora Studies* 8, no. 1 (2015): 66–79.

Padios, Jan. "Labor." In *Keywords for Gender and Sexuality Studies*, edited by the Feminist Collective, 140–144. New York: New York University Press, 2021.

Padurang, Mala. "Imaginings of Khoja, Maasai and Swahili Aesthetics in Artist Ethnographer Sultan Somjee's Narratives." *Eastern African Literary and Cultural Studies* 4, no. 3–4 (2018): 204–220.

Pandurang, Mala. "Scrutinising the Past: A Review of Socio-Literary Narratives of the East African Asian Diasporic Experience." *South Asian Diaspora* 1, no. 1 (2009): 47–61.

Paroo, Alia. "Aga Khan III and the British Empire: The Ismailis in Tanganyika, 1920–1957." PhD diss., York University, 2012.

Paroo, Alia. "Playing Politics with the Youth: Aga Khan III's Use of Colonial Education and the Ismaili Girl Guide Movement in British Colonial Tanganyika, 1920–1940." *Journal of World History* 30, no. 4 (2019): 533–557.

Paroo, Alia. "Knowing One Another: Honoring Our Women and Foremothers." *Critical Conversations, Ismaili Tariqa and Religious Education Board for USA,* March 7, 2021.

Paroo, Kassamali. "Pioneering Ismaili Settlement in East Africa." Private papers, January 1970.

Patel, Zarina. *Challenge to Colonialism: The Struggle of Alibhai Mulla Jeevanjee for Equal Rights in Kenya.* Nairobi: Zand Graphics, 1997.

Patney, Giga. *Ties of Bandhana: The Story of Alladin Bapu.* Scotts Valley, CA: CreateSpace Independent Publishing Platform, 2016.

Peña, Elaine. *Performing Piety: Making Space with the Virgin of Guadalupe.* Oakland: University of California Press, 2011.

Perkins, Alisa. *Muslim American City: Gender and Religion in Metro Detroit.* New York: New York University Press, 2020.

Pierce, Matthew. *Twelve Infallible Men: The Imams and the Making of Shi'ism.* Cambridge, MA: Harvard University Press, 2016.

Poor, Daryoush. *Authority without Territory: The Aga Khan Development Network and the Ismaili Imamate.* London: Palgrave, 2014.

Pradhan, Toral. "A Brief History of the Khoja Ismaili Community in Daman, India, from the Portuguese Period to the Present." *Simerg,* October 7, 2013. https://simerg.com/literary-readings/a-brief-history-of-the-khoja-ismaili-community-in-daman-india-from-the-portuguese-period-to-the-present/, accessed July 21, 2022.

Prasad, Leela. *Poetics of Conduct: Oral Narratives and Moral Being in a South Indian Town.* New York: Columbia University Press, 2006.

Premji, Zahra. "From Refugee to Canadian Citizen: A Ugandan Tells the Story of His 1972 Journey to Winnipeg." *Global News,* March 1, 2017. https://globalnews.ca/news/3281456/from-refugee-to-canadian-citizen-a-ugandan-tells-the-story-of-his-journey-to-winnipeg-in-1972/, accessed December 16, 2020.

Purohit, Teena. *The Aga Khan Case.* Cambridge, MA: Harvard University Press, 2012.

Qureshi, Regula. *Sufi Music of India and Pakistan: Sound, Context, and Meaning in Qawwali.* Cambridge: Cambridge University Press, 1986.

Raghuram, Parvati. "Locating Care Ethics beyond the Global North." *ACME: An International Journal for Critical Geographies* 15, no. 3 (2016): 511–533.

Rahemtulla, Nazlin. *RSVP Rice and Stew Very Plenty: The Story of an Ismaili Girl's Expulsion from Uganda and Acceptance in Canada.* Altona: FriesenPress, 2012.

Ray, Krishnendu. "Migration, Transnational Cuisines, and Invisible Ethnics." In *Food in Time and Place,* edited by Paul Freedman, Joyce E. Chaplin, and Ken Albala, 209–230. Oakland: University of California Press, 2014.

Reinhart, Kevin. *Lived Islam: Colloquial Religion in a Cosmopolitan Tradition.* Cambridge: Cambridge University Press, 2020.

Remtilla, Aliaa. *Ismaili Identity and Jamatkhanas in East Africa.* London, UK: Institute of Ismaili Studies, 2023.

Remtilla, Aliaa. "Re-producing Social Relations: Political and Economic Change and Islam in Post-Soviet Tajik Ishkashim." PhD diss., University of Manchester, 2012.

Renard, John. *Friends of God: Islamic Images of Piety, Commitment, and Servanthood.* Oakland: University of California Press, 2008.

Renard, John. *Islam and the Heroic Image.* Columbia: University of South Carolina Press, 1993.

Rhys-Taylor, Alex. "Disgust and Distinction: The Case of the Jellied Eel." *Sociological Review* 61, no. 2 (2013): 227–246.

Ritchey, Sara. *Acts of Care: Recovering Women in Late Medieval Health*. Ithaca, NY: Cornell University Press, 2021.

Rizvi, Seyyid, and Noel King. "Some East African Ithna-Asheri Jamaats (1840–1967)." *Journal of Religion in Africa* 5, no. 1 (1973): 12–22.

Roberts, Dorothy. "Spiritual and Menial Housework." *Yale Journal of Law and Feminism* 9, no. 51 (1997): 51–80.

Ross-Shariff, Fariyal, and Azim Nanji. "Islamic Identity, Family, and Community: The Case of the Nizari Ismaili Community." In *Muslim Families in North America*, edited by Earle Waugh, Sharon Abu-Laban, and Regula Qureshi, 101–117. Edmonton: University of Alberta Press, 1991.

Rupani, Abdul. "Immigration and Citizenship in Canada." *Ismaili Forum* 4, no. 1 (1979): 7–11.

Ruthven, Malise. "Aga Khan III and the Ismaili Renaissance." In *New Trends and Developments in the World of Islam*, edited by Peter Clarke, 371–395. London: Luzac Oriental, 1997.

Sack, Daniel. *Whitebread Protestants: Food and Religion in American Culture*. New York: St. Martin's Press, 2000.

Saikia, Yasmin. *Women and the Making of Bangladesh: Remembering 1971*. Durham, NC: Duke University Press, 2011.

Sajoo, Amyn. *Muslim Ethics: Emerging Vistas*. London: Macmillan-I. B. Tauris, 2004.

Saleh, Ayeleen. "Documenting Oral History: A Case Study of the Ismaili Jamat in Bangladesh." Unpublished paper.

Salvadori, Cynthia. *Through Open Doors: A View of Asian Cultures in Kenya*. Bristol: Kenway Publications, 1989.

Salvadori, Cynthia. *We Came in Dhows*. Vols. 1–3. Nairobi: Paperchase Kenya Ltd., 1996.

Sarkar, Sucharita. "Religious Recipes: Culinary Motherlines of Feasts and Fasts in India." In *Food, Faith, and Gender in South Asia*, edited by Usha Sanyal and Nita Kumar, 73–92. New York: Bloomsbury, 2020.

Schaefer, Donovan. *Religious Affects*. Durham, NC: Duke University Press, 2015.

Schielke, Samuli, and Zentrum Orient. "Second Thoughts about the Anthropology of Islam, or How to Make Sense of Grand Schemes in Everyday Life." ZMO working papers, 2010.

Schiller, Nina, and Ayse Çağlar. "Displacement, Emplacement and Migrant Newcomers: Rethinking Urban Sociabilities within Multiscalar Power." *Identities: Global Studies in Culture and Power* 23, no. 1 (2016): 17–34.

Schweiker, William, and David Clairmont. *Religious Ethics: Meaning and Method*. Hoboken, NJ: Wiley, 2019.

Seeman, Don. "Kinship as Ethical Relation: A Critique of the Spiritual Kinship Paradigm." In *New Directions in Spiritual Kinship*, edited by Todne Thomas, Asiya Malik, and Rose Wellman, 85–108. New York: Springer, 2017.

Seidenberg, Dana. *Mercantile Adventurers: The World of East African Asians 1750–1985*. New Delhi: New International, 1996.

Selim, Nasima. "Learning the Elsewhere of 'Inner Space.'" *Religion and Society: Advances in Research* 11, no. 1 (2020): 105–119.

Seremetakis, C. Nadia. "The Memory of the Senses: Historical Perception, Commensal Exchange, and Modernity." *Visual Anthropology Review* 9, no. 2 (1993): 2–18.

Shia Ismaili Tariqa Board for Pakistan. *Ginan Sharif with Translation*. Part I (Urdu). Karachi, Pakistan: Shia Ismaili Tariqa Board for Pakistan, 1992.

Shodhan, Amrita. "Legal Formulation of the Question of Community: Defining the Khoja Collective." *Indian Social Science Review* 1, no. 1 (1999): 137–151.

Sierschynski, Jarek. "Improvising Identity, Body, and Race." *Cultural Studies Critical Methodologies* 20, no. 5 (2019): 429–433.

Sila Khan, Dominique. *Crossing the Threshold: Understanding Religious Identities in South Asia*. London: I. B. Tauris, 2004.

Singleton, Andrew. "'Your Faith Has Made You Well': The Role of Storytelling in the Experience of Miraculous Healing." *Review of Religious Research* 43, no. 2 (2001): 121–138.

Smith, Mark. "Preface: Styling Sensory History." *Journal for Eighteenth-Century Studies* 35, no. 4 (2012): 469–472.

Somjee, Sultan. *Bead Bai*. Scotts Valley, CA: CreateSpace Independent Publishing Platform, 2012.

Somjee, Sultan. *Home between Crossings*. Scotts Valley, CA: CreateSpace Independent Publishing Platform, 2016.

Srinivas, Smriti. *In the Presence of Sai Baba*. Leiden: Brill, 2008.

Srivastsan, R. "Concept of 'Seva' and the 'Sevak' in the Freedom Movement." *Economic and Political Weekly* 41, no. 5 (2006): 427–438.

Star, Rodney, and Roger Finke. *Acts of Faith: Explaining the Human Side of Religion*. Oakland: University of California, 2000.

Steinberg, Jonah. *Isma'ili Modern: Globalization and Identity in a Muslim Community*. Chapel Hill: University of North Carolina Press, 2011.

Sterba, James. "For Hungry Bihari Refugees in Karachi, Future Is Bleak." *New York Times*, January 28, 1972.

Stewart, Tony. "In Search of Equivalence: Conceiving Muslim-Hindu Encounter through Translation Theory." *History of Religions* 40, no. 3 (2001): 261–288.

Sutton, David. *Remembrance of Repasts: An Anthropology of Food and Memory*. New York: Bloomsbury, 2001.

Tajddin, Mumtaz. *101 Ismaili Heroes*. Vol. 1, *Late 19th Century to Present Age*. Karachi: Islamic Book Publisher, 2003.

Tejpar, Azizeddin. "The Migration of Indians to Eastern Africa: A Case Study of the Ismaili Community, 1866–1966." Master's thesis, University of Central Florida, 2019.

Theophano, Janet. *Eat My Words: Reading Women's Lives through the Cookbooks They Wrote*. New York: St. Martin's Griffin, 2003.

Thomas, David. "Miracles in Islam." In *The Cambridge Companion to Miracles*, edited by Graham Twelftree, 199–215. Cambridge: Cambridge University Press, 2011.Thomas, Todne. *Kincraft: The Making of Black Evangelical Sociality*. Durham, NC: Duke University Press, 2021.

Thomas, Todne. "Rebuking the Ethnic Frame: Afro Caribbean and African American Evangelicals and Spiritual Kinship." In *New Directions in Spiritual Kinship*, edited by Todne Thomas, Asiya Malik, and Rose Wellman, 219–244. New York: Palgrave, 2017.

Thomas, Todne. "Strangers, Friends, and Kin: Negotiated Recognition in Ethnographic Relationships." *Anthropology and Humanism* 41, no. 1 (2016): 66–85.

Thomas, Todne, Asiya Malik, and Rose Wellman. *New Directions in Spiritual Kinship*. New York: Springer, 2017.

Thomson, Alistair. "Memory and Remembering in Oral History." In *The Oxford Handbook of Oral History*, edited by Donald Ritchie, 77–95. Oxford: Oxford University Press, 2010.

Thrift, Nigel. "But Malice Aforethought." *Transactions* 30, no. 2 (2005): 133–150.

Tobin, Sarah. "Self-Making in Exile." *Journal of Religious Ethics* 48, no. 4 (2020): 664–687.

Tomczak, Anna. "On Exile, Memory and Food: Yasmin Alibhai-Brown's *The Settler's Cookbook: A Memoir of Love, Migration and Food.*" In *Traumatic Memory and the Ethical, Political and Transhistorical Functions of Literature*, edited by Susana Onega, 229–249. London: Palgrave Macmillan, 2017.

Tompkins, Kyla. "Consider the Recipe." *Journal of Nineteenth-Century Americanists* 1, no. 2 (2013): 439–445.

Tompkins, Kyla. "Literary Approaches to Food Studies." *Food, Culture and Society* 8, no. 2 (2005): 243–258.

Tönnies, Ferdinan. *Community and Society*. New York: Harper and Row, 1963.

Trovão, Susana. "Doing Family, Gender, Religion and Raced Identities across Generations: A Narrative Ethnography on Ismaili Women of Indian East African Heritage." *Journal of Muslim Minority Affairs* 41, no. 1 (2021): 102–121.

Tuan, Yi-Fu. *Topophilia: A Study of Environmental Perception, Attitudes and Values*. New York: Columbia University Press, 1974.

Tweed, Thomas. *Our Lady of the Exile: Diasporic Religion at a Cuban Catholic Shrine in Miami*. Oxford: Oxford University Press, 1997.

Umedaly, Lella, and Muneera Spence. *Mamajee's Kitchen*. Vancouver, British Columbia: Umedaly Publishing, 2005.

Vang, Ma. "Rechronicling History." In *Claiming Place*, edited by Chia Youyee Vang, Ma Vang, and Faith G. Nibbs, 28–55. Minneapolis: University of Minnesota Press, 2016.

Vásquez, Manuel, and Kim Knott. "Three Dimensions of Religious Place Making in Diaspora." *Global Networks* 14, no. 3 (2014): 326–347.

Vellani, Shams. *People of Faith*. London: Institute of Ismaili Studies, 2020.

Virani, Shafique. "The Eagle Returns: Evidence of Continued Ismai'li Activity at Alamut and in the South Caspian Region Following the Mongol Conquests." *Journal of the American Oriental Society* 123, no. 2 (2003): 351–370.

Virani, Shafique. "Khwajah Sindhi (Khojki): Its Name, Manuscripts and Origin." In *Texts, Scribes and Transmission: Manuscript Cultures of the Ismaili Communities and Beyond*, edited by Wafi Momin, 275–301. London: I. B. Tauris, 2022.

Virani, Shafique. "Taqiyya and Identity in a South Asian Community." *Journal of Asian Studies* 70, no. 1 (2011): 99–139.

Walji, Shirin. "A History of the Ismaili Community in Tanzania." PhD diss., University of Wisconsin, 1974.

Walmsley, Emily. "Race, Place and Taste: Making Identities through Sensory Experience in Ecuador." *Etnofoor* 18, no. 1 (2005): 43–60.

Weddle, David. *Miracles: Wonder and Meaning in World Religions*. New York: New York University Press, 2010.

Wellman, Rose. "Substance, Spirit, and Sociality." In *New Directions in Spiritual Kinship*, edited by Todne Thomas, Asiya Malik, and Rose Wellman, 171–194. New York: Springer, 2017.

Wheaton, Barbara. "Finding Real Life in Cookbooks: The Adventures of a Culinary Historian." In *Food, Cookery and Culture, Working Papers in the Humanities*, edited by Leslie Howsam, 2–15. Windsor: University of Windsor, 1998.

Whyte, William. *The Social Life of Small Urban Spaces*. New York: Project for Public Spaces, (1980) 2018.

Winders, Jason. "Molloy: Reflecting on the Ugandan Refugee Movement." *Western News*, October 3, 2012. https://news.westernu.ca/2012/10/molloy-reflecting-on-the-ugan dan-refugee-movement/

Wu, Stephen, Stephen Ellingson, Paul Hagstrom, and Jaime Kucinskas. "Religion and Refugee Well-Being: The Importance of Inclusive Community." *Journal for the Scientific Study of Religion* 60, no. 2 (2021): 291–308.

Yazicioglu, Isra. *Understanding the Qur'anic Miracle Stories in the Modern Age*. University Park, PA: Penn State, 2015.

Zakaria, Anam. *1971: A People's History from Bangladesh, Pakistan and India*. New York: Penguin Random House, 2019.

Zargar, Cyrus. *The Polished Mirror: Storytelling and the Pursuit of Virtue in Islamic Philosophy and Sufism*. London: Oneworld Publications, 2017.

Zia-Shariff, Shelina. *Nairobi Days*. Indianapolis: Dog Ear Publishing, 2017.

Index

For the benefit of digital users, indexed terms that span two pages (e.g., 52–53) may, on occasion, appear on only one of those pages.

Figures are indicated by f following the page number